EDITED BOOK OF PHARMACOLOGY – III

[According to latest syllabus of B. Pharm – VI semester of Pharmacy Council of India]

Mrs. Priyanka Gupta

Associate Professor

Rajiv Gandhi Institute of Pharmacy,

AKS University

Satna (Madhya Pradesh)

Ms. Neha Goel

Associate Professor

Rajiv Gandhi Institute of Pharmacy,

AKS University

Satna (Madhya Pradesh).

Mr. Abu Tahir

Assistant Professor

Rajiv Gandhi Institute of Pharmacy,

AKS University

Satna (Madhya Pradesh).

NOTION PRESS

EDITED BOOK OF PHARMACOLOGY – III
ABOUT THE EDITORS

Mrs. Priyanka Gupta is working as Associate Professor in Rajiv Gandhi Institute of Pharmacy, AKS University, Satna (M.P.) & having 13 yrs experience in the teaching. She completed her M. Pharm in pharmacology from premier institute. She is actively engaged in teaching & research work & service to the pharmacy profession. She has participated in various national & international conferences & received best poster award. She has contributed to social awareness programs by counselling & motivating the students regarding the career opportunities in pharmacy profession.

Ms. Neha Goel is working as Associate Professor, Rajiv Gandhi Institute of Pharmacy, AKS University; Satna (M.P.). She has bagged first class academic degree M. Pharm from premier institute. She is actively participating in academic & research work & also involved in various extracurricular activity. She has participated in various conferences & received best poster award. With over 10 years of experience in teaching, she has established herself as a respected figure in the field of education. Her commitment to fostering a holistic learning environment underscores her dedication to the development of her students.

Mr. Abu Tahir is currently Assistant Professor, in AKS University, Satna (M.P.) He completed his M. Pharm in pharmacology. He is an academician and researcher, more than 5 years' experience in academic and is credited with having published his research as well as review articles more than 6 papers in ELSIVER journals and 60+ in Scopus and UGC journal. He has written various national and international book chapters with reputed publishers. He has also participated in various national and international conferences and received best paper presentation awards from Jamia hamdard university, Delhi and waiting for awarded Ph.D. in Pharmaceutical Sciences.

EDITED BOOK OF PHARMACOLOGY – III
NOTION PRESS
PREFACE

The authors feel great pleasure in presenting the first edition of the book **"Edited Book of Pharmacology – III"** for graduate and post graduate students. The present book on **Edited Book of Pharmacology – III** has been written according to the syllabus of B. Pharm – VI semester of Pharmacy Council of India and covers full course of the subject.

THE SALIENT FEATURES OF THE BOOK ARE: -

- *Easy to understand style of writing* which makes the book a self-study material.
- *Each new concept has been introduced through day-today problem of interest* to the students which makes the subject matter interesting.
- *The language of the book, on the whole, is lucid and easy to understand.*
- Wherever needed *neatly labeled figures have been drawn.*

The authors hope that the students, teachers and other readers will find the book interesting and to the point covering the course. We hope that the students will receive the book warmly.

I express a sincere thank you to the Management of GRY Institute of Pharmacy y, Guru Nanak Institute of Pharmacy, Indore institute of Pharmacy, Bhagwan Singh Institute of Pharmacy and United Institute of Pharmacy, for their support during the writing of this book.

Every effort is made to keep the book error free. The author will gratefully acknowledge the suggestions to improve the book to make it more useful.

Wishing our readers success in examination and life ahead. The authors feel that their efforts will be fully rewarded if the book serves the purpose for which it is written.

EDITED BOOK OF PHARMACOLOGY – III

CONTENT

	suppressant	Associate Professor Rajiv Gandhi Institute of Pharmacy, Faculty of Pharmaceutical Science & Technology, AKS University Satna, MP-India	
5.	Digestants and carminatives	Mr. Prabhakar Tiwari Associate Professor Rajiv Gandhi Institute of Pharmacy, Faculty of Pharmaceutical Science & Technology, AKS University Satna, MP-India	81
6.	Emetics and Anti – Emetics	Mrs. Priyanka Gupta Associate Professor Rajiv Gandhi Institute of Pharmacy, Faculty of Pharmaceutical Science & Technology, AKS University Satna, MP-India	95
7.	Chemotherapy – I	Ms. Neha Goel Associate Professor Rajiv Gandhi Institute of Pharmacy, Faculty of Pharmaceutical Science & Technology, AKS University Satna, MP-India	107
8.	Antibiotic	Mrs. Priya Diwedi	116

		Assistant Professor Rajiv Gandhi Institute of Pharmacy, Faculty of Pharmaceutical Science & Technology, AKS University Satna, MP-India	
9.	Antitubercular agents	Mrs. Pooja Chauhan Assistant Professor Rajiv Gandhi Institute of Pharmacy, Faculty of Pharmaceutical Science & Technology, AKS University Satna, MP-India	135
10.	Antileprotic agents	Mr. Satyendra Garg Assistant Professor Rajiv Gandhi Institute of Pharmacy, Faculty of Pharmaceutical Science & Technology, AKS University Satna, MP-India	145
11.	Antifungal agents	Mrs. Neelam Singh Assistant Professor Rajiv Gandhi Institute of Pharmacy, Faculty of Pharmaceutical Science & Technology, AKS University Satna, MP-India	154
12.	Antiviral drugs	Mr. Abu Tahir	167

		Assistant Professor Rajiv Gandhi Institute of Pharmacy, Faculty of Pharmaceutical Science & Technology, AKS University Satna, MP-India	
13.	Anthelmintics	Ms. Shikha Singh Assistant Professor Rajiv Gandhi Institute of Pharmacy, Faculty of Pharmaceutical Science & Technology, AKS University Satna, MP-India	177
14.	Antimalarial drugs	Dr. Gopal Garg Professor Rajiv Gandhi Institute of Pharmacy, Faculty of Pharmaceutical Science & Technology, AKS University Satna, MP-India	189
15.	Antiamoebic agents	Mrs. Neha Soni Assistant Professor Rajiv Gandhi Institute of Pharmacy, Faculty of Pharmaceutical Science & Technology, AKS University Satna, MP-India	206
16.	Chemotherapy – II	Mr. Sumit Kumar Pandey	220

		Assistant Professor Rajiv Gandhi Institute of Pharmacy, Faculty of Pharmaceutical Science & Technology, AKS University Satna, MP-India	
17.	Chemotherapy of Malignancy	Mrs. Durgesh Kumari Gupta Assistant Professor Rajiv Gandhi Institute of Pharmacy, Faculty of Pharmaceutical Science & Technology, AKS University Satna, MP-India	227
18.	Immunopharmacology	Mr. Santosh Kumar Assistant Professor Rajiv Gandhi Institute of Pharmacy, Faculty of Pharmaceutical Science & Technology, AKS University Satna, MP-India	240
19.	Principles of toxicology	Mr. Ram Prasad Sahu Assistant Professor Rajiv Gandhi Institute of Pharmacy, Faculty of Pharmaceutical Science & Technology, AKS University Satna, MP-India	258

| 20. | Chronopharmacology | Mr. Satyendra Garg
Assistant Professor
Rajiv Gandhi Institute of
Pharmacy, Faculty of
Pharmaceutical Science &
Technology, AKS
University Satna, MP-India | 273 |

CHAPTER – 1

PHARMACOLOGY OF DRUGS ACTING ON RESPIRATORY SYSTEM

Dr. Surya Prakash Gupta

Professor & Director, Rajiv Gandhi Institute of Pharmacy, Faculty of
Pharmaceutical Science & Technology, AKS University, Satna (M.P.)

ABSTRACT:

The pharmacology of drugs acting on the respiratory system encompasses a variety of agents designed to manage and treat respiratory conditions such as asthma, chronic obstructive pulmonary disease (COPD), allergic rhinitis, and cough. Bronchodilators, including beta-2 agonists, anticholinergics, and methylxanthines, are pivotal in relieving bronchoconstriction by relaxing the smooth muscles of the airways. Anti-inflammatory drugs, such as corticosteroids, leukotriene modifiers, and mast cell stabilizers, reduce airway inflammation and prevent exacerbations. Additionally, biologic agents targeting specific inflammatory pathways, like anti-IgE and anti-IL-5 antibodies, offer advanced treatment options for severe asthma. Expectorants and mucolytics facilitate the clearance of mucus, while antitussives suppress the cough reflex. Nasal decongestants alleviate nasal congestion by constricting blood vessels in the nasal mucosa. Respiratory stimulants, on the other hand, enhance the respiratory drive in cases of respiratory depression. Each drug class has a specific mechanism of action, therapeutic use, and potential side effects, making a comprehensive understanding of their pharmacology essential for optimizing respiratory care and improving patient outcomes.

Introduction:

Drugs acting on the respiratory system are used to treat various respiratory conditions such as asthma, chronic obstructive pulmonary disease (COPD), allergic rhinitis, and other related disorders. These drugs can be broadly classified into several categories based on their mechanisms of action and therapeutic uses.

Classification of Respiratory Drugs

1. **Bronchodilators**
   - **Beta-2 Agonists**: These drugs stimulate beta-2 adrenergic receptors in the bronchial smooth muscle, leading to bronchodilation. They can be short-acting (SABA) or long-acting (LABA).
     - **Short-acting beta-2 agonists (SABA)**: Albuterol (Salbutamol), Levalbuterol
     - **Long-acting beta-2 agonists (LABA)**: Salmeterol, Formoterol
   - **Anticholinergics**: These drugs block the muscarinic receptors in the bronchial smooth muscle, leading to bronchodilation.
     - **Short-acting**: Ipratropium bromide
     - **Long-acting**: Tiotropium bromide
   - **Methylxanthines**: These drugs inhibit phosphodiesterase, leading to an increase in cyclic AMP and bronchodilation.
     - Theophylline, Aminophylline
2. **Anti-inflammatory Drugs**
   - **Corticosteroids**: These drugs reduce inflammation by inhibiting multiple inflammatory cytokines.
     - **Inhaled corticosteroids (ICS)**: Beclomethasone, Budesonide, Fluticasone
     - **Systemic corticosteroids**: Prednisone, Methylprednisolone
   - **Leukotriene Modifiers**: These drugs inhibit leukotrienes, which are involved in the inflammatory process.

- **Leukotriene receptor antagonists**: Montelukast, Zafirlukast
- **5-lipoxygenase inhibitors**: Zileuton
o **Mast Cell Stabilizers**: These drugs prevent the release of histamine and other mediators from mast cells.
- Cromolyn sodium, Nedocromil

3. **Combination Drugs**
o These drugs combine bronchodilators and anti-inflammatory agents for a synergistic effect.
- Fluticasone/Salmeterol (Advair)
- Budesonide/Formoterol (Symbicort)

4. **Antihistamines**
o These drugs block histamine receptors and are used in allergic conditions.
- **First-generation**: Diphenhydramine, Chlorpheniramine
- **Second-generation**: Cetirizine, Loratadine, Fexofenadine

5. **Decongestants**
o These drugs reduce nasal congestion by vasoconstriction.
- **Sympathomimetics**: Pseudoephedrine, Phenylephrine

6. **Antitussives**
o These drugs suppress coughing.
- **Opioid antitussives**: Codeine, Hydrocodone
- **Non-opioid antitussives**: Dextromethorphan, Benzonatate

7. **Expectorants and Mucolytics**
o These drugs help in the removal of mucus from the respiratory tract.
- **Expectorants**: Guaifenesin
- **Mucolytics**: Acetylcysteine, Carbocisteine

Mechanisms of Action

1. **Bronchodilators**
   - **Beta-2 Agonists**: Activation of beta-2 adrenergic receptors leads to relaxation of bronchial smooth muscle.
   - **Anticholinergics**: Blockade of muscarinic receptors inhibits bronchoconstriction.
   - **Methylxanthines**: Inhibition of phosphodiesterase increases cAMP, leading to bronchodilation.
2. **Anti-inflammatory Drugs**
   - **Corticosteroids**: Suppress the production of inflammatory cytokines and reduce airway inflammation.
   - **Leukotriene Modifiers**: Block the effects of leukotrienes, reducing bronchoconstriction and inflammation.
   - **Mast Cell Stabilizers**: Prevent the release of mediators from mast cells.
3. **Antihistamines**
   - Block histamine receptors, reducing symptoms of allergic reactions.
4. **Decongestants**
   - Stimulate alpha-adrenergic receptors, causing vasoconstriction and reducing nasal congestion.
5. **Antitussives**
   - Suppress the cough reflex through central or peripheral mechanisms.
6. **Expectorants and Mucolytics**
   - Expectorants increase the volume and reduce the viscosity of bronchial secretions, facilitating their removal.

o   Mucolytics break down mucus, making it easier to clear from the airways.

Clinical Applications

- **Asthma**: Beta-2 agonists, corticosteroids, leukotriene modifiers, and mast cell stabilizers.
- **COPD**: Anticholinergics, beta-2 agonists, corticosteroids.
- **Allergic Rhinitis**: Antihistamines, corticosteroids, decongestants.
- **Cough**: Antitussives, expectorants, mucolytics.

Side Effects and Monitoring

1. **Beta-2 Agonists**
   o   Side effects: Tachycardia, tremors, nervousness.
   o   Monitoring: Heart rate, frequency of use.
2. **Anticholinergics**
   o   Side effects: Dry mouth, urinary retention, constipation.
   o   Monitoring: Signs of anticholinergic effects.
3. **Corticosteroids**
   o   Side effects: Oral thrush (inhaled), weight gain, osteoporosis (systemic).
   o   Monitoring: Adrenal function, bone density, signs of infection.
4. **Leukotriene Modifiers**
   o   Side effects: Headache, liver enzyme elevation.
   o   Monitoring: Liver function tests.
5. **Antihistamines**
   o   Side effects: Sedation (first-generation), dry mouth.
   o   Monitoring: Level of sedation, anticholinergic effects.
6. **Decongestants**

- o Side effects: Hypertension, insomnia.
- o Monitoring: Blood pressure, heart rate.

ANTI -ASTHMATIC DRUGS

Anti-asthmatic drugs are medications used to manage and treat asthma, a chronic respiratory condition characterized by airway inflammation, bronchoconstriction (narrowing of the airways), and increased mucus production. These drugs aim to relieve symptoms, reduce airway inflammation, and improve lung function. There are several classes of anti-asthmatic drugs, each with its own mechanism of action and specific role in asthma management. Some of the common classes of anti-asthmatic drugs include:

1. **Bronchodilators:**
   a. **Beta-2 Agonists:** These drugs, like albuterol and salmeterol, relax the smooth muscles in the airways, causing bronchodilation and rapid relief of acute asthma symptoms. They are commonly used as rescue inhalers for quick relief during asthma attacks.
   b. **Anticholinergics:** Medications like ipratropium bromide work by blocking the action of acetylcholine, a neurotransmitter that can cause airway constriction.

2. **Corticosteroids (Anti-Inflammatory Agents):**
   a. **Inhaled Corticosteroids:** Drugs like fluticasone and budesonide reduce airway inflammation and are used for long-term asthma control.
   b. **Oral Corticosteroids:** In severe asthma exacerbations, oral corticosteroids like prednisone may be prescribed to quickly reduce inflammation and symptoms.

3. **Leukotriene Modifiers:**
   a. These drugs, such as montelukast, zafirlukast, and zileuton, block the action of leukotrienes, which are inflammatory compounds involved in asthma. They help to reduce airway inflammation and constriction.

4. Mast Cell Stabilizers:

a. Cromolyn sodium and nedocromil sodium inhibit the release of inflammatory mediators from mast cells, which can help prevent asthma attacks by reducing airway inflammation.

5. Monoclonal Antibodies:

a. These biologic drugs target specific immune system molecules involved in asthma. Examples include omalizumab, mepolizumab, reslizumab, and benralizumab. They are used in severe, uncontrolled asthma cases.

6. Theophylline:

a. Theophylline is a bronchodilator with anti-inflammatory properties. It is used less frequently today due to the availability of other, more effective medications.

7. Long-Acting Beta-Agonists (LABAs):

a. Drugs like salmeterol and formoterol are used in combination with inhaled corticosteroids for long-term asthma control.

8. **Antitussives:** Some anti-asthmatic medications, like codeine or dextromethorphan, may be used to control coughing associated with asthma.

9. **Biologics:** Newer biologic therapies target specific pathways and molecules involved in asthma inflammation. They are often reserved for severe asthma cases that do not respond to traditional treatments.

DRUGS USED IN THE MANAGEMENT OF COPD

Anti-asthmatic drugs are medications used to treat and manage asthma, a chronic inflammatory disease of the airways characterized by recurrent episodes of wheezing, breathlessness, chest tightness, and coughing. These drugs aim to reduce inflammation, prevent bronchoconstriction, and relieve acute symptoms.

Classification of Anti-Asthmatic Drugs

Anti-asthmatic drugs can be classified into several categories based on their mechanisms of action and therapeutic uses:

1. **Bronchodilators**
   - **Beta-2 Agonists**
     - Short-acting beta-2 agonists (SABA)
     - Long-acting beta-2 agonists (LABA)
   - **Anticholinergics**
     - Short-acting muscarinic antagonists (SAMA)
     - Long-acting muscarinic antagonists (LAMA)
   - **Methylxanthines**
2. **Anti-inflammatory Drugs**
   - **Corticosteroids**
     - Inhaled corticosteroids (ICS)
     - Systemic corticosteroids
   - **Leukotriene Modifiers**
     - Leukotriene receptor antagonists
     - 5-lipoxygenase inhibitors
   - **Mast Cell Stabilizers**
3. **Biologic Agents**
   - Anti-IgE antibodies
   - Anti-IL-5 antibodies
   - Anti-IL-4/IL-13 antibodies
4. **Combination Drugs**
   - ICS/LABA combinations
   - ICS/LAMA/LABA combinations

Pharmacology of Anti-Asthmatic Drugs

1. Bronchodilators

Beta-2 Agonists

- **Short-acting beta-2 agonists (SABA)**
- o **Examples**: Albuterol (Salbutamol), Levalbuterol
- o **Mechanism of Action**: SABAs stimulate beta-2 adrenergic receptors in the bronchial smooth muscle, leading to muscle relaxation and bronchodilation. They provide rapid relief from acute bronchoconstriction.
- o **Uses**: Relief of acute asthma symptoms and prevention of exercise-induced bronchospasm.
- o **Side Effects**: Tachycardia, tremors, nervousness, hypokalemia.
- **Long-acting beta-2 agonists (LABA)**
- o **Examples**: Salmeterol, Formoterol
- o **Mechanism of Action**: LABAs provide prolonged stimulation of beta-2 adrenergic receptors, leading to sustained bronchodilation.
- o **Uses**: Maintenance therapy for chronic asthma, used in combination with inhaled corticosteroids.
- o **Side Effects**: Similar to SABAs, increased risk of asthma-related death when used alone.

Anticholinergics

- **Short-acting muscarinic antagonists (SAMA)**
- o **Example**: Ipratropium bromide
- o **Mechanism of Action**: SAMAs block muscarinic receptors in the bronchial smooth muscle, leading to bronchodilation and reduced mucus secretion.
- o **Uses**: Relief of acute asthma symptoms, often used in combination with SABAs.
- o **Side Effects**: Dry mouth, throat irritation, urinary retention.

- **Long-acting muscarinic antagonists (LAMA)**
    - **Example**: Tiotropium bromide
    - **Mechanism of Action**: LAMAs provide prolonged blockade of muscarinic receptors, leading to sustained bronchodilation.
    - **Uses**: Maintenance therapy for chronic asthma and COPD.
    - **Side Effects**: Similar to SAMAs, with potential for systemic anticholinergic effects.

Methylxanthines

- **Examples**: Theophylline, Aminophylline
- **Mechanism of Action**: Methylxanthines inhibit phosphodiesterase, leading to increased levels of cyclic AMP and bronchodilation. They also have anti-inflammatory effects.
- **Uses**: Maintenance therapy for chronic asthma, often as an add-on treatment.
- **Side Effects**: Nausea, vomiting, insomnia, arrhythmias, seizures (narrow therapeutic index).

2. Anti-inflammatory Drugs

Corticosteroids

- **Inhaled corticosteroids (ICS)**
    - **Examples**: Beclomethasone, Budesonide, Fluticasone
    - **Mechanism of Action**: ICS reduce airway inflammation by inhibiting the production of inflammatory cytokines, reducing airway hyperresponsiveness, and decreasing mucus production.
    - **Uses**: First-line maintenance therapy for chronic asthma.
    - **Side Effects**: Oral thrush, hoarseness, potential systemic effects with high doses.

- **Systemic corticosteroids**
- o **Examples**: Prednisone, Methylprednisolone
- o **Mechanism of Action**: Systemic corticosteroids reduce inflammation throughout the body, including the airways.
- o **Uses**: Short-term treatment of severe asthma exacerbations.
- o **Side Effects**: Weight gain, osteoporosis, adrenal suppression, hyperglycemia, increased risk of infection.

Leukotriene Modifiers

- **Leukotriene receptor antagonists**
- o **Examples**: Montelukast, Zafirlukast
- o **Mechanism of Action**: These drugs block leukotriene receptors, reducing bronchoconstriction, inflammation, and mucus production.
- o **Uses**: Maintenance therapy for chronic asthma, especially in patients with allergic components.
- o **Side Effects**: Headache, gastrointestinal disturbances, neuropsychiatric events (rare).
- **5-lipoxygenase inhibitors**
- o **Example**: Zileuton
- o **Mechanism of Action**: Inhibits 5-lipoxygenase, reducing the synthesis of leukotrienes.
- o **Uses**: Maintenance therapy for chronic asthma.
- o **Side Effects**: Liver enzyme elevation, headache.

Mast Cell Stabilizers

- **Examples**: Cromolyn sodium, Nedocromil
- **Mechanism of Action**: Prevent the release of histamine and other inflammatory mediators from mast cells.

- **Uses**: Maintenance therapy for mild persistent asthma, prevention of exercise-induced bronchospasm.
- **Side Effects**: Throat irritation, coughing.

3. Biologic Agents

Anti-IgE Antibodies

- **Example**: Omalizumab
- **Mechanism of Action**: Binds to IgE, preventing it from binding to its receptor on mast cells and basophils, reducing allergic inflammation.
- **Uses**: Severe allergic asthma not controlled by conventional therapies.
- **Side Effects**: Injection site reactions, anaphylaxis (rare).

Anti-IL-5 Antibodies

- **Examples**: Mepolizumab, Reslizumab, Benralizumab
- **Mechanism of Action**: Target and neutralize IL-5, reducing eosinophilic inflammation in the airways.
- **Uses**: Severe eosinophilic asthma.
- **Side Effects**: Injection site reactions, headache.

Anti-IL-4/IL-13 Antibodies

- **Example**: Dupilumab
- **Mechanism of Action**: Inhibits IL-4 and IL-13 signaling, reducing inflammation and mucus production.
- **Uses**: Moderate to severe asthma with an eosinophilic phenotype or corticosteroid-dependent asthma.
- **Side Effects**: Injection site reactions, conjunctivitis.

4. Combination Drugs

ICS/LABA Combinations

- **Examples**: Fluticasone/Salmeterol (Advair), Budesonide/Formoterol (Symbicort)
- **Mechanism of Action**: Provide both anti-inflammatory effects (ICS) and sustained bronchodilation (LABA).
- **Uses**: Maintenance therapy for moderate to severe asthma.
- **Side Effects**: Similar to individual components.

ICS/LAMA/LABA Combinations

- **Example**: Fluticasone/Umeclidinium/Vilanterol (Trelegy Ellipta)
- **Mechanism of Action**: Provide anti-inflammatory effects, bronchodilation, and reduced mucus secretion.
- **Uses**: Maintenance therapy for severe asthma and COPD.
- **Side Effects**: Similar to individual components.

EXPECTORANTS AND ANTITUSSIVES

Anti-asthmatic drugs are medications used to treat and manage asthma, a chronic inflammatory disease of the airways characterized by recurrent episodes of wheezing, breathlessness, chest tightness, and coughing. These drugs aim to reduce inflammation, prevent bronchoconstriction, and relieve acute symptoms.

Classification of Anti-Asthmatic Drugs

Anti-asthmatic drugs can be classified into several categories based on their mechanisms of action and therapeutic uses:

1. **Bronchodilators**
o **Beta-2 Agonists**
- Short-acting beta-2 agonists (SABA)

- Long-acting beta-2 agonists (LABA)
  - **Anticholinergics**
    - Short-acting muscarinic antagonists (SAMA)
    - Long-acting muscarinic antagonists (LAMA)
  - **Methylxanthines**

2. **Anti-inflammatory Drugs**
  - **Corticosteroids**
    - Inhaled corticosteroids (ICS)
    - Systemic corticosteroids
  - **Leukotriene Modifiers**
    - Leukotriene receptor antagonists
    - 5-lipoxygenase inhibitors
  - **Mast Cell Stabilizers**

3. **Biologic Agents**
  - Anti-IgE antibodies
  - Anti-IL-5 antibodies
  - Anti-IL-4/IL-13 antibodies

4. **Combination Drugs**
  - ICS/LABA combinations
  - ICS/LAMA/LABA combinations

Pharmacology of Anti-Asthmatic Drugs

1. Bronchodilators

Beta-2 Agonists

- **Short-acting beta-2 agonists (SABA)**
  - **Examples**: Albuterol (Salbutamol), Levalbuterol
  - **Mechanism of Action**: SABAs stimulate beta-2 adrenergic receptors in the bronchial smooth muscle, leading to muscle

relaxation and bronchodilation. They provide rapid relief from acute bronchoconstriction.

- o **Uses**: Relief of acute asthma symptoms and prevention of exercise-induced bronchospasm.
- o **Side Effects**: Tachycardia, tremors, nervousness, hypokalemia.
- **Long-acting beta-2 agonists (LABA)**
- o **Examples**: Salmeterol, Formoterol
- o **Mechanism of Action**: LABAs provide prolonged stimulation of beta-2 adrenergic receptors, leading to sustained bronchodilation.
- o **Uses**: Maintenance therapy for chronic asthma, used in combination with inhaled corticosteroids.
- o **Side Effects**: Similar to SABAs, increased risk of asthma-related death when used alone.

Anticholinergics

- **Short-acting muscarinic antagonists (SAMA)**
- o **Example**: Ipratropium bromide
- o **Mechanism of Action**: SAMAs block muscarinic receptors in the bronchial smooth muscle, leading to bronchodilation and reduced mucus secretion.
- o **Uses**: Relief of acute asthma symptoms, often used in combination with SABAs.
- o **Side Effects**: Dry mouth, throat irritation, urinary retention.
- **Long-acting muscarinic antagonists (LAMA)**
- o **Example**: Tiotropium bromide
- o **Mechanism of Action**: LAMAs provide prolonged blockade of muscarinic receptors, leading to sustained bronchodilation.
- o **Uses**: Maintenance therapy for chronic asthma and COPD.

o **Side Effects**: Similar to SAMAs, with potential for systemic anticholinergic effects.

Methylxanthines

- **Examples**: Theophylline, Aminophylline
- **Mechanism of Action**: Methylxanthines inhibit phosphodiesterase, leading to increased levels of cyclic AMP and bronchodilation. They also have anti-inflammatory effects.
- **Uses**: Maintenance therapy for chronic asthma, often as an add-on treatment.
- **Side Effects**: Nausea, vomiting, insomnia, arrhythmias, seizures (narrow therapeutic index).

2. Anti-inflammatory Drugs

Corticosteroids

- **Inhaled corticosteroids (ICS)**
    - o **Examples**: Beclomethasone, Budesonide, Fluticasone
    - o **Mechanism of Action**: ICS reduce airway inflammation by inhibiting the production of inflammatory cytokines, reducing airway hyperresponsiveness, and decreasing mucus production.
    - o **Uses**: First-line maintenance therapy for chronic asthma.
    - o **Side Effects**: Oral thrush, hoarseness, potential systemic effects with high doses.
- **Systemic corticosteroids**
    - o **Examples**: Prednisone, Methylprednisolone
    - o **Mechanism of Action**: Systemic corticosteroids reduce inflammation throughout the body, including the airways.
    - o **Uses**: Short-term treatment of severe asthma exacerbations.

- o **Side Effects**: Weight gain, osteoporosis, adrenal suppression, hyperglycemia, increased risk of infection.

Leukotriene Modifiers

- **Leukotriene receptor antagonists**
- o **Examples**: Montelukast, Zafirlukast
- o **Mechanism of Action**: These drugs block leukotriene receptors, reducing bronchoconstriction, inflammation, and mucus production.
- o **Uses**: Maintenance therapy for chronic asthma, especially in patients with allergic components.
- o **Side Effects**: Headache, gastrointestinal disturbances, neuropsychiatric events (rare).
- **5-lipoxygenase inhibitors**
- o **Example**: Zileuton
- o **Mechanism of Action**: Inhibits 5-lipoxygenase, reducing the synthesis of leukotrienes.
- o **Uses**: Maintenance therapy for chronic asthma.
- o **Side Effects**: Liver enzyme elevation, headache.

Mast Cell Stabilizers

- **Examples**: Cromolyn sodium, Nedocromil
- **Mechanism of Action**: Prevent the release of histamine and other inflammatory mediators from mast cells.
- **Uses**: Maintenance therapy for mild persistent asthma, prevention of exercise-induced bronchospasm.
- **Side Effects**: Throat irritation, coughing.

3. Biologic Agents

Anti-IgE Antibodies

- **Example**: Omalizumab
- **Mechanism of Action**: Binds to IgE, preventing it from binding to its receptor on mast cells and basophils, reducing allergic inflammation.
- **Uses**: Severe allergic asthma not controlled by conventional therapies.
- **Side Effects**: Injection site reactions, anaphylaxis (rare).

Anti-IL-5 Antibodies

- **Examples**: Mepolizumab, Reslizumab, Benralizumab
- **Mechanism of Action**: Target and neutralize IL-5, reducing eosinophilic inflammation in the airways.
- **Uses**: Severe eosinophilic asthma.
- **Side Effects**: Injection site reactions, headache.

Anti-IL-4/IL-13 Antibodies

- **Example**: Dupilumab
- **Mechanism of Action**: Inhibits IL-4 and IL-13 signaling, reducing inflammation and mucus production.
- **Uses**: Moderate to severe asthma with an eosinophilic phenotype or corticosteroid-dependent asthma.
- **Side Effects**: Injection site reactions, conjunctivitis.

4. Combination Drugs

ICS/LABA Combinations

- **Examples**: Fluticasone/Salmeterol (Advair), Budesonide/Formoterol (Symbicort)

- **Mechanism of Action**: Provide both anti-inflammatory effects (ICS) and sustained bronchodilation (LABA).
- **Uses**: Maintenance therapy for moderate to severe asthma.
- **Side Effects**: Similar to individual components.

ICS/LAMA/LABA Combinations

- **Example**: Fluticasone/Umeclidinium/Vilanterol (Trelegy Ellipta)
- **Mechanism of Action**: Provide anti-inflammatory effects, bronchodilation, and reduced mucus secretion.
- **Uses**: Maintenance therapy for severe asthma and COPD.
- **Side Effects**: Similar to individual components.

Drugs Used in the Management of Chronic Obstructive Pulmonary Disease (COPD)

Chronic Obstructive Pulmonary Disease (COPD) is a progressive respiratory disorder characterized by persistent airflow limitation and chronic respiratory symptoms. The management of COPD involves the use of various pharmacologic agents to relieve symptoms, improve lung function, reduce exacerbations, and enhance the overall quality of life.

Classification of Drugs for COPD

1. **Bronchodilators**
   - **Beta-2 Agonists**
     - Short-acting beta-2 agonists (SABA)
     - Long-acting beta-2 agonists (LABA)
   - **Anticholinergics**
     - Short-acting muscarinic antagonists (SAMA)
     - Long-acting muscarinic antagonists (LAMA)

- **Methylxanthines**

2. **Anti-inflammatory Drugs**
   - **Corticosteroids**
     - Inhaled corticosteroids (ICS)
     - Systemic corticosteroids
   - **Phosphodiesterase-4 (PDE4) Inhibitors**

3. **Combination Drugs**
   - LABA/ICS combinations
   - LAMA/LABA combinations
   - Triple therapy (LAMA/LABA/ICS)

4. **Other Therapies**
   - Antibiotics
   - Mucolytics and Expectorants
   - Oxygen therapy
   - Vaccinations

Pharmacology of Drugs for COPD

1. Bronchodilators

Beta-2 Agonists

- **Short-acting beta-2 agonists (SABA)**
  - **Examples**: Albuterol (Salbutamol), Levalbuterol
  - **Mechanism of Action**: SABAs stimulate beta-2 adrenergic receptors in the bronchial smooth muscle, leading to muscle relaxation and bronchodilation. They provide rapid relief from acute bronchoconstriction.
  - **Uses:** Relief of acute bronchospasm and as-needed symptom control.
  - **Side Effects**: Tachycardia, tremors, nervousness, hypokalemia.

- **Long-acting beta-2 agonists (LABA)**
o **Examples**: Salmeterol, Formoterol, Indacaterol
o **Mechanism of Action**: LABAs provide prolonged stimulation of beta-2 adrenergic receptors, leading to sustained bronchodilation.
o **Uses**: Maintenance therapy for chronic COPD, often in combination with other medications.
o **Side Effects**: Similar to SABAs, with increased risk of cardiovascular events in some patients.

Anticholinergics

- **Short-acting muscarinic antagonists (SAMA)**
o **Example**: Ipratropium bromide
o **Mechanism of Action**: SAMAs block muscarinic receptors in the bronchial smooth muscle, leading to bronchodilation and reduced mucus secretion.
o **Uses**: Relief of acute symptoms, often in combination with SABAs.
o **Side Effects**: Dry mouth, throat irritation, urinary retention.
- **Long-acting muscarinic antagonists (LAMA)**
o **Examples**: Tiotropium bromide, Aclidinium bromide, Glycopyrronium, Umeclidinium
o **Mechanism of Action**: LAMAs provide prolonged blockade of muscarinic receptors, leading to sustained bronchodilation.
o **Uses**: Maintenance therapy for chronic COPD.
o **Side Effects**: Similar to SAMAs, with potential for systemic anticholinergic effects.

Methylxanthines

- **Examples**: Theophylline, Aminophylline

- **Mechanism of Action**: Methylxanthines inhibit phosphodiesterase, leading to increased levels of cyclic AMP and bronchodilation. They also have anti-inflammatory effects.
- **Uses**: Maintenance therapy for chronic COPD, often as an add-on treatment.
- **Side Effects**: Nausea, vomiting, insomnia, arrhythmias, seizures (narrow therapeutic index).

2. Anti-inflammatory Drugs

Corticosteroids

- **Inhaled corticosteroids (ICS)**
    - **Examples**: Beclomethasone, Budesonide, Fluticasone
    - **Mechanism of Action**: ICS reduce airway inflammation by inhibiting the production of inflammatory cytokines, reducing airway hyperresponsiveness, and decreasing mucus production.
    - **Uses**: Maintenance therapy for chronic COPD, often in combination with LABAs.
    - **Side Effects**: Oral thrush, hoarseness, potential systemic effects with high doses.
- **Systemic corticosteroids**
    - **Examples**: Prednisone, Methylprednisolone
    - **Mechanism of Action**: Systemic corticosteroids reduce inflammation throughout the body, including the airways.
    - **Uses**: Short-term treatment of severe COPD exacerbations.
    - **Side Effects**: Weight gain, osteoporosis, adrenal suppression, hyperglycemia, increased risk of infection.

Phosphodiesterase-4 (PDE4) Inhibitors

- **Example**: Roflumilast
- **Mechanism of Action**: Inhibits PDE4, leading to increased levels of cyclic AMP, which reduces inflammation and relaxes smooth muscles in the airways.
  - **Uses**: Maintenance therapy for severe COPD with chronic bronchitis and a history of exacerbations.
  - **Side Effects**: Nausea, diarrhea, weight loss, psychiatric symptoms.

3. Combination Drugs

LABA/ICS Combinations

- **Examples**: Fluticasone/Salmeterol (Advair), Budesonide/Formoterol (Symbicort)
- **Mechanism of Action**: Provide both anti-inflammatory effects (ICS) and sustained bronchodilation (LABA).
- **Uses**: Maintenance therapy for moderate to severe COPD.
- **Side Effects**: Similar to individual components.

LAMA/LABA Combinations

- **Examples**: Tiotropium/Olodaterol (Stiolto Respimat), Umeclidinium/Vilanterol (Anoro Ellipta)
- **Mechanism of Action**: Provide dual bronchodilation by blocking muscarinic receptors and stimulating beta-2 adrenergic receptors.
- **Uses**: Maintenance therapy for moderate to severe COPD.
- **Side Effects**: Similar to individual components.

Triple Therapy (LAMA/LABA/ICS)

- **Examples**: Fluticasone/Umeclidinium/Vilanterol (Trelegy Ellipta)

- **Mechanism of Action**: Combines anti-inflammatory effects (ICS), muscarinic blockade (LAMA), and beta-2 stimulation (LABA).
- **Uses**: Maintenance therapy for severe COPD with frequent exacerbations.
- **Side Effects**: Similar to individual components.

4. Other Therapies

Antibiotics

- **Uses**: Treatment of bacterial infections and prevention of exacerbations in patients with frequent infections.
- **Examples**: Azithromycin, Doxycycline
- **Side Effects**: Gastrointestinal disturbances, antibiotic resistance.

Mucolytics and Expectorants

- **Examples**: Acetylcysteine, Carbocisteine
- **Mechanism of Action**: Reduce mucus viscosity, making it easier to expectorate.
- **Uses**: Maintenance therapy for chronic bronchitis.
- **Side Effects**: Gastrointestinal disturbances, hypersensitivity reactions.

Oxygen Therapy

- **Uses**: Long-term oxygen therapy for patients with chronic hypoxemia.
- **Benefits**: Improves survival, quality of life, and exercise capacity.
- **Side Effects**: Nasal dryness, potential for oxygen toxicity.

Vaccinations

- **Uses**: Prevention of respiratory infections.
- **Examples**: Influenza vaccine, Pneumococcal vaccine
- **Benefits**: Reduces the risk of infections and exacerbations.

EXPECTORANTS **AND** ANTITUSSIVES

Expectorants and **antitussives** are two classes of medications commonly used to manage symptoms of respiratory conditions such as cough, mucus production, and throat irritation.

- **Expectorants**: These drugs help to thin and loosen mucus in the airways, making it easier to cough up and expel from the respiratory tract.
- **Antitussives**: These drugs suppress the cough reflex, reducing the urge to cough, which can be beneficial in managing dry, non-productive coughs.

Classification

Expectorants

1. **Direct Expectorants**
   - **Examples**: Guaifenesin
   - **Mechanism**: Increase the hydration of the respiratory tract, reducing the viscosity of mucus and facilitating its removal through coughing.
2. **Mucolytics**
   - **Examples**: Acetylcysteine, Carbocisteine
   - **Mechanism**: Break down the chemical structure of mucus molecules, making mucus less thick and sticky, thereby easing its expulsion.

Antitussives

1. **Central Antitussives**
   - **Opioid Antitussives**
     - **Examples**: Codeine, Hydrocodone

- **Mechanism**: Act on the cough center in the brainstem to suppress the cough reflex.
  - ○ **Non-opioid Antitussives**
    - **Examples**: Dextromethorphan
    - **Mechanism**: Similar to opioids but without the analgesic and addictive properties.

2. **Peripheral Antitussives**
   - ○ **Examples**: Benzonatate
   - ○ **Mechanism**: Numb the stretch receptors in the respiratory tract, reducing the cough reflex.

Pharmacology of Expectorants and Antitussives

Expectorants

Guaifenesin

- **Mechanism of Action**: Increases the volume and reduces the viscosity of secretions in the trachea and bronchi, facilitating the removal of mucus by coughing.
- **Uses**: Relief of productive cough associated with common cold, bronchitis, and other respiratory conditions.
- **Side Effects**: Generally well-tolerated, but may cause nausea, vomiting, dizziness, and headache.

Acetylcysteine

- **Mechanism of Action**: Breaks disulfide bonds in mucus, reducing its viscosity and making it easier to expel.
- **Uses**: Management of chronic bronchitis, cystic fibrosis, and as an antidote for acetaminophen overdose.

- **Side Effects**: Nausea, vomiting, stomatitis, and hypersensitivity reactions.

Carbocisteine

- **Mechanism of Action**: Reduces the viscosity of bronchial mucus, facilitating its expulsion.
- **Uses**: Similar to acetylcysteine, used in chronic respiratory conditions with thick mucus.
- **Side Effects**: Gastrointestinal disturbances, skin rash, hypersensitivity reactions.

Antitussives

Codeine

- **Mechanism of Action**: Acts on the central nervous system to increase the threshold for coughing.
- **Uses**: Management of moderate to severe dry cough.
- **Side Effects**: Sedation, constipation, nausea, risk of dependence and respiratory depression.

Hydrocodone

- **Mechanism of Action**: Similar to codeine, suppresses the cough reflex by acting on the brainstem.
- **Uses**: Severe cough suppression.
- **Side Effects**: Similar to codeine, with a higher risk of dependence and respiratory depression.

Dextromethorphan

- **Mechanism of Action**: Acts centrally on the cough center in the medulla to suppress the cough reflex.
- **Uses**: Relief of non-productive cough.
- **Side Effects**: Dizziness, nausea, drowsiness, at high doses can cause dissociative hallucinations.

Benzonatate

- **Mechanism of Action**: Numbs the stretch receptors in the lungs and airways, reducing the cough reflex.
- **Uses**: Relief of cough.
- **Side Effects**: Nausea, constipation, drowsiness, and in rare cases, hypersensitivity reactions

NASAL DECONGESTANTS

Nasal decongestants are medications used to relieve nasal congestion, a common symptom of conditions such as the common cold, sinusitis, allergies, and rhinitis. They work by constricting the blood vessels in the nasal passages, which reduces swelling and congestion.

Classification of Nasal Decongestants

Nasal decongestants can be classified based on their route of administration and the duration of their action:

1. **Route of Administration**
   - **Topical (Nasal Sprays or Drops)**
   - **Oral**
2. **Duration of Action**
   - **Short-acting**
   - **Intermediate-acting**
   - **Long-acting**

Pharmacology of Nasal Decongestants

Mechanism of Action

Nasal decongestants primarily work by stimulating alpha-adrenergic receptors, which leads to vasoconstriction of the blood vessels in the nasal mucosa. This vasoconstriction reduces blood flow to the nasal passages, decreasing swelling and congestion.

Common Nasal Decongestants

1. **Topical Nasal Decongestants**

Short-acting

- **Examples**: Phenylephrine, Naphazoline
- **Mechanism of Action**: Directly stimulate alpha-adrenergic receptors in the nasal mucosa, causing vasoconstriction and reducing nasal congestion.
- **Duration of Action**: Typically lasts 4-6 hours.
- **Side Effects**: Rebound congestion (rhinitis medicamentosa) with prolonged use, local irritation, dryness of the nasal mucosa.

Intermediate-acting

- **Examples**: Tetrahydrozoline
- **Mechanism of Action**: Similar to short-acting decongestants, with a longer duration of action.
- **Duration of Action**: Typically lasts 6-8 hours.
- **Side Effects**: Similar to short-acting decongestants.

Long-acting

- **Examples**: Oxymetazoline, Xylometazoline
- **Mechanism of Action**: Provide prolonged stimulation of alpha-adrenergic receptors, leading to sustained vasoconstriction and decongestion.
- **Duration of Action**: Typically lasts 10-12 hours.
- **Side Effects**: Higher risk of rebound congestion with prolonged use, local irritation, dryness of the nasal mucosa.
2. **Oral Nasal Decongestants**

Examples

- **Pseudoephedrine**
    - **Mechanism of Action**: Indirectly stimulates alpha-adrenergic receptors by increasing the release of norepinephrine, leading to vasoconstriction and reduced nasal congestion.
    - **Duration of Action**: Typically lasts 4-6 hours (immediate release) or 12-24 hours (extended release).
    - **Side Effects**: Insomnia, nervousness, tachycardia, hypertension, potential for abuse (due to its use in the illicit manufacture of methamphetamine).
- **Phenylephrine**
    - **Mechanism of Action**: Directly stimulates alpha-adrenergic receptors, leading to vasoconstriction and reduced nasal congestion.
    - **Duration of Action**: Typically lasts 4-6 hours.
    - **Side Effects**: Less effective than pseudoephedrine, with similar but milder side effects including increased blood pressure, headache, dizziness.

Clinical Uses

- **Common Cold**: To relieve nasal congestion and improve breathing.
- **Allergic Rhinitis**: To reduce nasal congestion associated with allergies.
- **Sinusitis**: To decrease congestion and facilitate sinus drainage.
- **Eustachian Tube Dysfunction**: To relieve pressure and congestion in the middle ear.

Side Effects and Precautions

- **Rebound Congestion (Rhinitis Medicamentosa)**: Prolonged use of topical decongestants (more than 3-5 days) can lead to rebound nasal congestion, making the condition worse once the medication is stopped.
- **Systemic Side Effects (Oral Decongestants)**: Increased blood pressure, palpitations, nervousness, and insomnia.
- **Contraindications**: Patients with hypertension, cardiovascular disease, hyperthyroidism, diabetes, and prostate enlargement should use these medications with caution.
- **Drug Interactions**: Can interact with monoamine oxidase inhibitors (MAOIs), leading to hypertensive crisis, and may reduce the effectiveness of beta-blockers.

Pharmacology of Respiratory Stimulants

Central Respiratory Stimulants

1. **Medullary Stimulants**
   - **Examples**: Doxapram, Almitrine
   - **Mechanism of Action**: These drugs stimulate the respiratory centers in the medulla oblongata, increasing the rate and depth of respiration.

- o **Uses**: Treatment of acute respiratory failure, post-anesthesia respiratory depression, and chronic respiratory insufficiency.
- o **Side Effects**: Hypertension, tachycardia, anxiety, tremors, convulsions (at high doses).

2. **Cerebral Cortex Stimulants**
- o **Examples**: Caffeine, Theophylline, Aminophylline
- o **Mechanism of Action**: These drugs increase the sensitivity of the respiratory centers to carbon dioxide, thereby enhancing respiratory drive. They also inhibit phosphodiesterase, increasing cyclic AMP levels and leading to bronchodilation.
- o **Uses**: Management of neonatal apnea, COPD, asthma, and obstructive sleep apnea.
- o **Side Effects**: Insomnia, gastrointestinal disturbances, cardiac arrhythmias, seizures (at high doses).

3. **Carotid Body Stimulants**
- o **Examples**: Almitrine
- o **Mechanism of Action**: Stimulates peripheral chemoreceptors in the carotid bodies, enhancing respiratory drive by increasing sensitivity to hypoxia.
- o **Uses**: Treatment of chronic respiratory failure and hypoventilation syndromes.
- o **Side Effects**: Peripheral neuropathy, gastrointestinal disturbances, liver toxicity.

Peripheral Respiratory Stimulants

1. **Direct Respiratory Muscle Stimulants**
- o **Examples**: Epinephrine (Adrenaline)

- o **Mechanism of Action**: Acts on beta-adrenergic receptors to enhance the contractility of the respiratory muscles, including the diaphragm, thereby improving ventilation.
- o **Uses**: Emergency treatment of severe asthma and anaphylaxis, acute bronchospasm.
- o **Side Effects**: Tachycardia, hypertension, tremors, anxiety, palpitations.

Clinical Applications

- **Drug Overdose**: Respiratory stimulants can reverse respiratory depression caused by opioid or sedative overdose.
- **Neonatal Apnea**: Medications like caffeine are used to stimulate breathing in premature infants with apnea of prematurity.
- **Chronic Respiratory Conditions**: Used as an adjunct in the management of chronic respiratory failure, COPD, and central sleep apnea.
- **Post-Anesthesia**: To counteract respiratory depression following anesthesia and sedative administration.

Side Effects and Monitoring

- **Hypertension and Tachycardia**: Common with most respiratory stimulants, especially those that act on the adrenergic system.
- **Anxiety and Tremors**: Due to central nervous system stimulation.
- **Gastrointestinal Disturbances**: Nausea, vomiting, and abdominal discomfort.
- **Seizures**: High doses of central respiratory stimulants can lower the seizure threshold.

- **Peripheral Neuropathy and Liver Toxicity**: Specific to drugs like almitrine, requiring careful monitoring.

Contraindications and Precautions

- **Cardiovascular Disease**: Use with caution in patients with hypertension, arrhythmias, or ischemic heart disease.
- **Seizure Disorders**: Central stimulants can precipitate seizures, so they should be used cautiously in patients with a history of epilepsy.
- **Liver and Renal Impairment**: Adjust doses and monitor for toxicity in patients with compromised liver or kidney function.

CHAPTER – 2

ANTIULCER AGENTS

Dr. Gopal Garg

Professor, Rajiv Gandhi Institute of Pharmacy, Faculty of Pharmaceutical Science & Technology, AKS University Satna, MP-India

ABSTRACT:

Antiulcer agents are essential medications used to manage and treat conditions like peptic ulcers, gastroesophageal reflux disease (GERD), and other acid-related disorders of the gastrointestinal tract. These agents are classified into several categories based on their mechanisms of action: proton pump inhibitors (PPIs), H2-receptor antagonists (H2RAs), antacids, mucosal protective agents, antibiotics, and prostaglandin analogues. PPIs, such as omeprazole and lansoprazole, work by irreversibly inhibiting the hydrogen-potassium ATPase enzyme, significantly reducing gastric acid secretion. H2RAs, including ranitidine and famotidine, competitively inhibit histamine at H2 receptors, decreasing acid production. Antacids like magnesium hydroxide and calcium carbonate neutralize stomach acid, providing rapid symptomatic relief. Mucosal protective agents, such as sucralfate and bismuth subsalicylate, protect the gastric lining by forming a barrier or coating ulcers. Antibiotics like clarithromycin and amoxicillin are used in combination regimens to eradicate Helicobacter pylori, a common cause of peptic ulcers. Prostaglandin analogues, like misoprostol, enhance mucosal defenses by increasing mucus and bicarbonate secretion. Each of these agents has specific therapeutic uses and potential side effects, making them integral to the effective management of acid-related gastrointestinal conditions.

Introduction:

Antiulcer agents are medications used to treat and manage ulcers in the stomach and duodenum, as well as other gastrointestinal disorders associated with excessive gastric acid production. These agents help to reduce gastric acidity, protect the mucosal lining, and promote healing of the ulcerated tissue.

Classification of Antiulcer Agents

1. **Proton Pump Inhibitors (PPIs)**
2. **H2-Receptor Antagonists (H2RAs)**
3. **Antacids**
4. **Mucosal Protective Agents**
5. **Antibiotics**
6. **Prostaglandin Analogues**

Pharmacology of Antiulcer Agents

1. Proton Pump Inhibitors (PPIs)

Examples: Omeprazole, Lansoprazole, Pantoprazole, Esomeprazole

Mechanism of Action: PPIs irreversibly inhibit the hydrogen-potassium ATPase enzyme (proton pump) in the parietal cells of the stomach, leading to a significant reduction in gastric acid secretion. By blocking the final step in acid production, PPIs are highly effective in reducing both basal and stimulated gastric acid output.

Uses: Treatment of gastroesophageal reflux disease (GERD), peptic ulcer disease, Zollinger-Ellison syndrome, and eradication of Helicobacter pylori in combination with antibiotics.

Side Effects: Headache, gastrointestinal disturbances (nausea, diarrhea, abdominal pain), long-term use may be associated with increased risk of fractures, vitamin B12 deficiency, and potential renal issues.

2. H2-Receptor Antagonists (H2RAs)

Examples: Ranitidine, Famotidine, Cimetidine, Nizatidine
Mechanism of Action: H2RAs competitively inhibit the binding of histamine to H2 receptors on the parietal cells in the stomach, thereby reducing gastric acid secretion. They primarily reduce basal and nocturnal acid production.
Uses: Treatment of GERD, peptic ulcer disease, and prevention of stress ulcers.
Side Effects: Headache, dizziness, constipation or diarrhea, and in rare cases, mental confusion (more common in elderly patients). Cimetidine, in particular, can inhibit cytochrome P450 enzymes, leading to drug interactions.

3. Antacids

Examples: Aluminum hydroxide, Magnesium hydroxide, Calcium carbonate, Sodium bicarbonate
Mechanism of Action: Antacids neutralize stomach acid by increasing the pH of the gastric contents. They provide symptomatic relief of acid-related discomfort by buffering the acid.
Uses: Rapid relief of heartburn, indigestion, and mild cases of GERD.
Side Effects: Constipation (aluminum-containing antacids), diarrhea (magnesium-containing antacids), and potential metabolic alkalosis with excessive use (sodium bicarbonate).

4. Mucosal Protective Agents

Examples: Sucralfate, Bismuth subsalicylate, Misoprostol
Mechanism of Action:

- **Sucralfate**: Forms a protective barrier by adhering to the ulcer site, shielding it from acid and pepsin.
- **Bismuth subsalicylate**: Coats ulcers and erosions, has antimicrobial action against H. pylori, and anti-inflammatory properties.
- **Misoprostol**: A prostaglandin E1 analogue that increases the production of protective mucus and bicarbonate, and enhances mucosal blood flow.

Uses: Treatment and prevention of peptic ulcers, particularly in patients taking NSAIDs (misoprostol), and as part of H. pylori eradication regimens (bismuth subsalicylate).

Side Effects: Constipation (sucralfate), black stools and tongue (bismuth subsalicylate), diarrhea and uterine contractions (misoprostol).

5. Antibiotics

Examples: Clarithromycin, Amoxicillin, Metronidazole, Tetracycline

Mechanism of Action: These antibiotics are used in combination to eradicate H. pylori infection, which is a major cause of peptic ulcers. Each antibiotic targets the bacterium in a different way to ensure complete eradication and prevent resistance.

Uses: Part of combination therapy for H. pylori-associated peptic ulcer disease.

Side Effects: Gastrointestinal disturbances (nausea, diarrhea), antibiotic resistance, and specific side effects related to individual antibiotics (e.g., metallic taste with metronidazole).

6. Prostaglandin Analogues

Example: Misoprostol

Mechanism of Action: As mentioned earlier, misoprostol is a synthetic prostaglandin E1 analogue that mimics the protective effects of endogenous prostaglandins. It increases mucus and bicarbonate secretion and enhances mucosal blood flow, providing a protective effect on the gastric lining.

Uses: Prevention of NSAID-induced gastric ulcers, particularly in patients at high risk of complications.

Side Effects: Diarrhea, abdominal pain, uterine contractions (contraindicated in pregnancy).

OMEPRAZOLE (PRILOSEC):

1. **Mechanism of Action:** Omeprazole irreversibly inhibits the H+/K+ ATPase proton pump in the stomach's parietal cells. This action decreases the secretion of gastric acid, leading to reduced acidity in the stomach.

2. **Absorption:** Omeprazole is usually taken orally and is rapidly absorbed from the gastrointestinal tract. Its absorption is optimized when taken on an empty stomach.

3. **Metabolism:** Omeprazole is extensively metabolized in the liver by the cytochrome P450 enzyme system, primarily CYP2C19 and CYP3A4.

4. **Active Metabolite:** Omeprazole undergoes hepatic metabolism to form an active metabolite, 5-hydroxyomeprazole. This metabolite is responsible for the inhibition of the proton pump and is considered the pharmacologically active form.

5. **Duration of Action:** Omeprazole has a relatively long duration of action, and its effects can last for up to 24 hours.

6. **Therapeutic Uses:** Omeprazole is used to treat various conditions associated with excessive stomach acid, including GERD, peptic ulcers, Zollinger-Ellison syndrome, and as part of H. pylori eradication therapy in combination with antibiotics.

ESOMEPRAZOLE (NEXIUM):

1. **Mechanism of Action:** Esomeprazole is the S-isomer of omeprazole, and it also inhibits the H+/K+ ATPase proton pump in the stomach's parietal cells. Like omeprazole, it reduces gastric acid secretion.

2. **Absorption:** Esomeprazole is well-absorbed when taken orally, and it is available in both delayed-release capsules and intravenous formulations.

3. **Metabolism:** Esomeprazole is metabolized in the liver, primarily by the enzyme CYP2C19.

4. **Active Metabolite:** Esomeprazole has the same active metabolite, 5-hydroxyomeprazole, as omeprazole. However, esomeprazole may have a slightly higher systemic exposure compared to omeprazole.

5. **Duration of Action:** Esomeprazole, like omeprazole, has a relatively long duration of action and is typically dosed once daily.

6. **Therapeutic Uses:** Esomeprazole is used for the same indications as omeprazole, including the treatment of GERD, peptic ulcers, Zollinger-Ellison syndrome, and H. pylori eradication therapy.

LANSOPRAZOLE (PREVACID):

1. **Mechanism of Action:** Lansoprazole inhibits the H+/K+ ATPase proton pump in the stomach's parietal cells. By doing so, it decreases the secretion of gastric acid, leading to reduced acidity in the stomach.

2. **Absorption:** Lansoprazole is taken orally and is well-absorbed from the gastrointestinal tract. It is more stable in acidic conditions than omeprazole, which can be an advantage in some clinical situations.

3. **Metabolism:** Lansoprazole is metabolized in the liver, primarily by the enzyme CYP2C19, similar to Omeprazole.

4. **Active Metabolite:** Lansoprazole has an active metabolite, 5-hydroxylansoprazole, which is responsible for inhibiting the proton pump and is considered the pharmacologically active form.

5. **Duration of Action:** Lansoprazole has a relatively long duration of action, with its effects lasting up to 24 hours.

6. **Therapeutic Uses:** Lansoprazole is used to treat various conditions associated with excessive stomach acid, including gastroesophageal reflux disease (GERD), peptic ulcers, Zollinger-Ellison syndrome, and H. pylori eradication therapy in combination with antibiotics.

PANTOPRAZOLE (PROTONIX):

1. **Mechanism of Action:** Pantoprazole inhibits the H+/K+ ATPase proton pump in the parietal cells of the stomach, leading to decreased gastric acid production.

2. **Absorption:** Pantoprazole is taken orally and is absorbed from the gastrointestinal tract. It is available in both delayed-release tablet and intravenous formulations.

3. **Metabolism:** Pantoprazole is metabolized in the liver, primarily by the enzyme CYP2C19, similar to Omeprazole and Lansoprazole.

4. **Active Metabolite:** Unlike some other PPIs, Pantoprazole does not have an active metabolite. It acts directly as a prodrug in its active form.

5. **Duration of Action:** Pantoprazole has a relatively long duration of action and is typically dosed once daily.

6. **Therapeutic Uses:** Pantoprazole is used to treat conditions similar to other PPIs, such as GERD, peptic ulcers, Zollinger-Ellison syndrome, and H. pylori eradication therapy when used in combination with antibiotics.

FAMOTIDINE (PEPCID):

1. **Mechanism of Action:** Famotidine competitively inhibits histamine-2 receptors (H2 receptors) in the stomach's parietal cells. By doing so, it reduces the stimulation of these cells, leading to a decrease in the production of gastric acid.

2. **Absorption:** Famotidine is well-absorbed when taken orally, and it is available in both over-the-counter and prescription strengths.

3. **Metabolism:** Famotidine undergoes hepatic metabolism, mainly through oxidation, but it has a relatively low potential for drug interactions compared to some other medications.

4. **Duration of Action:** Famotidine has a relatively short duration of action compared to proton pump inhibitors (PPIs) like Omeprazole or Lansoprazole, requiring more frequent dosing for sustained acid suppression.

5. **Therapeutic Uses:** Famotidine is used for the short-term treatment and prevention of conditions associated with excessive stomach acid, including heartburn, indigestion, and certain gastrointestinal disorders like gastroesophageal reflux disease (GERD).

RANITIDINE (ZANTAC):

1. **Mechanism of Action:** Ranitidine also inhibits H2 receptors in the stomach's parietal cells. Like Famotidine, it reduces the stimulation of these cells and decreases gastric acid production.

2. **Absorption:** Ranitidine is well-absorbed when taken orally, and it is available in various formulations, including tablets, effervescent tablets, and syrup.

3. **Metabolism:** Ranitidine is metabolized in the liver, primarily through oxidation and conjugation with glucuronic acid.

4. **Duration of Action:** Ranitidine has a relatively short duration of action and requires more frequent dosing compared to PPIs, with most people taking it two times a day.

5. **Therapeutic Uses:** Ranitidine is used for the treatment and prevention of conditions associated with excess stomach acid, including peptic ulcers, GERD, and Zollinger-Ellison syndrome.

CIMETIDINE (TAGAMET):

1. **Mechanism of Action:** Cimetidine competitively inhibits H2 receptors in the stomach's parietal cells. By doing so, it decreases the stimulation of these cells, leading to a reduction in the production of gastric acid.

2. **Absorption:** Cimetidine is well-absorbed when taken orally. It is available in various formulations, including tablets and liquid forms.

3. **Metabolism:** Cimetidine is extensively metabolized in the liver, primarily through the cytochrome P450 enzyme system, with a notable impact on CYP2D6 and CYP3A4 enzymes. This can lead to significant drug interactions.

4. **Duration of Action:** Cimetidine has a relatively short duration of action, which requires more frequent dosing for sustained acid suppression, typically three to four times a day.

5. **Therapeutic Uses:** Cimetidine is used to treat conditions associated with excess stomach acid, including peptic ulcers, gastroesophageal reflux disease (GERD), and Zollinger-Ellison syndrome. It can also be used for the prevention and treatment of stress ulcers in critically ill patients.

NIZATIDINE (AXID):

1. **Mechanism of Action**: Nizatidine, like Cimetidine, is an H2 receptor antagonist. It inhibits H2 receptors in the stomach's parietal cells, leading to reduced gastric acid production.

2. **Absorption:** Nizatidine is well-absorbed when taken orally, and it is available in tablet and liquid forms.

3. **Metabolism:** Nizatidine is metabolized in the liver, but it has less potential for drug interactions compared to Cimetidine, as it has a more favorable profile regarding its effect on the cytochrome P450 enzyme system.

4. **Duration of Action:** Nizatidine has a relatively short duration of action, requiring more frequent dosing for sustained acid suppression, typically two times a day.

5. **Therapeutic Uses**: Nizatidine is used for the treatment of conditions associated with excessive stomach acid, including peptic ulcers, GERD, and heartburn.

ALUMINUM HYDROXIDE (AMPHOJEL):

1. **Mechanism of Action:** Aluminum hydroxide is an antacid that acts by neutralizing stomach acid through the formation of aluminum salts. It reacts with hydrochloric acid (HCl) in the stomach to produce aluminum chloride and water, thereby raising the pH in the stomach.

2. **Absorption:** Aluminum ions from aluminum hydroxide are not significantly absorbed from the gastrointestinal tract into the bloodstream. This makes it a relatively safe choice as an antacid, as systemic absorption is minimal.

3. **Onset of Action:** The onset of action is relatively slow, taking about 30 minutes to 2 hours to provide relief.

4. **Duration of Action:** The duration of action is relatively prolonged, and the effects can last for several hours.

5. **Potential Side Effects:** Chronic use of aluminum-containing antacids can lead to aluminum accumulation in the body, which may be harmful in individuals with impaired kidney function. This can lead to conditions like aluminum-induced osteomalacia and encephalopathy. Therefore, aluminum-containing antacids should be used with caution, especially in those with kidney disease

MAGNESIUM HYDROXIDE (MILK OF MAGNESIA):

1. **Mechanism of Action:** Magnesium hydroxide is another antacid that neutralizes stomach acid. It reacts with hydrochloric acid in the stomach to form magnesium chloride and water, raising the pH in the stomach.

2. **Absorption:** Unlike aluminum hydroxide, magnesium ions can be absorbed to some extent from the gastrointestinal tract into the bloodstream. This can lead to magnesium excess in the body, particularly in individuals with impaired kidney function.

3. **Onset of Action:** The onset of action is relatively rapid, usually within 30 minutes to 1 hour.

4. **Duration of Action:** The duration of action is moderate, and relief from symptoms can last for a few hours.

5. **Potential Side Effects:** Magnesium-containing antacids can lead to diarrhea and, in individuals with impaired kidney function, hypermagnesemia (excess magnesium in the blood). In severe cases, hypermagnesemia can be life-threatening.

CALCIUM CARBONATE (TUMS):

1. **Mechanism of Action:** Calcium carbonate is an antacid that works by directly neutralizing stomach acid through a chemical reaction. It reacts with hydrochloric acid (HCl) in the stomach to form calcium chloride, carbon dioxide, and water, raising the pH in the stomach.

2. **Absorption:** Calcium from calcium carbonate can be absorbed in the gastrointestinal tract, which can be both a benefit and a potential drawback. The absorbed calcium can contribute to the body's calcium levels, which may be useful for individuals with calcium deficiencies.

3. **Onset of Action:** The onset of action is relatively rapid, usually within a few minutes to half an hour.

4. **Duration of Action:** The duration of action is moderate, and relief from symptoms can last for a few hours.

5. **Potential Side Effects:** Chronic use of calcium-containing antacids like Tums can lead to excessive calcium intake, which may have adverse effects on calcium metabolism and potentially contribute to conditions like kidney stones.

SODIUM BICARBONATE (BAKING SODA):

1. **Mechanism of Action:** Sodium bicarbonate is an antacid that neutralizes stomach acid through a chemical reaction. It reacts with hydrochloric acid (HCl) in the stomach to form sodium chloride, carbon dioxide, and water, raising the pH in the stomach.

2. **Absorption:** Sodium bicarbonate is rapidly absorbed from the gastrointestinal tract, leading to an increase in systemic sodium levels. This can be a potential concern for individuals who need to restrict their sodium intake, such as those with hypertension or heart conditions.

3. **Onset of Action:** The onset of action is relatively rapid, usually within a few minutes.

4. **Duration of Action:** The duration of action is moderate, providing relief for a few hours.

5. **Potential Side Effects:** Excessive use of sodium bicarbonate can result in systemic alkalosis, leading to symptoms such as muscle twitching, hand tremors, and cognitive changes. In individuals with certain medical conditions, excessive sodium intake can worsen health issues, so it should be used with caution.

SUCRALFATE (CARAFATE):

1. **Mechanism of Action:** Sucralfate is a mucosal protective agent. It does not directly neutralize stomach acid but acts by forming a protective barrier over the ulcer or damaged mucosal lining in the stomach and duodenum. This barrier adheres to the ulcer site, providing a physical barrier that shields the tissue from stomach acid and other irritants.

2. **Absorption:** Sucralfate is not significantly absorbed from the gastrointestinal tract. It acts locally within the stomach and duodenum.

3. **Onset of Action:** The onset of action is relatively slow, as it requires time to bind to the damaged mucosal surface. Therefore, it may not provide immediate relief of symptoms.

4. **Duration of Action:** Sucralfate's protective barrier can last for several hours, which allows for extended protection of the ulcer site.

5. **Therapeutic Uses:** Sucralfate is used to treat and promote healing of peptic ulcers, including duodenal ulcers and gastric ulcers. It is also used to manage gastroesophageal reflux disease (GERD) and protect against further damage from stomach acid.

MISOPROSTOL (CYTOTEC):

1. **Mechanism of Action:** Misoprostol is a synthetic prostaglandin analogue. It acts by stimulating the production of mucus in the stomach lining, which enhances the protective mucus layer and increases bicarbonate secretion. This helps to reduce the risk of stomach ulcers by maintaining the mucosal barrier and decreasing the effects of gastric acid.

2. **Absorption:** Misoprostol is absorbed from the gastrointestinal tract and can have systemic effects, which may contribute to its therapeutic and side effects.

3. **Onset of Action:** The onset of action is relatively quick, with effects typically seen within an hour or so after administration.

4. **Duration of Action:** Misoprostol's effects on mucus production and bicarbonate secretion can last for several hours.

5. **Therapeutic Uses:** Misoprostol is used for the prevention and treatment of nonsteroidal anti-inflammatory drug (NSAID)-induced gastric ulcers. It is also used to induce labor and for medical abortion in some cases.

CLARITHROMYCIN:

1. **Mechanism of Action:** Clarithromycin is a macrolide antibiotic. It works by inhibiting bacterial protein synthesis. Specifically, it binds to the 50S ribosomal subunit of bacteria and interferes with the translation process, thus preventing the synthesis of new proteins and inhibiting bacterial growth.

2. **Spectrum of Activity:** Clarithromycin is effective against a wide range of Gram-positive and Gram-negative bacteria. It is commonly used to treat

respiratory tract infections, skin and soft tissue infections, and some gastrointestinal infections. Additionally, it is effective against certain atypical pathogens like Mycoplasma pneumoniae and Chlamydia pneumoniae.

3. **Absorption and Distribution:** Clarithromycin is well-absorbed when taken orally and achieves good tissue penetration. It can reach high concentrations in the lungs, making it suitable for the treatment of respiratory infections.

4. **Metabolism and Excretion**: Clarithromycin is metabolized in the liver, primarily through the cytochrome P450 enzyme system, particularly CYP3A4. It is excreted in both the urine and feces.

5. **Potential Side Effects:** Common side effects of Clarithromycin can include gastrointestinal symptoms, such as nausea and diarrhea. It may also interact with other medications that are metabolized by CYP3A4, potentially leading to drug interactions.

AMOXICILLIN:

1. **Mechanism of Action:** Amoxicillin is a penicillin-type antibiotic. It works by interfering with bacterial cell wall synthesis. Specifically, it inhibits the enzymes involved in cross-linking peptidoglycans, which are essential components of the bacterial cell wall. This results in weakened cell walls and ultimately leads to bacterial cell lysis.

2. **Spectrum of Activity:** Amoxicillin is effective against a wide range of Gram-positive and some Gram-negative bacteria. It is commonly used to treat respiratory tract infections, urinary tract infections, skin and soft tissue infections, and other bacterial infections. It is often used in combination with other antibiotics to treat more severe infections.

3. **Absorption and Distribution:** Amoxicillin is well-absorbed when taken orally and reaches high concentrations in many body tissues and fluids, making it effective for various types of infections.

4. **Metabolism and Excretion:** Amoxicillin is excreted primarily through the kidneys, and its elimination is largely unchanged in the urine. This is why it is often dosed multiple times a day to maintain therapeutic levels.

5. **Potential Side Effects:** Common side effects of Amoxicillin may include gastrointestinal symptoms like nausea, vomiting, and diarrhea. In some cases, individuals may experience allergic reactions, such as skin rashes or more severe hypersensitivity reactions.

METRONIDAZOLE:

1. **Mechanism of Action:** Metronidazole is an antibiotic with a unique mechanism of action. It is effective against anaerobic bacteria and certain parasites. Inside bacterial and protozoal cells, it undergoes chemical reduction and forms unstable intermediates that disrupt DNA structure and inhibit nucleic acid synthesis. This leads to bacterial cell death.

2. **Spectrum of Activity:** Metronidazole is particularly effective against anaerobic bacteria, making it useful for treating infections in environments with low oxygen levels. It is commonly used to treat infections in the gastrointestinal tract, gynecological infections, and parasitic infections, such as amebiasis and giardiasis.

3. **Absorption and Distribution:** Metronidazole is well-absorbed when taken orally or administered intravenously. It can penetrate various tissues and body fluids, including the central nervous system.

4. **Metabolism and Excretion:** Metronidazole is primarily metabolized in the liver and excreted in the urine.

5. **Potential Side Effects**: Common side effects of Metronidazole can include gastrointestinal symptoms like nausea and diarrhea. Prolonged use of Metronidazole can lead to peripheral neuropathy. It should not be taken with alcohol, as it can cause a disulfiram-like reaction with symptoms like nausea, vomiting, and headache.

TETRACYCLINE:

1. **Mechanism of Action:** Tetracycline is a broad-spectrum antibiotic that works by inhibiting bacterial protein synthesis. It does so by binding to the 30S ribosomal subunit, preventing the attachment of aminoacyl-tRNA to the mRNA-ribosome complex. This ultimately leads to the inhibition of protein production and bacterial growth.

2. **Spectrum of Activity:** Tetracycline is effective against a wide range of Gram-positive and Gram-negative bacteria. It is commonly used to treat respiratory tract infections, skin and soft tissue infections, and other bacterial infections. It is also used for the treatment of certain atypical pathogens like Mycoplasma pneumoniae and Chlamydia trachomatis.

3. **Absorption and Distribution:** Tetracycline is well-absorbed when taken orally, but its absorption can be affected by the presence of food, calcium, and antacids. It can penetrate many body tissues, including the respiratory tract, urinary tract, and skin.

4. **Metabolism and Excretion:** Tetracycline is primarily excreted in the urine and, to a lesser extent, in the bile.

5. **Potential Side Effects:** Common side effects of Tetracycline may include gastrointestinal symptoms, such as nausea, vomiting, and diarrhea. Prolonged use of Tetracycline can result in tooth discoloration, especially in children. It can also make the skin more sensitive to sunlight (photosensitivity), leading to sunburn.

REBAMIPIDE:

1. **Mechanism of Action:** Rebamipide is a mucosal protective agent. It exerts its effects by enhancing the production of mucus, bicarbonate, and prostaglandins in the stomach and small intestine. These actions help protect and promote the healing of the mucosal lining, making it more resistant to injury from factors like stomach acid and other irritants.

2. **Therapeutic Uses:** Rebamipide is primarily used to treat gastrointestinal conditions, such as peptic ulcers, gastritis, and gastroesophageal reflux disease (GERD). It is particularly useful for the treatment of mucosal damage caused by nonsteroidal anti-inflammatory drugs (NSAIDs) and Helicobacter pylori infection.

3. **Absorption and Distribution:** Rebamipide is well-absorbed when taken orally and undergoes rapid absorption and distribution to the gastrointestinal mucosa, where it exerts its protective effects.

4. **Metabolism and Excretion:** Rebamipide is metabolized in the liver and excreted in the urine.

5. **Potential Side Effects:** Common side effects of Rebamipide may include gastrointestinal symptoms like diarrhea and nausea.

CHAPTER – 3

DRUGS FOR CONSTIPATION AND DIARRHEA

Mrs. Kiran Shukla

Associate Professor, Rajiv Gandhi Institute of Pharmacy, Faculty of Pharmaceutical Science & Technology, AKS University Satna, MP-India

ABSTRACT:

Drugs for managing constipation and diarrhea are crucial in treating gastrointestinal disorders that disrupt normal bowel function. Constipation is commonly treated with laxatives, which are classified into several types based on their mechanisms of action: bulk-forming agents (e.g., psyllium), which increase stool bulk and promote peristalsis; osmotic laxatives (e.g., polyethylene glycol), which draw water into the bowel to soften stools; stimulant laxatives (e.g., bisacodyl), which stimulate intestinal motility; and stool softeners (e.g., docusate), which facilitate the mixing of water and fat with stools. On the other hand, diarrhea is managed with antidiarrheal agents like loperamide, which slows intestinal motility, and bismuth subsalicylate, which reduces inflammation and has antimicrobial properties. Additionally, probiotics can restore normal gut flora, and oral rehydration solutions (ORS) are used to prevent dehydration. Each class of these drugs has specific therapeutic uses and potential side effects, making it essential to tailor treatment based on the underlying cause and severity of the symptoms. Effective management of these conditions can significantly improve patient comfort and health outcomes.

Introduction:

Drugs for constipation are medications used to relieve and manage constipation, which is characterized by infrequent, difficult, or painful bowel movements. These drugs work by various mechanisms to stimulate bowel movements, soften stools, and promote regular defecation.

Drugs for Constipation:

1. Constipation is a condition characterized by infrequent bowel movements, hard stools, and difficulty in passing stool. Drugs used to treat constipation can be categorized into several classes, including:

a. **Laxatives:** These medications promote bowel movements by either softening the stool, increasing intestinal motility, or adding bulk to the stool. Common laxative types include bulk-forming laxatives (e.g., psyllium), osmotic laxatives (e.g., magnesium hydroxide), stimulant laxatives (e.g., bisacodyl), and lubricant laxatives (e.g., mineral oil).

b. **Stool softeners:** These drugs, such as docusate sodium, help make the stool easier to pass by increasing its moisture content.

c. **Prokinetics:** Some drugs, like prucalopride, can help increase intestinal motility and relieve constipation.

d. **Opioid receptor antagonists:** Medications like naloxegol and methylnaltrexone can be used to alleviate constipation caused by opioid pain medications.

CLASSIFICATION

Drugs for Constipation:

1. **Laxatives:**

a. **Bulk-Forming Laxatives:** These increase stool bulk and soften it. Examples include psyllium (Metamucil) and methylcellulose (Citrucel).

b. **Osmotic Laxatives:** They draw water into the intestines to soften stool and promote bowel movements. Examples include magnesium hydroxide (Milk of Magnesia) and polyethylene glycol (MiraLAX).

c. **Stimulant Laxatives:** These stimulate intestinal contractions, leading to bowel movements. Examples include bisacodyl (Dulcolax) and senna (Senokot).

d. **Lubricant Laxatives:** These help stool move more smoothly through the intestines. Mineral oil is an example.

2. **Stool Softeners:**

    a. **Docusate Sodium (Colace):** This medication helps soften the stool, making it easier to pass.

3. **Prokinetics:**

    a. **Prucalopride (Resolor):** It stimulates intestinal motility and can be used for chronic constipation.

4. **Opioid Receptor Antagonists:**

    a. **Naloxegol (Movantik) and Methylnaltrexone (Relistor):** These are used to treat opioid-induced constipation.

Classification of Drugs for Constipation

1. **Bulk-Forming Laxatives**
2. **Osmotic Laxatives**
3. **Stimulant Laxatives**
4. **Stool Softeners**
5. **Lubricant Laxatives**
6. **Prokinetic Agents**
7. **Chloride Channel Activators**
8. **Guanylate Cyclase-C Agonists**

Pharmacology of Drugs for Constipation

1. Bulk-Forming Laxatives

Examples: Psyllium, Methylcellulose, Polycarbophil

Mechanism of Action: Bulk-forming laxatives are indigestible fibers that absorb water in the intestine, increasing stool bulk and promoting peristalsis. The increased stool mass stimulates bowel movements.

Uses: Treatment of chronic constipation, irritable bowel syndrome (IBS) with constipation, and as a preventive measure for patients who should avoid straining during defecation.

Side Effects: Bloating, gas, and potential for intestinal obstruction if not taken with adequate fluids.

2. Osmotic Laxatives

Examples: Polyethylene glycol (PEG), Lactulose, Magnesium hydroxide, Sorbitol

Mechanism of Action: Osmotic laxatives draw water into the bowel lumen by osmosis, increasing the water content of stools and promoting bowel movements.

Uses: Short-term relief of constipation, bowel preparation before diagnostic procedures, and management of chronic constipation.

Side Effects: Bloating, diarrhea, electrolyte imbalance (with prolonged use), and dehydration.

3. Stimulant Laxatives

Examples: Bisacodyl, Senna, Cascara sagrada

Mechanism of Action: Stimulant laxatives increase intestinal motility by directly stimulating the enteric nerves, and they also promote the accumulation of water and electrolytes in the bowel lumen.

Uses: Short-term relief of acute constipation and bowel preparation before diagnostic procedures.

Side Effects: Abdominal cramping, diarrhea, electrolyte imbalance, and potential for dependency with prolonged use.

4. Stool Softeners

Examples: Docusate sodium, Docusate calcium

Mechanism of Action: Stool softeners act as surfactants, reducing the surface tension of stools and allowing water and fats to penetrate and soften them, making bowel movements easier.

Uses: Prevention of constipation in patients who should avoid straining, such as those recovering from surgery or childbirth.

Side Effects: Generally well-tolerated, but may cause mild abdominal cramping and diarrhea.

5. Lubricant Laxatives

Examples: Mineral oil

Mechanism of Action: Lubricant laxatives coat the stool and the intestinal lining with a waterproof film, which helps retain moisture in the stool and ease its passage through the intestines.

Uses: Short-term relief of constipation, especially in patients with anal fissures or hemorrhoids.

Side Effects: Risk of lipid pneumonia if aspirated, decreased absorption of fat-soluble vitamins (A, D, E, K), and potential anal leakage.

6. Prokinetic Agents

Examples: Prucalopride

Mechanism of Action: Prokinetic agents stimulate serotonin receptors (5-HT4) in the gastrointestinal tract, enhancing peristalsis and promoting bowel movements.

Uses: Treatment of chronic constipation, particularly in patients with slow-transit constipation.

Side Effects: Headache, abdominal pain, nausea, and diarrhea.

7. Chloride Channel Activators

Examples: Lubiprostone

Mechanism of Action: Chloride channel activators increase the secretion of chloride ions into the intestinal lumen, followed by sodium and water, resulting in softer stools and increased bowel movements.

Uses: Treatment of chronic idiopathic constipation and IBS with constipation.

Side Effects: Nausea, diarrhea, abdominal pain, and headache.

8. Guanylate Cyclase-C Agonists

Examples: Linaclotide, Plecanatide

Mechanism of Action: These drugs activate guanylate cyclase-C receptors on the luminal surface of the intestinal epithelium, increasing cyclic GMP levels, which stimulates chloride and bicarbonate secretion into the intestinal lumen, resulting in increased intestinal fluid and accelerated transit.

Uses: Treatment of chronic idiopathic constipation and IBS with constipation.

Side Effects: Diarrhea, abdominal pain, flatulence, and bloating.

Drugs for Diarrhea:

1. Diarrhea is characterized by frequent and loose bowel movements. Drugs for treating diarrhea can be grouped as follows:

a. **Anti-diarrheal agents:** These drugs aim to slow down bowel movements and reduce the frequency of loose stools. Loperamide (Imodium) is a common over-the-counter anti-diarrheal medication.

b. **Antispasmodic agents:** Medications like dicyclomine can help alleviate cramps and abdominal pain associated with diarrhea.

c. **Antibiotics:** In cases of infectious diarrhea caused by bacteria, specific antibiotics may be prescribed to treat the underlying infection.

Drugs for Diarrhea:

1. **Anti-Diarrheal Agents:**

   a. **Loperamide (Imodium):** It slows down bowel movements and reduces diarrhea.

   b. **Bismuth Subsalicylate (Pepto-Bismol):** It can relieve symptoms of traveler's diarrhea and mild gastrointestinal distress.

2. **Antispasmodic Agents:**

   a. **Dicyclomine (Bentyl):** It helps alleviate abdominal cramps and discomfort associated with diarrhea.

3. **Antibiotics:**

   a. Antibiotics may be used to treat infectious diarrhea caused by specific bacteria, such as ciprofloxacin for travelers' diarrhea.

DRUGS FOR DIARRHEA:

Loperamide (Imodium):

1. **Mechanism of Action:**

   a. Loperamide is an opioid receptor agonist, but it acts primarily on the mu-opioid receptors in the intestines, which are distinct from the mu-opioid receptors in the brain.

   b. It reduces peristalsis (intestinal contractions) and increases the tone of the intestinal muscles, leading to a decrease in stool frequency and improved stool consistency.

2. **Effect on Diarrhea:**

   a. Loperamide slows down the transit time of stool through the intestines, allowing for more water absorption and leading to firmer stools.

   b. This results in the reduction of diarrhea symptoms and the normalization of bowel movements.

3. **Clinical Indications:**

a. Loperamide is used to manage acute and chronic diarrhea, including traveler's diarrhea and irritable bowel syndrome with diarrhea (IBS-D).

Bismuth Subsalicylate (Pepto-Bismol):

1. Mechanism of Action:

a. Bismuth subsalicylate has multiple mechanisms of action, including antimicrobial and anti-inflammatory effects.

b. It helps reduce inflammation in the gastrointestinal tract and inhibit the growth of certain bacteria that can cause diarrhea.

2. Effect on Diarrhea:

a. Bismuth subsalicylate has a multifaceted approach to managing diarrhea. It can decrease the frequency and volume of stools by addressing the underlying causes.

b. Additionally, it can provide a coating or protective layer over the irritated intestinal mucosa, reducing discomfort and symptoms of diarrhea.

3. Clinical Indications:

a. Bismuth subsalicylate is used to relieve symptoms associated with acute, traveler's, and infectious diarrhea. It can also provide relief from stomach upset, indigestion, and nausea.

Dicyclomine (Bentyl):

1. Mechanism of Action:

a. Dicyclomine is an anticholinergic medication that acts as a muscarinic receptor antagonist.

b. It blocks the action of acetylcholine, a neurotransmitter, on muscarinic receptors in the smooth muscles of the gastrointestinal tract.

2. Effect on Gastrointestinal Muscles:

a. Dicyclomine helps to relax and reduce the spasms of the gastrointestinal muscles.

b. By blocking the muscarinic receptors, it decreases the uncontrolled contractions of the gastrointestinal muscles, which can cause cramps and abdominal pain.

3. **Clinical Indications:**

a. Dicyclomine is primarily used for the relief of irritable bowel syndrome (IBS) symptoms, including abdominal pain, cramps, and gastrointestinal muscle spasms.

Ciprofloxacin:

1. **Mechanism of Action:**

a. Ciprofloxacin is a broad-spectrum fluoroquinolone antibiotic.

b. It works by inhibiting the action of bacterial DNA gyrase and topoisomerase IV, enzymes necessary for DNA replication and repair in bacteria.

2. **Effect on Bacterial Growth:**

a. Ciprofloxacin kills or inhibits the growth of susceptible bacteria by disrupting their DNA replication and repair processes.

b. It is effective against a wide range of bacteria, making it useful for treating various bacterial infections.

3. **Clinical Indications:**

a. Ciprofloxacin is used to treat a variety of bacterial infections, including urinary tract infections, respiratory tract infections, gastrointestinal infections, skin and soft tissue infections, and certain sexually transmitted infections.

CHAPTER – 4

APPETITE STIMULANTS AND SUPPRESSANT

Mrs. Shaily Goyal

Associate Professor, Rajiv Gandhi Institute of Pharmacy, Faculty of Pharmaceutical Science & Technology, AKS University Satna, MP-India

ABSTRACT:

Appetite stimulants and suppressants are medications used to manage weight-related conditions by either increasing or decreasing appetite. Appetite stimulants, such as megestrol acetate and cyproheptadine, are often used in patients experiencing significant weight loss due to chronic illnesses like cancer or HIV/AIDS. These drugs work by interacting with hormones and neurotransmitters that regulate hunger, helping to improve nutritional intake and body weight. On the other hand, appetite suppressants, like phentermine and liraglutide, are used to aid weight loss in obese patients. These medications act on the central nervous system to reduce hunger signals, promoting a feeling of fullness and decreasing caloric intake. Both types of drugs play vital roles in managing weight but must be used cautiously due to potential side effects. Stimulants can cause edema and hormonal imbalances, while suppressants may lead to increased heart rate, insomnia, and gastrointestinal issues. Understanding the pharmacology of these agents is essential for their safe and effective use in treating appetite and weight disorders, ensuring that the benefits outweigh the risks for each patient.

Appetite Stimulants:

1. **Megestrol Acetate (Megace):** A synthetic progestin used to stimulate appetite and weight gain in individuals with involuntary weight loss.

2. **Dronabinol (Marinol):** It contains synthetic cannabinoids and is used to stimulate appetite, particularly in patients with cancer or AIDS-related anorexia.

3. **Mirtazapine (Remeron):** An antidepressant that can increase appetite as a side effect and may be prescribed to individuals with depression and poor appetite.

Appetite Suppressants:

1. **Phentermine (Adipex-P, Suprenza):** A central nervous system stimulant that reduces appetite and is used for short-term weight loss.

2. **Orlistat (Alli, Xenical):** This medication inhibits the absorption of dietary fats and is used to promote weight loss by reducing calorie intake.

3. **Lorcaserin (Belviq):** A serotonin receptor agonist that helps control appetite and is used for weight management in obese or overweight individuals. Please note that lorcaserin was voluntarily withdrawn from the market in February 2020 due to safety concerns.

Appetite Stimulants:

Appetite stimulants are medications used to increase appetite and promote weight gain in individuals experiencing significant weight loss or poor appetite due to medical conditions such as cancer, HIV/AIDS, chronic illnesses, or certain psychological disorders. These medications help enhance the desire to eat and can improve nutritional intake and overall health.

Classification of Appetite Stimulants

1. Hormonal Agents
   - Megestrol Acetate
   - Corticosteroids
2. Antihistamines
   - Cyproheptadine

3. Antidepressants

o Mirtazapine

4. Cannabinoids

o Dronabinol

5. Other Agents

o Anabolic Steroids

Pharmacology of Appetite Stimulants

1. Hormonal Agents

Megestrol Acetate

- Mechanism of Action: Megestrol acetate is a synthetic progestin that increases appetite through its effects on the hypothalamus and its potential to modulate various hormones involved in appetite regulation.
- Uses: Treatment of anorexia, cachexia, and significant weight loss in patients with cancer or HIV/AIDS.
- Side Effects: Weight gain, edema, thromboembolic events, and hormonal imbalances.

Corticosteroids

- Examples: Prednisone, Dexamethasone
- Mechanism of Action: Corticosteroids increase appetite by reducing inflammation and modulating the hypothalamic-pituitary-adrenal (HPA) axis, which can influence hunger signals.
- Uses: Short-term appetite stimulation in patients with cancer or chronic inflammatory diseases.
- Side Effects: Hyperglycemia, osteoporosis, hypertension, and increased risk of infection.

2. Antihistamines

Cyproheptadine

- Mechanism of Action: Cyproheptadine is a first-generation antihistamine with antiserotonergic properties. It increases appetite by antagonizing serotonin receptors that suppress hunger.
- Uses: Appetite stimulation in patients with anorexia or weight loss due to chronic illness.
- Side Effects: Sedation, dry mouth, dizziness, and weight gain.

3. Antidepressants

Mirtazapine

- Mechanism of Action: Mirtazapine is a tetracyclic antidepressant that increases appetite by antagonizing central presynaptic alpha-2 adrenergic receptors, serotonin receptors (5-HT2 and 5-HT3), and histamine receptors.
- Uses: Treatment of depression with concurrent appetite stimulation and weight gain.
- Side Effects: Sedation, increased appetite, weight gain, and dry mouth.

4. Cannabinoids

Dronabinol

- Mechanism of Action: Dronabinol is a synthetic form of delta-9-tetrahydrocannabinol (THC), the active component of cannabis. It stimulates appetite by activating cannabinoid receptors in the brain.
- Uses: Appetite stimulation in patients with AIDS-related anorexia and chemotherapy-induced nausea and vomiting.

- Side Effects: Euphoria, dizziness, paranoia, and potential for abuse.

5. Other Agents

Anabolic Steroids

- Examples: Oxandrolone
- Mechanism of Action: Anabolic steroids promote muscle growth and weight gain by increasing protein synthesis and muscle mass.
- Uses: Treatment of severe weight loss and muscle wasting in patients with chronic diseases.
- Side Effects: Liver toxicity, hormonal imbalances, and potential for abuse.

Appetite Suppressants:

Appetite suppressants are medications or substances that reduce hunger, decrease food intake, and aid in weight loss. These agents are commonly used as part of a comprehensive weight management program for individuals with obesity or overweight conditions. Appetite suppressants work by influencing the central nervous system to decrease appetite or increase feelings of fullness.

Classification of Appetite Suppressants

1. Central Nervous System Stimulants
o Sympathomimetic Amines
o Serotonin-Norepinephrine Reuptake Inhibitors (SNRIs)
2. Serotonin Agonists
o Selective Serotonin 5-HT2C Receptor Agonists
3. Glucagon-Like Peptide-1 (GLP-1) Receptor Agonists
o GLP-1 Agonists
4. Combination Drugs

    o Combination of Central Nervous System Stimulants and Other Agents

Pharmacology of Appetite Suppressants

1. Central Nervous System Stimulants

Sympathomimetic Amines

Examples: Phentermine, Diethylpropion

Mechanism of Action: These drugs stimulate the release of norepinephrine and dopamine in the hypothalamus, leading to reduced appetite and increased energy expenditure by activating the "fight or flight" response.

Uses: Short-term treatment of obesity.

Side Effects: Increased heart rate, elevated blood pressure, insomnia, nervousness, and potential for abuse and dependence.

Serotonin-Norepinephrine Reuptake Inhibitors (SNRIs)

Example: Sibutramine (withdrawn from the market due to cardiovascular risks)

Mechanism of Action: These drugs inhibit the reuptake of serotonin and norepinephrine, increasing their levels in the brain and promoting a feeling of satiety.

Uses: (Previously used) Treatment of obesity.

Side Effects: Increased heart rate, elevated blood pressure, dry mouth, constipation, and insomnia.

2. Serotonin Agonists

Selective Serotonin 5-HT2C Receptor Agonists

Example: Lorcaserin (withdrawn from the market due to cancer risk concerns)

Mechanism of Action: Lorcaserin selectively activates serotonin 5-HT2C receptors in the brain, which helps increase feelings of fullness and reduce food intake.

Uses: (Previously used) Treatment of obesity.

Side Effects: Headache, dizziness, fatigue, nausea, and potential psychiatric effects.

3. Glucagon-Like Peptide-1 (GLP-1) Receptor Agonists

GLP-1 Agonists

Examples: Liraglutide, Semaglutide

Mechanism of Action: These drugs mimic the action of GLP-1, a hormone that promotes insulin secretion, slows gastric emptying, and increases feelings of fullness, thereby reducing appetite.

Uses: Treatment of obesity and type 2 diabetes.

Side Effects: Nausea, vomiting, diarrhea, constipation, and potential risk of pancreatitis.

4. Combination Drugs

Examples: Phentermine/Topiramate (Qsymia), Bupropion/Naltrexone (Contrave)

Mechanism of Action: Combination drugs use multiple mechanisms to reduce appetite and promote weight loss. For example:

- Phentermine/Topiramate: Combines the appetite-suppressing effects of phentermine with the anticonvulsant and weight-loss-promoting effects of topiramate.
- Bupropion/Naltrexone: Combines bupropion's effects on dopamine and norepinephrine with naltrexone's effects on the opioid system, both contributing to appetite suppression and weight loss.

Uses: Treatment of obesity.

Side Effects: Depends on the individual components but may include increased heart rate, elevated blood pressure, insomnia, dry mouth, dizziness, and gastrointestinal disturbances.

APPETITE STIMULANTS:

Megestrol Acetate:

1. **Mechanism of Action:**
   a. Megestrol acetate is a synthetic progestin, a type of hormone related to progesterone.
   b. It binds to and activates progesterone receptors in the body, influencing various physiological processes.

2. **Effect on Appetite and Weight Gain:**
   a. One of the primary uses of megestrol acetate is as an appetite stimulant.
   b. It is thought to work by increasing appetite and promoting weight gain, particularly in individuals with involuntary weight loss, such as those with cancer or HIV/AIDS.

3. **Clinical Indications:**
   a. Megestrol acetate is prescribed to stimulate appetite and facilitate weight gain in patients with conditions leading to cachexia (severe muscle wasting) or anorexia.

Dronabinol:

1. **Mechanism of Action:**
   a. Dronabinol is a synthetic form of delta-9-tetrahydrocannabinol (THC), the active compound found in cannabis.
   b. It acts on cannabinoid receptors in the central nervous system.

2. **Effect on Appetite and Nausea:**
   a. Dronabinol has appetite-stimulating properties and can alleviate nausea.

b. It is used to boost appetite and reduce nausea and vomiting in patients undergoing chemotherapy or experiencing weight loss associated with conditions like AIDS.

3. Clinical Indications:

a. Dronabinol is primarily prescribed for the management of chemotherapy-**induced** nausea and vomiting, as well as for stimulating appetite in HIV/AIDS patients with associated weight loss.

Mirtazapine:

1. Mechanism of Action:

a. Mirtazapine is an atypical antidepressant that affects various neurotransmitter systems in the brain.

b. It enhances the release of norepinephrine and serotonin while blocking certain serotonin receptors.

2. Effect on Appetite:

a. One of the side effects of mirtazapine is an increase in appetite.

b. This medication can cause weight gain due to its influence on appetite and metabolism.

3. Clinical Indications:

a. Mirtazapine is primarily used to treat depression and other mood disorders. Its appetite-stimulating side effect may be useful for individuals with depression who have reduced appetite and weight loss.

APPETITE SUPPRESSANTS:

Phentermine:

1. Mechanism of Action:

a. Phentermine is a sympathomimetic amine that acts as an appetite suppressant.

b. It primarily works by stimulating the release of norepinephrine in the brain, which leads to decreased appetite and increased feelings of fullness.

2. Effect on Appetite and Weight Loss:

a. Phentermine reduces appetite and promotes weight loss by influencing the central nervous system to decrease hunger and food intake.

b. It may also increase energy expenditure by its sympathomimetic actions.

3. Clinical Indications:

a. Phentermine is prescribed for short-term weight management in individuals with obesity as part of a comprehensive weight loss program, typically for a few weeks to a few months.

Orlistat:

1. Mechanism of Action:

a. Orlistat is a lipase inhibitor.

b. It works by inhibiting pancreatic lipase, an enzyme that breaks down dietary fat in the digestive tract, thus reducing fat absorption.

2. Effect on Fat Absorption and Weight Loss:

a. Orlistat decreases the absorption of dietary fats, leading to a reduced caloric intake from fat.

b. This leads to weight loss and may also result in improvements in lipid profiles.

3. Clinical Indications:

a. Orlistat is used for long-term weight management in individuals with obesity. It is intended for use in conjunction with a reduced-calorie diet and a comprehensive weight loss plan.

Lorcaserin:

1. Mechanism of Action:

a. Lorcaserin is a selective serotonin 5-HT2C receptor agonist.

b. It specifically activates the 5-HT2C receptors in the brain, which play a role in appetite control and satiety.

2. Effect on Appetite and Weight Loss:

a. Lorcaserin works by enhancing the feeling of fullness and reducing hunger.

b. It helps individuals consume fewer calories by moderating their appetite, thus promoting weight loss.

3. Clinical Indications:

a. Lorcaserin was used to treat obesity as an adjunct to diet and exercise. However, it was voluntarily withdrawn from the market in February 2020 due to safety concerns.

CHAPTER – 5

DIGESTANTS AND CARMINATIVES

Mr. Prabhakar Tiwari

Associate Professor, Rajiv Gandhi Institute of Pharmacy, Faculty of Pharmaceutical Science & Technology, AKS University Satna, MP-India

ABSTRCT:

Digestants and carminatives are two categories of medications that aid in the digestive process and alleviate gastrointestinal discomfort, respectively. Digestants, such as pancreatic enzymes and bile salts, help in the breakdown and absorption of food nutrients by supplementing endogenous digestive enzymes. They are particularly useful in conditions like pancreatic insufficiency and bile acid deficiency. Carminatives, on the other hand, are agents that help in expelling gas from the stomach and intestines, thereby relieving bloating and flatulence. Common carminatives include herbs like peppermint, ginger, and fennel, which work by relaxing the gastrointestinal muscles and reducing gas formation. These agents are often used in functional gastrointestinal disorders like irritable bowel syndrome (IBS). Both digestants and carminatives play crucial roles in managing digestive health, improving nutrient absorption, and enhancing overall gastrointestinal comfort. Understanding their uses and mechanisms can help optimize treatment for patients experiencing digestive issues.

Introduction:

Digestants are substances that promote the digestion of food by supplementing or enhancing the action of the body's natural digestive enzymes. They are used to improve the breakdown and absorption of nutrients in patients with digestive disorders where normal enzyme production or function is compromised.

Classification of Digestants

1. **Pancreatic Enzymes**
   o Pancrelipase
   o Pancreatin
2. **Bile Salts**
   o Ursodeoxycholic acid (UDCA)
   o Chenodeoxycholic acid (CDCA)
3. **Acidifying Agents**
   o Hydrochloric acid (Betaine HCl)
   o Glutamic acid hydrochloride
4. **Pepsin Preparations**

Pharmacology of Digestants

1. Pancreatic Enzymes

Pancrelipase

- **Mechanism of Action**: Pancrelipase is a combination of digestive enzymes, including lipase, amylase, and protease, derived from porcine pancreas. These enzymes help break down fats, carbohydrates, and proteins, respectively, facilitating their absorption in the small intestine.
- **Uses**: Treatment of exocrine pancreatic insufficiency (EPI) due to conditions such as cystic fibrosis, chronic pancreatitis, and pancreatectomy.
- **Side Effects**: Gastrointestinal disturbances (nausea, diarrhea, abdominal pain), hyperuricemia, and potential for allergic reactions in patients with pork protein sensitivity.

Pancreatin

- **Mechanism of Action**: Similar to pancrelipase, pancreatin contains a mixture of digestive enzymes that assist in the breakdown of dietary macronutrients.
- **Uses**: Treatment of pancreatic insufficiency and as a digestive aid in patients with malabsorption syndromes.
- **Side Effects**: Similar to pancrelipase, with gastrointestinal discomfort and risk of allergic reactions.

2. Bile Salts

Ursodeoxycholic Acid (UDCA)

- **Mechanism of Action**: UDCA is a naturally occurring bile acid that reduces cholesterol absorption and improves bile flow. It helps dissolve cholesterol gallstones and improves liver function in certain liver diseases.
- **Uses**: Treatment of primary biliary cholangitis, dissolution of small cholesterol gallstones, and as adjunctive therapy in certain liver disorders.
- **Side Effects**: Diarrhea, nausea, abdominal pain, and rare liver toxicity.

Chenodeoxycholic Acid (CDCA)

- **Mechanism of Action**: CDCA is another primary bile acid that helps dissolve cholesterol gallstones by reducing cholesterol saturation in bile.
- **Uses**: Dissolution of cholesterol gallstones and as part of therapy in certain bile acid synthesis disorders.
- **Side Effects**: Diarrhea, liver toxicity, and elevated cholesterol levels.

3. Acidifying Agents

Hydrochloric Acid (Betaine HCl)

- **Mechanism of Action**: Betaine HCl supplements the stomach's natural hydrochloric acid, enhancing the acidic environment necessary for the activation of pepsin and effective protein digestion.
- **Uses**: Treatment of hypochlorhydria (low stomach acid) and as a digestive aid.
- **Side Effects**: Potential for gastrointestinal irritation, peptic ulcers, and acid reflux.

Glutamic Acid Hydrochloride

- **Mechanism of Action**: Similar to betaine HCl, it provides additional hydrochloric acid to aid in the digestion of proteins by activating pepsin.
- **Uses**: Treatment of hypochlorhydria and as a digestive aid.
- **Side Effects**: Similar to betaine HCl, with risk of gastrointestinal irritation.

4. Pepsin Preparations

Pepsin

- **Mechanism of Action**: Pepsin is a proteolytic enzyme that breaks down proteins into smaller peptides in the acidic environment of the stomach.
- **Uses**: Supplementation in cases of pepsin deficiency or as a digestive aid.
- **Side Effects**: Generally well-tolerated, but excessive use can lead to gastrointestinal irritation.

DIGESTANTS:

Amylase:

1. Mechanism of Action:

a. Amylase is an enzyme that plays a crucial role in the digestion of carbohydrates, specifically starches and complex carbohydrates.

b. It works by breaking down long chains of carbohydrates into shorter chains and individual sugar molecules (glucose, maltose, and others).

2. **Pharmacological Use:**

a. Exogenous (supplemental) amylase is not commonly used in pharmacology because the body naturally produces amylase in the salivary glands and pancreas.

b. However, in some medical conditions, such as pancreatic insufficiency, where the pancreas does not produce sufficient amylase, pancreatic enzyme replacement therapy (PERT) may be prescribed to aid in digestion.

3. **Administration:**

a. Amylase is typically administered orally in the form of digestive enzyme supplements, which may contain various enzymes, including amylase, protease, and lipase.

Protease:

1. **Mechanism of Action:**

a. Protease is an enzyme responsible for the digestion of proteins into smaller peptides and individual amino acids.

b. It breaks the peptide bonds between amino acids in proteins, cleaving them into smaller fragments that can be absorbed in the small intestine.

2. **Pharmacological Use:**

a. Exogenous protease is not commonly used as a medication.

b. However, protease enzymes are included in digestive enzyme supplements, especially in cases where individuals have difficulty digesting proteins due to pancreatic insufficiency or other gastrointestinal disorders.

3. Administration:

a. Protease is typically administered orally, often in combination with other digestive enzymes like amylase and lipase, to support the digestion of proteins.

4. Clinical Considerations:

a. The use of exogenous amylase and protease is mainly seen in conditions where the natural production of these enzymes by the body is compromised. This can occur in diseases like cystic fibrosis, chronic pancreatitis, or after certain surgical procedures that affect the pancreas.

Salivary Amylase:

1. Mechanism of Action:

a. Salivary amylase, also known as α-amylase, is an enzyme produced in the salivary glands.

b. Its primary function is to initiate the digestion of carbohydrates, particularly starches.

c. Salivary amylase breaks down complex carbohydrates into simpler sugars like maltose and dextrin by cleaving the alpha-1,4 glycosidic bonds in the starch molecules.

2. Pharmacological Use:

a. Salivary amylase itself is not typically used as a pharmacological agent.

b. However, some pharmaceuticals or medical conditions may affect salivary amylase production, and treatments may be directed toward improving salivary function or managing conditions that reduce salivary flow.

3. Administration:

a. In cases where salivary flow is compromised due to conditions like Sjögren's syndrome or medication side effects, treatments may include artificial saliva (saliva substitutes) or medications that stimulate salivary flow.

Pepsin:

1. Mechanism of Action:

    a. Pepsin is an enzyme produced in the stomach, particularly in its chief cells.

    b. Its primary function is to break down proteins into smaller peptides by cleaving peptide bonds.

    c. Pepsin works optimally in the acidic environment of the stomach, helping to digest dietary proteins into smaller fragments that can be further broken down in the small intestine.

2. Pharmacological Use:

    a. Pharmacologically, pepsin itself is not typically used as a medication.

    b. However, pepsin inhibitors may be considered in cases of gastric disorders associated with excessive stomach acid production.

3. Clinical Considerations:

    a. Pepsin inhibitors or proton pump inhibitors (PPIs) are sometimes used to reduce excessive gastric acid production and, indirectly, pepsin activity in conditions like gastroesophageal reflux disease (GERD) or peptic ulcers.

Intestinal Lipase:

1. Mechanism of Action:

    a. Intestinal lipase, also known as pancreatic lipase or pancreatic triglyceride lipase, is an enzyme produced in the pancreas.

    b. Its primary function is to break down dietary fats (triglycerides) into fatty acids and glycerol.

    c. Intestinal lipase works in the small intestine and is especially important for the absorption of dietary fats, which are then absorbed into the bloodstream.

2. Pharmacological Use:

a. Exogenous (supplemental) intestinal lipase is not commonly used in pharmacology because the body naturally produces it.

b. However, in some medical conditions like pancreatic insufficiency, where the pancreas does not produce sufficient enzymes, pancreatic enzyme replacement therapy (PERT) may be prescribed, which includes lipase.

Digestive Enzyme Supplements:

Digestive enzyme supplements are medications or dietary supplements that provide additional digestive enzymes to aid in the breakdown and absorption of nutrients. These supplements are used to manage conditions where the body's natural production of digestive enzymes is insufficient, leading to malabsorption and digestive discomfort.

Classification of Digestive Enzyme Supplements

1. **Pancreatic Enzyme Supplements**
   - Pancrelipase
   - Pancreatin
2. **Proteolytic Enzyme Supplements**
   - Bromelain
   - Papain
3. **Lactase Supplements**
   - Lactase
4. **Other Specific Enzyme Supplements**
   - Alpha-Galactosidase
   - Lipase

Pharmacology of Digestive Enzyme Supplements

1. Pancreatic Enzyme Supplements

Pancrelipase

- **Mechanism of Action**: Pancrelipase is a mixture of digestive enzymes (lipase, amylase, and protease) derived from porcine pancreas. It helps digest fats, carbohydrates, and proteins, improving nutrient absorption in the small intestine.
- **Uses**: Treatment of exocrine pancreatic insufficiency (EPI) due to cystic fibrosis, chronic pancreatitis, pancreatectomy, and other conditions.
- **Side Effects**: Gastrointestinal disturbances (nausea, diarrhea, abdominal pain), potential for allergic reactions, and hyperuricemia.

Pancreatin

- **Mechanism of Action**: Similar to pancrelipase, pancreatin contains a combination of lipase, amylase, and protease enzymes. It aids in the digestion of dietary fats, carbohydrates, and proteins.
- **Uses**: Treatment of pancreatic insufficiency and malabsorption syndromes.
- **Side Effects**: Gastrointestinal discomfort, risk of allergic reactions, and potential for hyperuricemia.

2. Proteolytic Enzyme Supplements

Bromelain

- **Mechanism of Action**: Bromelain is a mixture of proteolytic enzymes derived from pineapple stems. It aids in the digestion of proteins by breaking them down into smaller peptides and amino acids.
- **Uses**: Digestive aid, anti-inflammatory agent, and treatment of digestive disorders.

- **Side Effects**: Gastrointestinal upset, allergic reactions (especially in individuals allergic to pineapple), and increased risk of bleeding.

Papain

- **Mechanism of Action**: Papain is a proteolytic enzyme derived from papaya fruit. It breaks down proteins into smaller peptides and amino acids, facilitating their digestion.
- **Uses**: Digestive aid and treatment of protein digestion disorders.
- **Side Effects**: Gastrointestinal irritation, allergic reactions, and potential for mouth and throat irritation if taken in large quantities.

3. Lactase Supplements

Lactase

- **Mechanism of Action**: Lactase is an enzyme that breaks down lactose, a sugar found in milk and dairy products, into glucose and galactose. It helps individuals with lactose intolerance digest lactose and reduce symptoms such as bloating, gas, and diarrhea.
- **Uses**: Treatment of lactose intolerance.
- **Side Effects**: Generally well-tolerated, but excessive use may cause gastrointestinal discomfort.

4. Other Specific Enzyme Supplements

Alpha-Galactosidase

- **Mechanism of Action**: Alpha-galactosidase breaks down complex carbohydrates, such as those found in beans and vegetables, into simpler sugars, reducing gas production and digestive discomfort.

- **Uses**: Prevention of gas and bloating associated with consumption of gas-producing foods.
- **Side Effects**: Generally well-tolerated, but excessive use may cause gastrointestinal discomfort.

Lipase

- **Mechanism of Action**: Lipase is an enzyme that breaks down dietary fats into fatty acids and glycerol, aiding in fat digestion and absorption.
- **Uses**: Treatment of fat malabsorption syndromes and as part of pancreatic enzyme replacement therapy.
- **Side Effects**: Gastrointestinal discomfort and potential for allergic reactions.

CARMINATIVES:

Definition

Carminatives are substances that help expel gas from the gastrointestinal tract, thereby relieving bloating, flatulence, and abdominal discomfort. They work by relaxing the intestinal muscles, reducing gas production, and facilitating the expulsion of gas.

Classification of Carminatives

1. **Herbal Carminatives**
   - Peppermint
   - Fennel
   - Ginger
   - Caraway
   - Anise
   - Chamomile

2. **Pharmaceutical Carminatives**

o Simethicone

Pharmacology of Carminatives

1. Herbal Carminatives

Peppermint (Mentha piperita)

- **Mechanism of Action**: Peppermint contains menthol, which relaxes the smooth muscles of the gastrointestinal tract and has antispasmodic properties. This reduces spasms and allows trapped gas to pass more easily.
- **Uses**: Treatment of irritable bowel syndrome (IBS), indigestion, and flatulence.
- **Side Effects**: Heartburn, allergic reactions, and in some cases, exacerbation of gastroesophageal reflux disease (GERD).

Fennel (Foeniculum vulgare)

- **Mechanism of Action**: Fennel contains anethole, which relaxes the smooth muscles of the intestines and has mild diuretic properties. It also stimulates bile flow, aiding digestion.
- **Uses**: Relief of bloating, flatulence, colic in infants, and digestive discomfort.
- **Side Effects**: Allergic reactions, photosensitivity, and potential estrogenic effects.

Ginger (Zingiber officinale)

- **Mechanism of Action**: Ginger contains gingerols and shogaols, which have carminative and anti-inflammatory properties. It enhances gastric motility and accelerates gastric emptying, reducing bloating and gas.
- **Uses**: Treatment of nausea, indigestion, and flatulence.
- **Side Effects**: Heartburn, diarrhea, and potential interactions with anticoagulant medications.

Caraway (Carum carvi)

- **Mechanism of Action**: Caraway contains carvone and limonene, which have antispasmodic and carminative properties. It helps relax gastrointestinal muscles and promotes the expulsion of gas.
- **Uses**: Relief of bloating, flatulence, and digestive discomfort.
- **Side Effects**: Allergic reactions, especially in individuals allergic to other plants in the Apiaceae family.

Anise (Pimpinella anisum)

- **Mechanism of Action**: Anise contains anethole, which has carminative, antispasmodic, and mild sedative effects. It helps relax the gastrointestinal tract and reduce gas.
- **Uses**: Treatment of indigestion, flatulence, and colic.
- **Side Effects**: Allergic reactions and potential estrogenic effects.

Chamomile (Matricaria chamomilla)

- **Mechanism of Action**: Chamomile contains bisabolol and flavonoids, which have anti-inflammatory, antispasmodic, and carminative properties. It soothes the gastrointestinal tract and reduces gas.
- **Uses**: Treatment of indigestion, bloating, and colic.

- **Side Effects**: Allergic reactions, especially in individuals allergic to ragweed, chrysanthemums, marigolds, or daisies.

2. Pharmaceutical Carminatives

Simethicone

- **Mechanism of Action**: Simethicone is an anti-foaming agent that reduces the surface tension of gas bubbles in the gastrointestinal tract, causing them to coalesce and be expelled more easily.
- **Uses**: Relief of bloating, pressure, and discomfort associated with excess gas in the stomach and intestines.
- **Side Effects**: Generally well-tolerated, with rare side effects including mild gastrointestinal disturbances.

CHAPTER – 6

EMETICS AND ANTI-EMETICS

Mrs. Priyanka Gupta

Associate Professor, Rajiv Gandhi Institute of Pharmacy, Faculty of

Pharmaceutical Science & Technology, AKS University Satna, MP-India

ABSTRACT:

Emetics and antiemetics are two classes of medications that serve opposite purposes in managing nausea and vomiting. Emetics, such as ipecac syrup, induce vomiting and are used primarily in certain poisoning cases to expel ingested toxins from the stomach. However, their use has declined due to the potential risks and the availability of more effective treatments. Antiemetics, on the other hand, are used to prevent or alleviate nausea and vomiting associated with various conditions, including chemotherapy, postoperative recovery, and motion sickness. These medications are classified based on their mechanisms of action, including serotonin (5-HT3) receptor antagonists like ondansetron, dopamine antagonists like metoclopramide, antihistamines like diphenhydramine, and anticholinergics like scopolamine. Each class targets different pathways involved in the vomiting reflex, providing comprehensive management options for different causes of nausea. Understanding the pharmacology, therapeutic uses, and potential side effects of emetics and antiemetics is essential for effective and safe treatment of nausea and vomiting, enhancing patient comfort and outcomes in various clinical scenarios.

Intoduction:

Emetics are substances or medications that induce vomiting in individuals. They are typically used to help remove ingested toxins or irritants from the stomach by triggering the body's natural reflex to expel the contents of the stomach through the mouth. Emetics are sometimes administered in cases of accidental poisoning or overdose.

Anti-emetics, on the other hand, are medications or treatments designed to prevent or alleviate nausea and vomiting. They are often used in various clinical settings, such as to manage side effects of chemotherapy, control motion sickness, or relieve nausea associated with pregnancy (morning sickness) or post-operative recovery. Anti-emetics work by blocking or reducing the signals that trigger the vomiting reflex in the body, helping individuals feel more comfortable and avoid vomiting.

Emetics

Definition

Emetics are medications that induce vomiting. They are used in certain medical situations to empty the stomach contents, such as in cases of specific types of poisoning or overdose. The use of emetics has become less common with the advent of safer and more effective treatments for poisoning.

Classification of Emetics

1. **Central Acting Emetics**
   - Apomorphine
2. **Peripheral Acting Emetics**
   - Ipecac Syrup

Pharmacology of Emetics

1. Central Acting Emetics

Apomorphine

- **Mechanism of Action**: Apomorphine is a dopamine agonist that stimulates the dopamine receptors in the chemoreceptor trigger zone (CTZ) of the brain, leading to the induction of vomiting.

- **Uses**: Induction of vomiting in cases of poisoning when the patient is conscious and alert.
- **Side Effects**: Respiratory depression, hypotension, sedation, and potential for abuse. It is typically administered via injection and should be used under medical supervision.
- **Contraindications**: Not recommended for use in patients with impaired consciousness, respiratory distress, or those who have ingested corrosive substances or hydrocarbons.

2. Peripheral Acting Emetics

Ipecac Syrup

- **Mechanism of Action**: Ipecac syrup contains emetine and cephaeline, which irritate the gastric mucosa and stimulate the vomiting center in the brain. The combined effect induces vomiting.
- **Uses**: Historically used to induce vomiting in cases of certain poisonings.
- **Side Effects**: Diarrhea, abdominal cramps, prolonged vomiting, and potential for cardiac toxicity with excessive use. It is generally considered outdated and is rarely recommended in modern clinical practice.
- **Contraindications**: Should not be used in patients who are unconscious, have ingested corrosive substances or hydrocarbons, or in cases where vomiting is contraindicated (e.g., risk of aspiration).

Antiemetics

Definition

Antiemetics are medications used to prevent or alleviate nausea and vomiting. These symptoms can be caused by various conditions, including motion sickness, chemotherapy, postoperative recovery, gastrointestinal disorders, and more. Antiemetics work through different mechanisms to target the pathways involved in the vomiting reflex.

Classification of Antiemetics

1. **Serotonin (5-HT3) Receptor Antagonists**
   o Ondansetron
   o Granisetron
   o Palonosetron
2. **Dopamine Antagonists**
   o Metoclopramide
   o Prochlorperazine
   o Domperidone
3. **Antihistamines (H1 Receptor Antagonists)**
   o Diphenhydramine
   o Meclizine
   o Dimenhydrinate
4. **Anticholinergics**
   o Scopolamine
5. **Neurokinin-1 (NK1) Receptor Antagonists**
   o Aprepitant
   o Fosaprepitant
6. **Cannabinoids**
   o Dronabinol
   o Nabilone
7. **Corticosteroids**
   o Dexamethasone
8. **Benzodiazepines**
   o Lorazepam

Pharmacology of Antiemetics

1. Serotonin (5-HT3) Receptor Antagonists

Ondansetron

- **Mechanism of Action**: Ondansetron blocks the serotonin 5-HT3 receptors in the central nervous system and the gastrointestinal tract, preventing nausea and vomiting.
- **Uses**: Prevention and treatment of chemotherapy-induced nausea and vomiting (CINV), postoperative nausea and vomiting (PONV), and radiation-induced nausea and vomiting.
- **Side Effects**: Headache, constipation, dizziness, and QT prolongation.

Granisetron

- **Mechanism of Action**: Similar to ondansetron, granisetron blocks 5-HT3 receptors.
- **Uses**: CINV, PONV, and radiation-induced nausea and vomiting.
- **Side Effects**: Headache, constipation, and potential QT prolongation.

Palonosetron

- **Mechanism of Action**: A newer 5-HT3 receptor antagonist with a longer half-life, it effectively blocks serotonin receptors.
- **Uses**: CINV, PONV.
- **Side Effects**: Headache, constipation, and less potential for QT prolongation compared to older 5-HT3 antagonists.

2. Dopamine Antagonists

Metoclopramide

- **Mechanism of Action**: Blocks dopamine D2 receptors in the chemoreceptor trigger zone (CTZ) and enhances gastrointestinal motility.
- **Uses**: PONV, CINV, gastroparesis, and GERD.
- **Side Effects**: Extrapyramidal symptoms (EPS), drowsiness, fatigue, and diarrhea.

Prochlorperazine

- **Mechanism of Action**: Blocks dopamine D2 receptors in the CTZ.
- **Uses**: Severe nausea and vomiting, migraine-associated nausea.
- **Side Effects**: EPS, sedation, hypotension, and anticholinergic effects.

Domperidone

- **Mechanism of Action**: Blocks peripheral dopamine receptors and increases gastrointestinal motility.
- **Uses**: Nausea and vomiting associated with gastroparesis and other gastrointestinal disorders.
- **Side Effects**: QT prolongation, dry mouth, and abdominal cramps.

3. Antihistamines (H1 Receptor Antagonists)

Diphenhydramine

- **Mechanism of Action**: Blocks H1 receptors in the vestibular system and the CTZ, providing antiemetic effects.
- **Uses**: Motion sickness, vertigo, and PONV.
- **Side Effects**: Sedation, dry mouth, blurred vision, and urinary retention.

Meclizine

- **Mechanism of Action**: Similar to diphenhydramine, it blocks H1 receptors.

- **Uses**: Motion sickness, vertigo.
- **Side Effects**: Drowsiness, dry mouth, and dizziness.

Dimenhydrinate

- **Mechanism of Action**: Combines diphenhydramine and theophylline, blocking H1 receptors.
- **Uses**: Motion sickness, nausea, and vomiting.
- **Side Effects**: Drowsiness, dry mouth, and blurred vision.

4. Anticholinergics

Scopolamine

- **Mechanism of Action**: Blocks muscarinic receptors in the vestibular system and the CTZ, preventing motion sickness.
- **Uses**: Motion sickness, PONV.
- **Side Effects**: Dry mouth, blurred vision, drowsiness, and urinary retention.

5. Neurokinin-1 (NK1) Receptor Antagonists

Aprepitant

- **Mechanism of Action**: Blocks NK1 receptors in the brain, preventing nausea and vomiting.
- **Uses**: CINV, PONV.
- **Side Effects**: Fatigue, hiccups, dizziness, and potential drug interactions.

Fosaprepitant

- **Mechanism of Action**: Prodrug of aprepitant, blocks NK1 receptors.
- **Uses**: CINV, PONV.

- **Side Effects**: Similar to aprepitant, with infusion-related reactions.

6. Cannabinoids

Dronabinol

- **Mechanism of Action**: Activates cannabinoid receptors in the brain, reducing nausea and increasing appetite.
- **Uses**: CINV, anorexia in patients with AIDS.
- **Side Effects**: Euphoria, dizziness, confusion, and potential for abuse.

Nabilone

- **Mechanism of Action**: Synthetic cannabinoid, similar to dronabinol.
- **Uses**: CINV, anorexia.
- **Side Effects**: Similar to dronabinol.

7. Corticosteroids

Dexamethasone

- **Mechanism of Action**: Reduces inflammation and has antiemetic properties, although the exact mechanism is not fully understood.
- **Uses**: CINV, PONV, and as an adjunct to other antiemetics.
- **Side Effects**: Insomnia, increased blood sugar, increased risk of infection, and adrenal suppression with long-term use.

8. Benzodiazepines

Lorazepam

- **Mechanism of Action**: Enhances the inhibitory effects of GABA in the central nervous system, providing anxiolytic and antiemetic effects.

- **Uses**: Anticipatory nausea and vomiting associated with chemotherapy.
- **Side Effects**: Sedation, dizziness, respiratory depression, and potential for dependence.

Dexamethasone:

1. **Pharmacological class**: Dexamethasone is a synthetic corticosteroid and belongs to the class of glucocorticoids.

2. **Mechanism of action:** Dexamethasone exerts its antiemetic effects through multiple mechanisms. It reduces inflammation and suppresses the immune response, particularly in the central nervous system. This anti-inflammatory and immunosuppressive action can help prevent nausea and vomiting caused by chemotherapy.

3. **Clinical uses:** Dexamethasone is commonly used as part of a combination regimen to prevent and treat chemotherapy-induced nausea and vomiting. It is often administered along with other antiemetic medications, such as serotonin (5-HT3) receptor antagonists (e.g., ondansetron) and NK1 receptor antagonists (e.g., aprepitant).

4. **Adverse effects:** Common side effects of dexamethasone can include increased appetite, weight gain, fluid retention, mood changes, and increased risk of infection. Prolonged or high-dose use of corticosteroids like dexamethasone can lead to various side effects, including immune suppression and metabolic changes.

Aprepitant:

1. **Pharmacological class:** Aprepitant is a neurokinin-1 (NK1) receptor antagonist.

2. **Mechanism of action:** Aprepitant works by blocking the action of substance P, a neurotransmitter involved in the emetic (vomiting) reflex. By antagonizing NK1 receptors in the central nervous system, it helps prevent nausea and vomiting, particularly during the delayed phase after chemotherapy.

3. **Clinical uses:** Aprepitant is used in combination with other antiemetic medications to prevent both acute and delayed chemotherapy-induced nausea and vomiting, especially for highly emetogenic chemotherapy regimens.

4. **Adverse effects:** Common side effects of aprepitant can include fatigue, hiccups, and changes in liver enzyme levels. It can also interact with various medications, so it's important for healthcare providers to consider potential drug interactions when prescribing it.

Lorazepam:

1. **Pharmacological class:** Lorazepam is a benzodiazepine, which acts as a central nervous system depressant.

2. **Mechanism of action:** Lorazepam enhances the inhibitory action of gamma-aminobutyric acid (GABA), a neurotransmitter that reduces neuronal excitability. By binding to GABA receptors in the brain, lorazepam increases the calming and sedating effects of GABA, resulting in reduced anxiety and muscle relaxation.

3. **Clinical uses:** Lorazepam is primarily used for its anxiolytic (anxiety-reducing) and sedative properties. It is commonly prescribed to manage anxiety disorders, acute panic attacks, and as a preoperative or perioperative medication to reduce anxiety and induce relaxation. It may also be used as an anti-emetic in some cases, particularly for nausea and vomiting related to anxiety.

4. **Adverse effects:** Common side effects of lorazepam can include drowsiness, dizziness, confusion, and impaired coordination. It may also cause a risk of tolerance, dependence, and withdrawal if used over an extended period or in higher doses.

Dronabinol (THC):

1. **Pharmacological class:** Dronabinol is a synthetic form of tetrahydrocannabinol (THC), the active component in cannabis (marijuana).

2. **Mechanism of action:** Dronabinol, like natural THC, acts on the endocannabinoid system. It binds to cannabinoid receptors, primarily CB1 receptors in the central nervous system. By activating these receptors, it can have various effects, including reducing nausea and vomiting and increasing appetite.

3. **Clinical uses:** Dronabinol is used to manage chemotherapy-induced nausea and vomiting, particularly when other anti-emetic treatments have proven ineffective. It can also be used to stimulate appetite in individuals with AIDS-related anorexia and for managing chronic pain and muscle spasticity in certain medical conditions.

4. **Adverse effects:** Common side effects of dronabinol can include dizziness, euphoria, confusion, and alterations in mood and perception. It may also cause increased heart rate, dry mouth, and in some cases, anxiety or paranoia. As with natural THC, it can have psychotropic effects, and its use may be subject to regulatory restrictions in many regions.

Ginger:

1. **Active compounds:** The active compounds in ginger include gingerol and shogaol, which are responsible for its medicinal properties.

2. **Mechanism of action:** Ginger has several pharmacological actions, including antiemetic (anti-nausea and vomiting), anti-inflammatory, and prokinetic effects on the gastrointestinal tract. It is thought to exert its antiemetic properties by acting on serotonin receptors (specifically the 5-HT3 receptor) and by reducing gut spasms. The exact mechanisms are not fully understood.

3. **Clinical uses:** Ginger is commonly used to manage nausea and vomiting associated with various conditions, including pregnancy (morning sickness), motion sickness, and chemotherapy-induced nausea. It can also help alleviate digestive discomfort and reduce inflammation.

4. **Adverse effects**: Ginger is generally well-tolerated, and side effects are rare. Some individuals may experience mild gastrointestinal symptoms such as heartburn, gas, or diarrhea.

Peppermint:

1. **Active compounds:** Peppermint contains menthol, the primary active compound responsible for its medicinal properties.

2. **Mechanism of action:** Peppermint has several pharmacological effects, including muscle relaxation and the reduction of spasms in the gastrointestinal tract. Menthol can act as a smooth muscle relaxant and may help reduce gastrointestinal discomfort.

3. **Clinical uses:** Peppermint is used to manage various gastrointestinal symptoms, including indigestion, bloating, and irritable bowel syndrome (IBS). It can help relieve discomfort related to gas and spasms in the digestive tract.

4. **Adverse effects:** Peppermint is generally well-tolerated, but it may cause heartburn or mild allergic reactions in some individuals. In some cases, concentrated peppermint oil can cause a burning sensation in the mouth or throat.

CHAPTER – 7

CHEMOTHERAPY – I

Ms. Neha Goel

Associate Professor, Rajiv Gandhi Institute of Pharmacy, Faculty of
Pharmaceutical Science & Technology, AKS University Satna, MP-India

ABSTRACT:

Chemotherapy is a treatment modality used primarily to combat various forms of cancer. It involves the administration of chemical agents that target rapidly dividing cancer cells, aiming to destroy or inhibit their growth. This approach can be used alone or in combination with other treatments like surgery, radiation therapy, and immunotherapy. Chemotherapy drugs can be administered orally, intravenously, or through other routes depending on the type and location of the cancer. While it is highly effective in targeting cancer cells, chemotherapy also affects healthy cells that divide rapidly, such as those in the bone marrow, digestive tract, and hair follicles. This can lead to a range of side effects, including nausea, fatigue, hair loss, and increased susceptibility to infections. Advances in chemotherapy have led to the development of more targeted therapies, which aim to minimize damage to healthy cells and reduce side effects. Personalized treatment plans are often created based on the specific type and stage of cancer, as well as the patient's overall health and response to previous treatments. Despite its challenges, chemotherapy remains a cornerstone of cancer treatment, significantly improving survival rates and quality of life for many patients. Continuous research and innovation are driving the development of new chemotherapeutic agents and delivery methods, offering hope for more effective and less toxic cancer treatments in the future.

Introduction:

Chemotherapy is a medical treatment that involves the use of powerful drugs or medications to treat various diseases, primarily cancer. The term "chemotherapy" often refers to the treatment of cancer, but it can also be used to manage other conditions, such as autoimmune disorders. The primary goal of chemotherapy is to destroy or inhibit the growth of rapidly dividing and abnormal cells, including cancer cells, which are characterized by uncontrolled growth and division.

Chemotherapy drugs work by interfering with various stages of the cell cycle or by targeting specific aspects of cell division and replication. They can be administered orally or intravenously and may be used as a standalone treatment or in combination with other therapies like surgery, radiation therapy, or targeted therapies.

While chemotherapy is effective in killing cancer cells, it can also affect normal, healthy cells, leading to side effects. The choice of chemotherapy drugs, treatment regimens, and dosages depends on the type and stage of the disease, the patient's overall health, and other individual factors. Chemotherapy is an essential component of cancer treatment and is often integrated into a comprehensive care plan, aiming to achieve remission, control the spread of cancer, alleviate symptoms, and improve a patient's quality of life.

GENERAL PRINCIPLES OF CHEMOTHERAPY:

Chemotherapy uses drugs to treat diseases, especially cancer. Here are the key principles and concepts:

1. **Cytotoxic Action:** Chemotherapy drugs kill or stop the growth of rapidly dividing cells, like cancer cells. However, they can also harm normal cells, causing side effects.

2. **Cell Cycle Specific vs. Non-Specific Drugs:** Some drugs work at specific stages of the cell cycle, while others work at any stage.

3. **Combination Therapy:** Using multiple drugs together can target cancer cells in different ways and reduce the chance of resistance.

4. **Dose Intensity:** The right dose and schedule are crucial for success, balancing effectiveness and side effects.

5. **Adjuvant and Neoadjuvant Therapy:** Chemotherapy can be given after surgery or radiation to kill remaining cancer cells (adjuvant) or before surgery to shrink tumors (neoadjuvant).

6. **Induction and Maintenance Therapy:** Initial treatment (induction) aims to put cancer into remission, while ongoing treatment (maintenance) prevents relapse.

7. **Scheduled Rest Periods:** Chemotherapy is given in cycles with breaks to allow normal cells to recover.

8. **Careful Monitoring:** Regular tests and check-ups are needed to track treatment progress and manage side effects.

9. **Targeted Therapies:** These drugs focus on specific molecules or pathways in cancer cells, often with fewer side effects.

10. **Combating Drug Resistance:** Changing drug combinations and developing new drugs help overcome cancer cell resistance.

11. **Patient Education:** Patients need to understand their treatment, potential side effects, and the importance of following the regimen.

12. **Supportive Care:** Managing side effects and keeping the patient healthy is crucial. This includes medications for nausea, growth factors for blood cells, and pain management.

13. **Quality of Life:** The goal is to extend life and improve quality of life, including palliative care for symptom control and emotional support.

14. **Multidisciplinary Approach:** A team of specialists, including doctors, nurses, and pharmacists, work together to provide comprehensive care.

15. **Personalized Medicine:** Advances in genetics allow treatments to be tailored to the individual's specific cancer characteristics.

16. **Ethical Considerations:** Decisions involve balancing benefits and risks, respecting patient choices, and ensuring informed consent.

17.**Clinical Trials:** Participation in trials is essential for developing new chemotherapy options and improving patient outcomes.

SULFONAMIDES AND COTRIMOXAZOLE:

SULFONAMIDES:

Sulfonamides, also known as sulfa drugs, are a class of synthetic antibiotics that are used to treat various bacterial infections. They work by inhibiting the growth and replication of bacteria by interfering with the synthesis of folic acid, which is essential for bacterial DNA and protein production. Sulfonamides are bacteriostatic, meaning they stop the growth of bacteria, allowing the body's immune system to effectively eliminate the infection. Some common sulfonamide antibiotics include sulfamethoxazole, sulfadiazine, and sulfisoxazole.

Sulfonamides are a class of synthetic antibiotics with a mechanism of action primarily related to their ability to inhibit bacterial folate synthesis. They work by interfering with the production of folic acid, an essential component for the synthesis of nucleic acids (DNA and RNA) in bacteria. Here is an overview of the pharmacology of sulfonamides:

Pharmacology of Sulfonamides

1. Mechanism of Action: Sulfonamides are antibacterial agents that work by inhibiting the synthesis of folic acid in bacteria. They competitively inhibit the enzyme dihydropteroate synthase, which is involved in the production of dihydrofolic acid, a precursor to folic acid. Since bacteria cannot obtain folic acid from the environment and must synthesize it, this inhibition is lethal to them.

2. Spectrum of Activity: Sulfonamides have a broad spectrum of activity against many Gram-positive and Gram-negative bacteria. However, their use has declined due to the development of bacterial resistance and the availability of more effective antibiotics.

3. Pharmacokinetics: Sulfonamides are well-absorbed from the gastrointestinal tract and distributed widely throughout body tissues and fluids, including the central nervous system and cerebrospinal fluid. They are metabolized in the liver and excreted primarily through the kidneys. The half-life of sulfonamides can vary significantly among different drugs in this class.

4. Clinical Uses: Sulfonamides are used to treat various bacterial infections, including urinary tract infections, certain types of meningitis, and respiratory infections. They are also used in combination with other drugs to treat specific conditions like toxoplasmosis and Pneumocystis jirovecii pneumonia.

5. Adverse Effects: Common side effects of sulfonamides include gastrointestinal disturbances, such as nausea and vomiting, as well as hypersensitivity reactions like rashes and fever. Severe adverse effects can include Stevens-Johnson syndrome, toxic epidermal necrolysis, and blood disorders such as agranulocytosis, aplastic anemia, and hemolytic anemia, particularly in individuals with glucose-6-phosphate dehydrogenase (G6PD) deficiency.

6. Resistance Mechanisms: Bacterial resistance to sulfonamides can occur through several mechanisms, including the production of an altered dihydropteroate synthase enzyme, increased production of para-aminobenzoic acid (PABA, which competes with the drug), and reduced drug uptake by the bacterial cells.

7. Drug Interactions: Sulfonamides can interact with several other medications. For example, they can potentiate the effects of oral anticoagulants, sulfonylurea hypoglycemic agents, and anticonvulsants. They can also displace drugs like methotrexate and bilirubin from plasma proteins, leading to increased toxicity or adverse effects.

8. Specific Agents: Commonly used sulfonamides include sulfamethoxazole (often combined with trimethoprim as co-trimoxazole), sulfadiazine, and sulfasalazine. Each of these agents has specific indications and pharmacokinetic properties that influence their clinical use.

9. Contraindications: Sulfonamides are contraindicated in patients with known hypersensitivity to the drugs, in pregnant women at term, in nursing mothers, and in infants less than two months of age due to the risk of kernicterus (bilirubin-induced brain damage).

10. Monitoring: Patients on sulfonamides should be monitored for signs of adverse reactions, particularly skin reactions and blood dyscrasias. Renal function should be monitored as well, especially in patients with pre-existing kidney disease. Regular blood counts may be necessary to detect potential hematologic toxicity.

COTRIMOXAZOLE:

Cotrimoxazole, also known as trimethoprim-sulfamethoxazole, is a combination antibiotic used to treat a variety of bacterial infections. It consists of two active ingredients, trimethoprim and sulfamethoxazole, which work synergistically to inhibit different steps in the folic acid synthesis pathway, effectively targeting a broad spectrum of bacteria. Here is an overview of the pharmacology of cotrimoxazole:

Composition and Mechanism of Action: Co-trimoxazole is a combination of two antibiotics: sulfamethoxazole and trimethoprim. This combination works synergistically to inhibit bacterial folic acid synthesis at two different steps. Sulfamethoxazole inhibits dihydropteroate synthase, while trimethoprim inhibits dihydrofolate reductase. This dual blockade results in a sequential inhibition of folic acid synthesis, making it more effective than either drug alone.

2. Spectrum of Activity: Co-trimoxazole has a broad spectrum of antibacterial activity against both Gram-positive and Gram-negative bacteria. It is particularly effective against urinary tract infections, respiratory infections, gastrointestinal infections, and certain types of pneumonia such as Pneumocystis jirovecii pneumonia (PCP).

3. Pharmacokinetics:

- **Absorption:** Co-trimoxazole is well-absorbed from the gastrointestinal tract when taken orally.
- **Distribution:** It is widely distributed throughout the body, including the central nervous system, lungs, kidneys, and tissues. It also crosses the placenta and is present in breast milk.
- **Metabolism:** Both sulfamethoxazole and trimethoprim are metabolized in the liver.
- **Excretion:** The metabolites and unchanged drugs are excreted primarily by the kidneys. The elimination half-lives of sulfamethoxazole and trimethoprim are approximately 10-12 hours and 8-10 hours, respectively.

4. Clinical Uses: Co-trimoxazole is used to treat various bacterial infections, including:

- Urinary tract infections (UTIs)
- Acute and chronic bronchitis
- Pneumocystis jirovecii pneumonia (PCP)
- Traveler's diarrhea
- Shigellosis
- Ear infections (otitis media)
- Certain types of bacterial prostatitis

5. Adverse Effects: Common side effects include:

- Gastrointestinal disturbances (nausea, vomiting, diarrhea)
- Skin reactions (rash, itching, photosensitivity)
- Blood disorders (anemia, leukopenia, thrombocytopenia)
- Hyperkalemia
- Rare but serious side effects can include Stevens-Johnson syndrome, toxic epidermal necrolysis, and severe allergic reactions.

6. Resistance Mechanisms: Bacterial resistance to co-trimoxazole can develop through several mechanisms, such as:

- Mutations in dihydropteroate synthase or dihydrofolate reductase enzymes, reducing drug binding.
- Increased production of PABA, bypassing the inhibitory effect of sulfamethoxazole.
- Enhanced efflux or reduced uptake of the drug by bacterial cells.

7. Drug Interactions:

- **Anticoagulants:** Co-trimoxazole can enhance the effects of warfarin, increasing the risk of bleeding.
- **Phenytoin:** Trimethoprim can inhibit the metabolism of phenytoin, increasing its levels and potential toxicity.
- **Methotrexate:** Co-trimoxazole can increase the risk of methotrexate toxicity.
- **Oral hypoglycemics:** Co-trimoxazole can potentiate the effects of sulfonylureas, increasing the risk of hypoglycemia.

8. Specific Considerations:

- **Renal Impairment:** Dosage adjustment is necessary in patients with renal impairment to prevent accumulation and toxicity.
- **Pregnancy and Lactation:** Co-trimoxazole is generally avoided during pregnancy, especially in the first trimester and near term, due to the risk of congenital abnormalities and neonatal kernicterus. It is also excreted in breast milk and should be used with caution in breastfeeding mothers.
- **G6PD Deficiency:** Use with caution in patients with G6PD deficiency due to the risk of hemolytic anemia.

9. Monitoring: Patients on co-trimoxazole should be monitored for:

- Signs of adverse reactions, especially severe skin reactions and blood dyscrasias.
- Blood counts, especially if the treatment is prolonged.

- Renal function, particularly in patients with existing kidney disease.
- Serum potassium levels, to detect hyperkalemia.

10. Contraindications: Co-trimoxazole is contraindicated in patients with:

- Known hypersensitivity to sulfonamides or trimethoprim.
- Severe renal or liver disease.
- Megaloblastic anemia due to folate deficiency.
- Infants less than two months old, due to the risk of kernicterus.

CHAPTER – 8

ANTIBIOTIC

Mrs. Priya Diwedi

Assistant Professor, Rajiv Gandhi Institute of Pharmacy, Faculty of

Pharmaceutical Science & Technology, AKS University Satna, MP-India

ABSTRACT:

Antibiotics are powerful medications used to treat infections caused by bacteria. They work by either killing the bacteria or inhibiting their growth, thus helping the body's immune system to combat the infection. Different antibiotics target specific bacterial processes, such as cell wall synthesis, protein production, or DNA replication. Common classes of antibiotics include penicillins, cephalosporins, tetracyclines, macrolides, and aminoglycosides, each with distinct mechanisms of action and spectra of activity. Antibiotics are typically prescribed based on the type of bacteria causing the infection and the location of the infection in the body. However, the overuse and misuse of antibiotics have led to the growing problem of antibiotic resistance, where bacteria evolve to withstand the effects of these drugs. This makes it increasingly challenging to treat common infections and underscores the importance of using antibiotics judiciously. Side effects of antibiotics can range from mild, such as gastrointestinal discomfort, to severe, including allergic reactions and antibiotic-associated colitis. Healthcare providers must carefully consider the appropriate antibiotic choice, dosage, and duration of therapy to ensure effectiveness and minimize the risk of resistance and side effects. Research continues to develop new antibiotics and strategies to combat resistant bacterial strains, but the prudent use of existing antibiotics remains crucial in safeguarding their efficacy for future generations.

Introduction:

Antibiotics are a class of drugs or substances that are used to treat bacterial infections. They work by either killing bacteria or inhibiting their growth and reproduction, ultimately helping the body's immune system to overcome the infection. Antibiotics are specific to bacteria and do not work against viral infections. They have been a crucial tool in modern medicine for treating various bacterial diseases and have significantly contributed to improving human health and increasing life expectancy. Antibiotics can be prescribed by healthcare professionals, and their use should be strictly monitored to prevent the development of antibiotic-resistant bacteria.

PENICILLINS

Penicillins are a group of antibiotics that are derived from the mold Penicillium. They were the first antibiotics to be discovered and have played a crucial role in the treatment of bacterial infections. The discovery of penicillin by Sir Alexander Fleming in 1928 marked a significant milestone in the field of medicine, as it introduced an effective treatment for a wide range of bacterial diseases.

Classification of Penicillins

Penicillins are classified based on their spectrum of activity, resistance to beta-lactamase, and their pharmacokinetic properties. Here is a detailed classification:

1. Natural Penicillins

Natural penicillins are the original penicillins derived from the Penicillium mold. They are primarily effective against Gram-positive organisms.

- **Penicillin G (Benzylpenicillin):** Usually administered parenterally due to poor oral absorption.

- **Penicillin V (Phenoxymethylpenicillin):** Acid-stable and can be taken orally.

2. Penicillinase-Resistant Penicillins (Antistaphylococcal Penicillins)

These penicillins are resistant to degradation by beta-lactamase enzymes produced by Staphylococcus aureus.

- **Methicillin:** No longer used clinically due to nephrotoxicity.
- **Nafcillin:** Used for serious staphylococcal infections.
- **Oxacillin:** Similar to nafcillin, used in treating staphylococcal infections.
- **Dicloxacillin:** Oral formulation, used for staphylococcal infections.
- **Cloxacillin:** Similar to dicloxacillin, available in oral and parenteral forms.

3. Aminopenicillins

Aminopenicillins have a broader spectrum of activity, including some Gram-negative organisms. They are susceptible to beta-lactamase.

- **Ampicillin:** Can be administered orally or parenterally; used for various infections including respiratory and urinary tract infections.
- **Amoxicillin:** Better oral absorption compared to ampicillin; commonly used for respiratory infections, otitis media, and as part of the regimen for H. pylori eradication.

4. Extended-Spectrum Penicillins (Antipseudomonal Penicillins)

These penicillins have an extended spectrum of activity, including activity against Pseudomonas aeruginosa and other Gram-negative bacteria.

- **Carboxypenicillins:**

- o **Carbenicillin:** Effective against Pseudomonas and other Gram-negative organisms; rarely used today.
  - o **Ticarcillin:** Often used in combination with clavulanate to broaden the spectrum.
- **Ureidopenicillins:**
  - o **Piperacillin:** Effective against a wide range of Gram-negative organisms, including Pseudomonas; often used in combination with tazobactam.
  - o **Mezlocillin:** Similar to piperacillin but less commonly used.

5. Beta-Lactamase Inhibitor Combinations

These combinations include a penicillin antibiotic and a beta-lactamase inhibitor, which extends the spectrum of activity by protecting the penicillin from degradation by beta-lactamase enzymes.

- **Amoxicillin/Clavulanate (Augmentin):** Broad-spectrum antibiotic used for respiratory infections, UTIs, skin infections, etc.
- **Ampicillin/Sulbactam (Unasyn):** Used for intra-abdominal infections, gynecological infections, and skin infections.
- **Piperacillin/Tazobactam (Zosyn):** Used for severe infections, including intra-abdominal, skin, and respiratory infections.
- **Ticarcillin/Clavulanate (Timentin):** Used for severe infections, particularly those caused by resistant Gram-negative organisms.

Pharmacology of Penicillins

1. Mechanism of Action: Penicillins are beta-lactam antibiotics that inhibit bacterial cell wall synthesis. They bind to and inactivate penicillin-binding proteins (PBPs), which are essential for the cross-linking of the bacterial cell wall peptidoglycan. This leads to a weakened cell wall and ultimately causes bacterial cell lysis and death, particularly during cell division.

2. Spectrum of Activity: Penicillins are effective against a variety of Gram-positive bacteria and some Gram-negative bacteria. They are particularly potent against Streptococcus species, Neisseria meningitidis, and some anaerobes.

3. Pharmacokinetics: Penicillins are absorbed from the gastrointestinal tract, though some are destroyed by gastric acid. They distribute widely in body tissues and fluids but have limited penetration into the cerebrospinal fluid except when the meninges are inflamed. They are primarily excreted by the kidneys, with a short half-life requiring frequent dosing.

4. Clinical Uses: Penicillins are used to treat infections such as streptococcal pharyngitis, syphilis, meningitis, and infections caused by susceptible staphylococci and pneumococci.

5. Adverse Effects: Common side effects include allergic reactions (rash, anaphylaxis), gastrointestinal disturbances, and rarely, interstitial nephritis and hematologic toxicity.

6. Resistance Mechanisms: Bacterial resistance to penicillins can occur via the production of beta-lactamase enzymes that hydrolyze the beta-lactam ring, altering PBPs, and reducing drug uptake.

Pharmacology of Cephalosporins

1. Mechanism of Action: Cephalosporins, like penicillins, are beta-lactam antibiotics that inhibit bacterial cell wall synthesis by binding to PBPs, leading to cell lysis and death.

2. Spectrum of Activity: Cephalosporins have a broader spectrum of activity compared to penicillins, and their spectrum varies by generation:

- **First-generation:** Effective mainly against Gram-positive cocci and some Gram-negative rods.
- **Second-generation:** Increased activity against Gram-negative bacteria, including Haemophilus influenzae and Enterobacter species.
- **Third-generation:** Broad-spectrum activity, including Pseudomonas aeruginosa and better CNS penetration.

- **Fourth-generation:** Broad-spectrum activity with improved stability against beta-lactamases.
- **Fifth-generation:** Effective against MRSA and resistant Gram-negative bacteria.

3. Pharmacokinetics: Cephalosporins are well absorbed orally and parenterally, widely distributed in body tissues and fluids, and some can penetrate the CNS. They are primarily excreted by the kidneys.

4. Clinical Uses: Cephalosporins treat a variety of infections, including pneumonia, skin infections, urinary tract infections, septicemia, and meningitis.

5. Adverse Effects: Similar to penicillins, cephalosporins can cause allergic reactions, gastrointestinal disturbances, and in rare cases, nephrotoxicity and hematologic abnormalities.

6. Resistance Mechanisms: Resistance mechanisms include beta-lactamase production, altered PBPs, and reduced permeability to the drug.

Pharmacology of Chloramphenicol

1. Mechanism of Action: Chloramphenicol inhibits bacterial protein synthesis by binding to the 50S ribosomal subunit, preventing peptide bond formation. This action is bacteriostatic, meaning it inhibits bacterial growth without killing the cells.

2. Spectrum of Activity: Chloramphenicol has a broad spectrum of activity, effective against many Gram-positive and Gram-negative bacteria, rickettsiae, and anaerobes. It is particularly useful for treating infections where other antibiotics are ineffective.

3. Pharmacokinetics: Chloramphenicol is well absorbed orally, widely distributed in body tissues and fluids, including the CNS, and metabolized in the liver. It is excreted in the urine primarily as inactive metabolites.

4. Clinical Uses: Chloramphenicol is used to treat serious infections like typhoid fever, meningitis, and rickettsial infections when other antibiotics are contraindicated or ineffective.

5. Adverse Effects: Chloramphenicol can cause serious side effects, including bone marrow suppression leading to aplastic anemia, dose-related anemia, and gray baby syndrome in neonates. Other side effects include gastrointestinal disturbances and hypersensitivity reactions.

6. Resistance Mechanisms: Resistance to chloramphenicol can occur through the production of chloramphenicol acetyltransferase, which inactivates the drug, as well as through efflux pumps and ribosomal mutations.

CEPHALOSPORINS

Cephalosporins are a class of antibiotics that are structurally related to penicillins and are used to treat a wide range of bacterial infections. They are classified into different generations based on their spectrum of activity and characteristics. Here's a definition of cephalosporins with their classification:

Definition:

Cephalosporins are a group of beta-lactam antibiotics that inhibit the synthesis of bacterial cell walls by binding to penicillin-binding proteins (PBPs), ultimately leading to bacterial cell death. They are used to treat various bacterial infections, including respiratory tract infections, urinary tract infections, skin and soft tissue infections, and more.

Classification of Cephalosporins by Generation:

1. **First-generation cephalosporins:** These antibiotics are effective against Gram-positive bacteria, including some Streptococcus and Staphylococcus species. They also have some activity against a limited number of Gram-negative bacteria. Examples include cephalexin and cefazolin.

2. **Second-generation cephalosporins:** This generation offers a broader spectrum of activity, with improved coverage of Gram-negative bacteria. They are often used to treat respiratory and urinary tract infections. Examples include cefuroxime and cefoxitin.

3. **Third-generation cephalosporins:** These antibiotics have an even wider spectrum of activity against both Gram-positive and Gram-negative bacteria, including some that are resistant to earlier-generation cephalosporins. They are commonly used to treat serious infections. Examples include ceftriaxone and cefotaxime.

4. **Fourth-generation cephalosporins:** This generation retains a broad spectrum of activity and exhibits increased resistance to certain beta-lactamases. They are often used to treat infections caused by multidrug-resistant bacteria. An example of a fourth-generation cephalosporin is cefepime.

5. **Fifth-generation cephalosporins:** Fifth-generation cephalosporins have an even broader spectrum of activity, including enhanced activity against multidrug-resistant Gram-negative bacteria. They are often used in complex hospital-acquired infections. An example of a fifth-generation cephalosporin is ceftolozane/tazobactam.

Classification of Macrolides

1. Based on Structure and Spectrum of Activity:

- **14-membered Ring Macrolides:**
    - **Erythromycin:** The prototype macrolide, used for respiratory and skin infections.
    - **Clarithromycin:** Similar to erythromycin but with better absorption and a broader spectrum.
    - **Roxithromycin:** Improved gastrointestinal tolerance compared to erythromycin.
- **15-membered Ring Macrolides (Azalides):**
    - **Azithromycin:** Enhanced tissue penetration and prolonged half-life, effective for respiratory and sexually transmitted infections.
- **16-membered Ring Macrolides:**

- o **Spiramycin:** Used in toxoplasmosis and some respiratory infections.
- o **Josamycin:** Effective for respiratory and skin infections, with a broader spectrum against Gram-positive bacteria.

2. Based on Generations:

- **First Generation:**
- o Erythromycin
- **Second Generation:**
- o Clarithromycin
- o Azithromycin
- o Roxithromycin

Classification of Quinolones

1. Based on Generations:

- **First Generation (Non-fluorinated Quinolones):**
- o **Nalidixic Acid:** Primarily used for urinary tract infections.
- **Second Generation (Early Fluoroquinolones):**
- o **Ciprofloxacin:** Broad spectrum, effective against Gram-negative bacteria and some Gram-positive bacteria, used for UTIs, respiratory, and gastrointestinal infections.
- o **Norfloxacin:** Primarily used for UTIs and prostatitis.
- **Third Generation (Extended Spectrum Fluoroquinolones):**
- o **Levofloxacin:** Improved activity against Gram-positive bacteria, used for respiratory and urinary tract infections.
- o **Sparfloxacin:** Enhanced activity against Gram-positive bacteria and atypical pathogens.
- **Fourth Generation (Advanced Spectrum Fluoroquinolones):**
- o **Moxifloxacin:** Broad spectrum, effective against Gram-positive, Gram-negative, and anaerobic bacteria, used for respiratory and skin infections.

- o **Trovafloxacin:** Broad spectrum, effective against Gram-positive, Gram-negative, and anaerobic bacteria, used for respiratory and skin infections.

Pharmacology of Macrolides

1. Mechanism of Action: Macrolides inhibit bacterial protein synthesis by binding to the 50S ribosomal subunit. This binding prevents the translocation step of protein synthesis, effectively stopping the growth of bacteria. Macrolides are typically bacteriostatic but can be bactericidal at higher concentrations or against certain bacteria.

2. Spectrum of Activity: Macrolides have a broad spectrum of activity, particularly effective against Gram-positive cocci (e.g., Streptococcus and Staphylococcus species), some Gram-negative bacteria (e.g., Haemophilus influenzae, Bordetella pertussis), and atypical pathogens (e.g., Mycoplasma, Chlamydia, and Legionella).

3. Pharmacokinetics: Macrolides are well absorbed from the gastrointestinal tract, though food can affect absorption. They are widely distributed in body tissues and fluids but have limited penetration into the cerebrospinal fluid. They are metabolized in the liver and excreted in bile and urine.

4. Clinical Uses: Macrolides are used to treat respiratory tract infections, skin infections, sexually transmitted infections (e.g., chlamydia), and Helicobacter pylori infections in combination therapy. They are also an alternative for patients allergic to penicillins.

5. Adverse Effects: Common side effects include gastrointestinal disturbances (nausea, vomiting, diarrhea), hepatotoxicity, and ototoxicity. Macrolides can also prolong the QT interval, increasing the risk of cardiac arrhythmias.

6. Resistance Mechanisms: Resistance can develop through modification of the ribosomal target site (methylation), efflux pumps, and enzymatic inactivation of the drug.

Classification of Quinolones

1. Based on Generations:

- **First Generation (Non-fluorinated Quinolones):**
  - **Nalidixic Acid:** Primarily used for urinary tract infections.
- **Second Generation (Early Fluoroquinolones):**
  - **Ciprofloxacin:** Broad spectrum, effective against Gram-negative bacteria and some Gram-positive bacteria, used for UTIs, respiratory, and gastrointestinal infections.
  - **Norfloxacin:** Primarily used for UTIs and prostatitis.
- **Third Generation (Extended Spectrum Fluoroquinolones):**
  - **Levofloxacin:** Improved activity against Gram-positive bacteria, used for respiratory and urinary tract infections.
  - **Sparfloxacin:** Enhanced activity against Gram-positive bacteria and atypical pathogens.
- **Fourth Generation (Advanced Spectrum Fluoroquinolones):**
  - **Moxifloxacin:** Broad spectrum, effective against Gram-positive, Gram-negative, and anaerobic bacteria, used for respiratory and skin infections.
  - **Trovafloxacin:** Broad spectrum, effective against Gram-positive, Gram-negative, and anaerobic bacteria, used for respiratory and skin infections.

Classification of Fluoroquinolones

1. Based on Generations:

- **Second Generation (Early Fluoroquinolones):**
  - Ciprofloxacin
  - Norfloxacin
  - Ofloxacin
- **Third Generation (Respiratory Fluoroquinolones):**
  - Levofloxacin
  - Sparfloxacin

- **Fourth Generation (Enhanced Activity Against Gram-positive and Anaerobes):**
    - Moxifloxacin
    - Trovafloxacin
    - Gemifloxacin

2. Based on Spectrum of Activity:

- **Gram-negative Activity:**
    - Ciprofloxacin
    - Norfloxacin
- **Respiratory Pathogens:**
    - Levofloxacin
    - Moxifloxacin
- **Anaerobic Activity:**
    - Moxifloxacin
    - Trovafloxacin

Pharmacology of Quinolones

1. Mechanism of Action: Quinolones inhibit bacterial DNA synthesis by targeting the bacterial enzymes DNA gyrase (topoisomerase II) and topoisomerase IV. This inhibition prevents the supercoiling of DNA, leading to breaks in the DNA strands and ultimately bacterial cell death. Quinolones are bactericidal.

2. Spectrum of Activity: Quinolones have a broad spectrum of activity against Gram-negative bacteria (e.g., Enterobacteriaceae, Pseudomonas aeruginosa) and limited activity against Gram-positive bacteria. They are also effective against some atypical bacteria and mycobacteria.

3. Pharmacokinetics: Quinolones are well absorbed orally, with excellent bioavailability. They are widely distributed in body tissues and fluids, including the prostate and bone. Quinolones are primarily excreted by the kidneys, with some liver metabolism.

4. Clinical Uses: Quinolones are used to treat urinary tract infections, gastrointestinal infections, respiratory tract infections, skin infections, and sexually transmitted infections. They are also used in the treatment of anthrax.

5. Adverse Effects: Side effects include gastrointestinal disturbances, CNS effects (headache, dizziness, seizures), tendonitis and tendon rupture, and photosensitivity. Quinolones can also prolong the QT interval.

6. Resistance Mechanisms: Resistance can occur through mutations in DNA gyrase or topoisomerase IV, efflux pumps, and decreased drug permeability.

Classification of Fluoroquinolones

1. Based on Generations:

- **Second Generation (Early Fluoroquinolones):**
  o Ciprofloxacin
  o Norfloxacin
  o Ofloxacin
- **Third Generation (Respiratory Fluoroquinolones):**
  o Levofloxacin
  o Sparfloxacin
- **Fourth Generation (Enhanced Activity Against Gram-positive and Anaerobes):**
  o Moxifloxacin
  o Trovafloxacin
  o Gemifloxacin

2. Based on Spectrum of Activity:

- **Gram-negative Activity:**
  o Ciprofloxacin
  o Norfloxacin
- **Respiratory Pathogens:**
  o Levofloxacin
  o Moxifloxacin

- **Anaerobic Activity:**
    - Moxifloxacin
    - Trovafloxacin

Pharmacology of Fluoroquinolones

1. Mechanism of Action: Fluoroquinolones, a subclass of quinolones, also inhibit bacterial DNA synthesis by targeting DNA gyrase and topoisomerase IV. They are more potent and have a broader spectrum of activity compared to the earlier quinolones. Fluoroquinolones are bactericidal.

2. Spectrum of Activity: Fluoroquinolones have an expanded spectrum of activity that includes both Gram-negative and Gram-positive bacteria, as well as atypical pathogens. They are particularly effective against Gram-negative bacteria, including Pseudomonas aeruginosa, and some Gram-positive bacteria like Streptococcus pneumoniae.

3. Pharmacokinetics: Fluoroquinolones are well absorbed orally, with high bioavailability. They distribute widely in body tissues and fluids, including the lungs, kidneys, and prostate. Most fluoroquinolones are excreted renally, although some are metabolized in the liver.

4. Clinical Uses: Fluoroquinolones are used to treat a wide range of infections, including urinary tract infections, respiratory tract infections, gastrointestinal infections, bone and joint infections, and certain sexually transmitted infections. They are also used in the treatment of anthrax and multi-drug-resistant tuberculosis.

5. Adverse Effects: Adverse effects are similar to those of other quinolones, including gastrointestinal disturbances, CNS effects, tendonitis and tendon rupture, photosensitivity, and QT interval prolongation. They may also cause dysglycemia (both hyperglycemia and hypoglycemia).

6. Resistance Mechanisms: Resistance mechanisms include mutations in the genes encoding DNA gyrase and topoisomerase IV, efflux pumps, and reduced drug permeability. Cross-resistance between fluoroquinolones and other quinolones is common.

Tetracyclines

Introduction

Tetracyclines are a class of broad-spectrum antibiotics that inhibit bacterial protein synthesis. They are derived from Streptomyces bacteria and were first discovered in the 1940s. Tetracyclines are widely used to treat a variety of infections caused by susceptible organisms.

Classification

1. Natural Tetracyclines:

- **Tetracycline**
- **Chlortetracycline**
- **Oxytetracycline**

2. Semisynthetic Tetracyclines:

- **Doxycycline:** More lipid-soluble, better absorption and longer half-life.
- **Minocycline:** Enhanced tissue penetration and longer half-life.
- **Methacycline**

3. Glycylcyclines:

- **Tigecycline:** A newer derivative with a broader spectrum of activity, including some tetracycline-resistant bacteria.

Pharmacology

1. Mechanism of Action: Tetracyclines bind to the 30S ribosomal subunit, preventing the attachment of aminoacyl-tRNA to the ribosome, thereby inhibiting protein synthesis. This action is bacteriostatic, meaning it stops the growth of bacteria rather than killing them directly.

2. Spectrum of Activity: Tetracyclines are effective against a wide range of Gram-positive and Gram-negative bacteria, as well as atypical organisms such as Rickettsia, Chlamydia, Mycoplasma, and certain protozoa.

3. Pharmacokinetics:

- **Absorption:** Oral absorption is variable; doxycycline and minocycline have better absorption compared to tetracycline.
- **Distribution:** Widely distributed in the body, including bones and teeth. They can cross the placenta and are excreted in breast milk.
- **Metabolism and Excretion:** Primarily excreted in the urine and feces, with doxycycline and minocycline being primarily excreted in the feces.

4. Clinical Uses:

- Respiratory tract infections
- Acne vulgaris
- Sexually transmitted infections (e.g., Chlamydia)
- Rickettsial infections (e.g., Rocky Mountain spotted fever)
- Lyme disease
- Malaria prophylaxis

5. Adverse Effects:

- Gastrointestinal disturbances (nausea, vomiting, diarrhea)
- Photosensitivity

- Discoloration of teeth and inhibition of bone growth in children
- Hepatotoxicity
- Vestibular toxicity (with minocycline)

6. Resistance Mechanisms: Resistance can occur via efflux pumps, ribosomal protection proteins, and enzymatic inactivation.

Aminoglycosides

Introduction

Aminoglycosides are a class of antibiotics derived from Streptomyces and Micromonospora species. They are primarily used to treat serious infections caused by Gram-negative bacteria. Aminoglycosides are bactericidal and work by inhibiting bacterial protein synthesis.

Classification

1. Natural Aminoglycosides:

- **Streptomycin:** Used for tuberculosis and certain other infections.
- **Neomycin:** Used topically and orally for bowel decontamination.

2. Semisynthetic Aminoglycosides:

- **Gentamicin:** Widely used for severe Gram-negative infections.
- **Tobramycin:** Similar to gentamicin, with enhanced activity against Pseudomonas aeruginosa.
- **Amikacin:** Resistant to many aminoglycoside-inactivating enzymes, broader spectrum.

Pharmacology

1. Mechanism of Action: Aminoglycosides bind to the 30S ribosomal subunit, causing misreading of mRNA and inhibiting protein synthesis. This results in the production of defective proteins and leads to bacterial cell death.

2. Spectrum of Activity: Aminoglycosides are primarily active against aerobic Gram-negative bacteria, including Pseudomonas aeruginosa, Escherichia coli, and Klebsiella species. They also have some activity against Gram-positive bacteria when used in combination with other antibiotics.

3. Pharmacokinetics:

- **Absorption:** Poorly absorbed from the gastrointestinal tract; administered parenterally (intravenous or intramuscular).
- **Distribution:** Distributes mainly in extracellular fluid, limited penetration into the cerebrospinal fluid. Concentrates in renal cortical and inner ear tissues.
- **Excretion:** Excreted unchanged in the urine, necessitating dose adjustment in renal impairment.

4. Clinical Uses:

- Severe Gram-negative infections (e.g., septicemia, respiratory tract infections, intra-abdominal infections)
- Endocarditis (in combination with beta-lactams or glycopeptides)
- Tuberculosis (streptomycin)
- Pseudomonas infections (tobramycin)

5. Adverse Effects:

- Nephrotoxicity (renal toxicity)
- Ototoxicity (hearing loss and balance issues)

- Neuromuscular blockade (rare)

- Allergic reactions (rare)

6. Resistance Mechanisms: Resistance can develop through enzymatic inactivation by aminoglycoside-modifying enzymes, alteration of the ribosomal binding site, and decreased uptake or increased efflux of the drug.

CHAPTER – 9

ANTITUBERCULAR AGENTS

Mrs. Pooja Chauhan

Assistant Professor, Rajiv Gandhi Institute of Pharmacy, Faculty of
Pharmaceutical Science & Technology, AKS University Satna, MP-India

ABSTRACT:

Antitubercular agents are medications used to treat tuberculosis (TB), a serious infectious disease caused by Mycobacterium tuberculosis. These agents are categorized into first-line and second-line drugs based on their efficacy, toxicity, and role in TB treatment regimens. First-line antitubercular drugs, such as isoniazid, rifampin, pyrazinamide, and ethambutol, are the cornerstone of TB therapy due to their high potency and relative safety. These drugs are usually administered in combination to prevent the development of drug resistance and to effectively eradicate the bacteria. Treatment typically lasts for at least six months, with an initial intensive phase followed by a continuation phase. Second-line drugs, including fluoroquinolones and injectable agents like amikacin, are used when the first-line drugs are ineffective due to resistance or intolerance. The prolonged duration and complexity of TB treatment can lead to challenges with patient adherence, which is critical for preventing the spread of resistant TB strains. Advances in TB research aim to shorten treatment duration, improve drug efficacy, and reduce side effects. Additionally, public health strategies, including Directly Observed Therapy (DOT), are implemented to ensure compliance and successful treatment outcomes.

Introduction to Antitubercular Agents

Antitubercular agents are medications specifically used to treat tuberculosis (TB), an infectious disease caused by the bacterium Mycobacterium tuberculosis. TB primarily affects the lungs but can also impact other parts of the body, such as the kidneys, spine, and brain. The disease is a major global health issue, and effective treatment requires a combination of drugs to ensure the complete eradication of the bacteria and to prevent the development of drug-resistant TB strains. Antitubercular agents are divided into first-line and second-line drugs based on their effectiveness, toxicity, and role in treatment regimens.

Classification of Antitubercular Agents

1. First-Line Antitubercular Drugs

First-line drugs are the most effective and least toxic options for treating TB. They form the core of standard treatment regimens.

- **Isoniazid (INH):** A bactericidal drug that inhibits mycolic acid synthesis, crucial for the bacterial cell wall. Example: Isoniazid.
- **Rifampin (RIF):** A bactericidal antibiotic that inhibits bacterial RNA synthesis by binding to RNA polymerase. Example: Rifampin.
- **Pyrazinamide (PZA):** A bactericidal drug effective in acidic environments, such as within the macrophages where M. tuberculosis resides. Example: Pyrazinamide.
- **Ethambutol (EMB):** A bacteriostatic drug that inhibits cell wall synthesis by obstructing arabinosyl transferases. Example: Ethambutol.
- **Streptomycin:** An aminoglycoside antibiotic used in certain cases, particularly in severe TB infections. Example: Streptomycin.

2. Second-Line Antitubercular Drugs

Second-line drugs are used when first-line drugs are ineffective due to drug resistance or intolerance. They are generally more toxic and less effective than first-line drugs.

- **Fluoroquinolones:**
  - **Levofloxacin:** Example: Levofloxacin.
  - **Moxifloxacin:** Example: Moxifloxacin.
- **Injectable Agents:**
  - **Amikacin:** Example: Amikacin.
  - **Capreomycin:** Example: Capreomycin.
- **Other Second-Line Drugs:**
  - **Ethionamide:** Example: Ethionamide.
  - **Cycloserine:** Example: Cycloserine.
  - **Para-aminosalicylic acid (PAS):** Example: PAS.
  - **Bedaquiline:** Example: Bedaquiline, used for multi-drug-resistant TB (MDR-TB).
  - **Delamanid:** Example: Delamanid, another option for MDR-TB.

3. Newer and Repurposed Drugs

Newer drugs and repurposed drugs are being developed and tested to improve TB treatment outcomes, especially for drug-resistant TB.

- **Bedaquiline:** Used for multi-drug-resistant TB (MDR-TB).
- **Delamanid:** Also used for MDR-TB.
- **Linezolid:** Originally an antibiotic for Gram-positive bacteria, now repurposed for drug-resistant TB.

Examples of Treatment Regimens

Standard TB Treatment Regimen:

- **Intensive Phase (2 months):** Isoniazid, Rifampin, Pyrazinamide, Ethambutol.
- **Continuation Phase (4-7 months):** Isoniazid, Rifampin.

MDR-TB Treatment Regimen:

- **Customized based on resistance patterns:** May include second-line drugs such as fluoroquinolones (Levofloxacin, Moxifloxacin), injectable agents (Amikacin, Capreomycin), and newer drugs (Bedaquiline, Delamanid).

ISONIAZID (INH):

1. **Mechanism of Action:** Isoniazid primarily inhibits the synthesis of mycolic acids, a key component of the mycobacterial cell wall. This disruption weakens the cell wall's structural integrity, making it more susceptible to damage and lysis by the immune system.

2. **Absorption and Bioavailability:** INH is well-absorbed from the gastrointestinal tract after oral administration. Its bioavailability is high, ranging from 60% to 100%. It achieves therapeutic levels in blood and tissues, including the lungs where TB infection occurs.

3. **Metabolism:** INH is metabolized in the liver by the enzyme N-acetyltransferase (NAT). Genetic variations in NAT can affect the rate of metabolism, leading to slow or fast acetylators. Slow acetylators are at an increased risk of INH toxicity.

4. **Excretion:** Metabolized INH and its acetyl derivatives are primarily excreted in the urine. The rate of excretion can vary based on NAT acetylator status.

5. **Drug Interactions:** INH can interact with other medications, including certain antiretroviral drugs, so it's important to be aware of potential drug interactions when treating patients with both TB and HIV.

Rifampin (RIF):

1. **Mechanism of Action:** Rifampin inhibits RNA synthesis by binding to the bacterial RNA polymerase, thereby preventing transcription of RNA from

DNA. This disruption interferes with the production of vital bacterial proteins.

2. **Absorption and Bioavailability:** Rifampin is well-absorbed from the gastrointestinal tract, and its oral bioavailability is around 95%. It distributes well in various tissues, including the lungs and cerebrospinal fluid, making it effective against TB in different body compartments.

3. **Metabolism:** Rifampin is extensively metabolized in the liver, primarily through the cytochrome P450 enzyme system. It induces its own metabolism and can also induce the metabolism of other drugs, which may lead to decreased drug levels of co-administered medications.

4. **Excretion:** Metabolized rifampin is excreted in bile, and some reabsorption occurs in the small intestine. Only a small fraction of the drug is excreted in the urine.

5. **Drug Interactions:** Rifampin is known for its potent induction of cytochrome P450 enzymes, which can accelerate the metabolism of numerous drugs. This can lead to significant drug interactions, especially when co-administered with other medications. Clinicians need to be vigilant when prescribing rifampin alongside other drugs.

Ethambutol (EMB):

1. **Mechanism of Action:** Ethambutol disrupts the synthesis of the mycobacterial cell wall by inhibiting the formation of arabinogalactan, an essential component of the cell wall. It targets the enzyme arabinosyl transferase.

2. **Absorption and Bioavailability**: Ethambutol is well-absorbed from the gastrointestinal tract after oral administration, and its bioavailability is approximately 80%.

3. **Distribution:** Ethambutol distributes throughout various body tissues, including the lungs, where TB infection is prevalent.

4. **Metabolism:** Ethambutol is not significantly metabolized in the body.

5. **Excretion:** Ethambutol is primarily excreted unchanged in the urine, making it suitable for patients with impaired liver function.

6. **Adverse Effects:** Ethambutol can cause ocular toxicity, primarily affecting the optic nerve. Patients on EMB should be monitored for changes in vision, particularly color vision, and regular eye examinations are recommended to detect and prevent optic neuropathy.

Pyrazinamide (PZA):

1. **Mechanism of Action:** The exact mechanism of action of Pyrazinamide is not fully understood, but it is believed to disrupt the synthesis of mycolic acids in the mycobacterial cell wall and create an acidic environment within the bacterial cell, which impairs its function.

2. **Absorption and Bioavailability:** Pyrazinamide is rapidly and well-absorbed from the gastrointestinal tract. It achieves high concentrations in the tissues, including the lungs, where TB infection occurs.

3. **Distribution:** Pyrazinamide has good penetration into various body tissues, making it effective against intracellular mycobacteria.

4. **Metabolism:** Pyrazinamide is extensively metabolized in the liver, primarily by amidase enzymes, to its active form, pyrazinoic acid. The active metabolite is excreted in the urine.

5. **Excretion:** Both the parent drug and its metabolites are excreted in the urine, mainly in their conjugated forms.

6. **Adverse Effects:** Pyrazinamide can cause hepatotoxicity, and liver function should be monitored during treatment. It may also lead to hyperuricemia and gout in some patients.

Amikacin:

1. **Mechanism of Action:** Amikacin is an aminoglycoside antibiotic that inhibits protein synthesis in the bacterial cell by binding to the 30S ribosomal subunit. This binding disrupts the translation process, leading to faulty protein production and bacterial cell death.

2. **Administration:** Amikacin is typically administered intravenously (IV) or intramuscularly (IM). In the context of TB treatment, it is generally used as part of a combination regimen for multidrug-resistant TB (MDR-TB) and extensively drug-resistant TB (XDR-TB).

3. **Absorption and Distribution:** After IV or IM administration, amikacin is rapidly absorbed and distributed widely throughout the body, including the lungs, where TB infection occurs.

4. **Metabolism and Excretion**: Amikacin is excreted unchanged by the kidneys. Its elimination depends on renal function, and dose adjustments are necessary in patients with impaired kidney function.

5. **Adverse Effects:** Amikacin can cause nephrotoxicity (kidney damage) and ototoxicity (hearing loss and vestibular dysfunction). Monitoring kidney function and hearing is crucial during treatment.

Capreomycin:

1. **Mechanism of Action:** Capreomycin is a cyclic peptide antibiotic that disrupts protein synthesis by binding to the 70S ribosomal subunit in bacteria. This binding inhibits the translocation step in protein synthesis, leading to the accumulation of nonfunctional proteins and bacterial cell death.

2. **Administration:** Capreomycin is typically administered by intramuscular (IM) injection. It is used as a second-line drug for the treatment of MDR-TB and XDR-TB.

3. **Absorption and Distribution:** After IM injection, capreomycin is absorbed and distributed in various body tissues, including the lungs.

4. **Metabolism and Excretion:** Capreomycin is primarily excreted unchanged in the urine. Dose adjustments are necessary for patients with impaired kidney function.

5. **Adverse Effects:** Capreomycin can cause ototoxicity, nephrotoxicity, and neuromuscular blockade. Regular monitoring of kidney function and hearing

is essential, and neuromuscular blockade may require the administration of calcium and/or neostigmine to reverse its effects.

Levofloxacin:

1. **Mechanism of Action:** Levofloxacin is a fluoroquinolone antibiotic that interferes with bacterial DNA replication and repair by inhibiting DNA gyrase and topoisomerase IV. This disruption leads to the inhibition of bacterial growth and cell division.

2. **Administration:** Levofloxacin is usually administered orally. It is used as part of combination therapy for multidrug-resistant tuberculosis (MDR-TB) and extensively drug-resistant tuberculosis (XDR-TB).

3. **Absorption and Distribution:** Levofloxacin is well-absorbed from the gastrointestinal tract, and it achieves good distribution throughout the body, including the lungs where TB infection occurs.

4. **Metabolism and Excretion**: Levofloxacin is primarily excreted unchanged in the urine. Dose adjustments may be required for individuals with impaired renal function.

5. **Adverse Effects:** Levofloxacin can cause various side effects, including gastrointestinal symptoms, central nervous system effects, and, in rare cases, tendon rupture. Patients receiving levofloxacin should be monitored for any adverse reactions, and they should be educated about the potential risks of tendon damage.

Ethionamide:

1. **Mechanism of Action:** Ethionamide disrupts mycobacterial cell wall synthesis by inhibiting the enzyme InhA, which is involved in the synthesis of mycolic acids. This disruption weakens the bacterial cell wall, making it more susceptible to damage and lysis.

2. **Administration:** Ethionamide is administered orally. It is used as part of multidrug regimens for the treatment of drug-resistant TB.

3. **Absorption and Distribution:** Ethionamide is well-absorbed from the gastrointestinal tract, and it distributes throughout various body tissues.

4. **Metabolism and Excretion:** Ethionamide is metabolized in the liver. One of its metabolites, the active form of the drug, is excreted in the urine.

5. **Adverse Effects:** Ethionamide can cause gastrointestinal side effects, including nausea, vomiting, and anorexia. Additionally, it may lead to hepatotoxicity and neurotoxicity. Patients should be closely monitored for these adverse effects, and liver function tests should be conducted regularly.

Streptomycin:

1. **Mechanism of Action:** Streptomycin is an aminoglycoside antibiotic that disrupts bacterial protein synthesis by binding to the 30S ribosomal subunit, causing misreading of the genetic code and preventing the correct assembly of proteins in the bacterial cell.

2. **Administration:** Streptomycin is typically administered by intramuscular (IM) injection. It is used in combination with other drugs for the treatment of multidrug-resistant tuberculosis (MDR-TB).

3. **Absorption and Distribution:** After IM injection, streptomycin is absorbed and distributed in various body tissues, including the lungs, where TB infection occurs.

4. **Metabolism and Excretion:** Streptomycin is primarily excreted unchanged in the urine. Dose adjustments are necessary for patients with impaired kidney function.

5. **Adverse Effects:** Streptomycin can cause nephrotoxicity (kidney damage), ototoxicity (hearing loss and vestibular dysfunction), and neuromuscular blockade. Regular monitoring of kidney function and hearing is essential, and neuromuscular blockade may require the administration of calcium and/or neostigmine to reverse its effects.

Bedaquiline:

1. **Mechanism of Action:** Bedaquiline is a diarylquinoline antibiotic that inhibits ATP synthase, a key enzyme in mycobacterial energy metabolism. This disruption impairs the production of ATP, leading to bacterial cell death.

2. **Administration:** Bedaquiline is administered orally. It is used in the treatment of multidrug-resistant tuberculosis (MDR-TB) when other treatment options are limited.

3. **Absorption and Distribution:** Bedaquiline is well-absorbed from the gastrointestinal tract, and it achieves good distribution in various body tissues, including the lungs.

4. **Metabolism and Excretion:** Bedaquiline is primarily metabolized in the liver, primarily by cytochrome P450 enzymes, and is excreted in the feces. It has a long half-life, which allows for less frequent dosing.

5. **Adverse Effects:** Bedaquiline can cause QT interval prolongation on electrocardiograms, which may increase the risk of arrhythmias. Monitoring of cardiac function and regular ECG assessments are necessary during treatment. Additionally, it may lead to hepatotoxicity, arthralgia, and mild nausea.

CHAPTER – 10

ANTILEPROTIC AGENTS

Mr. Satyendra Garg

Assistant Professor, Rajiv Gandhi Institute of Pharmacy, Faculty of Pharmaceutical Science & Technology, AKS University Satna, MP-India

ABSTRACT:

Antileprotic agents are medications used to treat leprosy, also known as Hansen's disease, which is caused by the bacterium Mycobacterium leprae. These agents are essential for controlling the disease, preventing its spread, and reducing the risk of complications. The cornerstone of leprosy treatment is multi-drug therapy (MDT), which typically includes a combination of dapsone, rifampicin, and clofazimine. This combination is effective in killing the bacteria and preventing drug resistance. Dapsone acts by inhibiting folic acid synthesis, while rifampicin inhibits bacterial RNA synthesis, and clofazimine has both anti-inflammatory and antimicrobial properties. Treatment duration can vary from six months to a year or longer, depending on the form and severity of the disease. Early diagnosis and consistent treatment are crucial in preventing the physical deformities and disabilities associated with leprosy. Additionally, monitoring and managing side effects, such as skin discoloration from clofazimine and hemolytic anemia from dapsone, are important for patient compliance and overall treatment success. Advances in understanding the disease and improving drug regimens continue to enhance the management of leprosy, aiming for complete eradication of this ancient disease.

Introduction to Antileprotic Agents

Leprosy, also known as Hansen's disease, is a chronic infectious disease caused by the bacterium *Mycobacterium leprae*. This disease primarily affects the skin, peripheral nerves, mucosa of the upper respiratory tract, and eyes. Antileprotic agents are drugs used to treat leprosy by either killing the causative bacteria or inhibiting its growth.

Classification of Antileprotic Agents

Antileprotic agents can be classified based on their mechanism of action and chemical structure. The main categories include:

1. **Sulfone Drugs**

2. **Antibiotics**

3. **Clofazimine**

4. **Other Agents**

1. Sulfone Drugs

Example: Dapsone (DDS)

Mechanism of Action: Dapsone acts by inhibiting bacterial dihydropteroate synthase, an enzyme involved in the synthesis of dihydrofolic acid, which is essential for bacterial growth.

Clinical Use: Dapsone is often used as a first-line treatment for leprosy and is usually part of a multidrug therapy (MDT) regimen to prevent the development of drug resistance.

2. Antibiotics

Example: Rifampicin

Mechanism of Action: Rifampicin inhibits DNA-dependent RNA polymerase in bacterial cells, thereby suppressing RNA synthesis and bacterial replication.

Clinical Use: Rifampicin is a crucial component of MDT for leprosy. It is highly bactericidal against *Mycobacterium leprae*.

Example: Ofloxacin

Mechanism of Action: Ofloxacin is a fluoroquinolone antibiotic that inhibits bacterial DNA gyrase and topoisomerase IV, leading to disruption of DNA replication and cell division.

Clinical Use: Ofloxacin is used in cases where resistance to other antileprotic drugs is suspected or as part of an alternative regimen.

3. Clofazimine

Example: Clofazimine

Mechanism of Action: Clofazimine binds to bacterial DNA and interferes with its replication and transcription. It also has anti-inflammatory properties, which help reduce the immune response associated with leprosy.

Clinical Use: Clofazimine is used in MDT for leprosy and is particularly useful in treating patients with erythema nodosum leprosum, a severe inflammatory complication of leprosy.

4. Other Agents

Example: Minocycline

Mechanism of Action: Minocycline is a tetracycline antibiotic that inhibits bacterial protein synthesis by binding to the 30S ribosomal subunit.

Clinical Use: Minocycline is used as an alternative treatment for leprosy, particularly in patients who cannot tolerate standard MDT.

Example: Clarithromycin

Mechanism of Action: Clarithromycin is a macrolide antibiotic that inhibits bacterial protein synthesis by binding to the 50S ribosomal subunit.

Clinical Use: Clarithromycin can be used as part of an alternative regimen for leprosy, especially in cases of drug resistance or intolerance to standard therapy.

Pharmacology of Dapsone (DDS)

Chemical   Structure:
Dapsone is a sulfone compound chemically known as 4,4'-diaminodiphenylsulfone.

Mechanism   of   Action:
Dapsone inhibits dihydropteroate synthase, an enzyme involved in the synthesis of folic acid in bacteria. This inhibition disrupts the production of folic acid, which is essential for bacterial DNA synthesis and cell replication. By hindering folic acid synthesis, dapsone exerts a bacteriostatic effect, particularly against *Mycobacterium leprae.*

Pharmacokinetics:

- **Absorption:** Dapsone is well absorbed from the gastrointestinal tract after oral administration.
- **Distribution:** It is widely distributed in the body tissues, with significant concentrations found in the skin, muscle, liver, and kidneys. It crosses the placenta and is present in breast milk.
- **Metabolism:** Dapsone is primarily metabolized in the liver through N-acetylation and hydroxylation. The N-acetylated metabolite is pharmacologically inactive.
- **Excretion:** It is excreted mainly in the urine, both as unchanged drug and as metabolites. The half-life of dapsone ranges from 20 to 30 hours.

Therapeutic Uses:

- Treatment of leprosy as part of multidrug therapy (MDT).
- Management of dermatitis herpetiformis, a chronic blistering skin condition.
- Prophylaxis and treatment of Pneumocystis jirovecii pneumonia (PCP) in immunocompromised patients, particularly those with HIV/AIDS.

Adverse Effects:

- Hematologic: Hemolysis, particularly in individuals with glucose-6-phosphate dehydrogenase (G6PD) deficiency, and methemoglobinemia.
- Dermatologic: Skin rashes, including severe reactions like erythema multiforme and toxic epidermal necrolysis.
- Gastrointestinal: Nausea, vomiting, and abdominal pain.
- Neurologic: Peripheral neuropathy and headache.
- Others: Dapsone syndrome (a hypersensitivity reaction characterized by fever, rash, and lymphadenopathy).

Pharmacology of Rifampicin (RIF)

Chemical Structure:

Rifampicin is a member of the rifamycin group of antibiotics. Its chemical name is 3-[[(4-methyl-1-piperazinyl)imino]methyl]rifamycin.

Mechanism of Action:

Rifampicin inhibits DNA-dependent RNA polymerase in bacterial cells, thereby blocking the transcription of RNA. This inhibition prevents bacterial protein synthesis and results in a bactericidal effect against a wide range of bacteria, including *Mycobacterium leprae* and *Mycobacterium tuberculosis*.

Pharmacokinetics:

- **Absorption:** Rifampicin is well absorbed from the gastrointestinal tract after oral administration. However, its absorption can be reduced by food.
- **Distribution:** It is widely distributed in the body, including the cerebrospinal fluid (CSF) and intracellular compartments. It crosses the placenta and is excreted in breast milk.
- **Metabolism:** Rifampicin is metabolized in the liver, primarily by deacetylation. The metabolite retains antimicrobial activity.
- **Excretion:** It is excreted mainly in bile and, to a lesser extent, in urine. The half-life of rifampicin ranges from 3 to 5 hours.

Therapeutic Uses:

- Treatment of tuberculosis (TB) as part of combination therapy.
- Treatment of leprosy as part of multidrug therapy (MDT).
- Prophylaxis against meningococcal meningitis.
- Treatment of other bacterial infections, such as brucellosis and Legionnaires' disease.

Adverse Effects:

- Hepatotoxicity: Elevated liver enzymes and, in severe cases, hepatitis.
- Gastrointestinal: Nausea, vomiting, abdominal pain, and diarrhea.
- Dermatologic: Rash and pruritus.
- Hematologic: Thrombocytopenia, leukopenia, and hemolytic anemia.

- Flu-like Syndrome: Fever, chills, and myalgia, especially with intermittent dosing.
- Discoloration of Body Fluids: Rifampicin can cause a red-orange discoloration of urine, sweat, tears, and other body fluids.

Drug Interactions: Rifampicin is a potent inducer of cytochrome P450 enzymes, leading to significant drug interactions. It can reduce the effectiveness of oral contraceptives, anticoagulants, antiretroviral drugs, and other medications metabolized by the liver.

CLOFAZIMINE:

1. Pharmacodynamics:

a. Clofazimine is a lipophilic, fat-soluble compound that exhibits both antimicrobial and anti-inflammatory properties.

b. It is believed to disrupt bacterial cell membrane integrity and affect the respiratory chain in mycobacteria, including Mycobacterium leprae, the causative agent of leprosy.

c. Clofazimine's exact mechanism of action is not fully understood, but it is thought to create free radicals that damage bacterial DNA and proteins, leading to bacterial death.

d. Additionally, clofazimine has anti-inflammatory effects, which can help in reducing tissue inflammation associated with conditions like leprosy reactions.

2. Pharmacokinetics:

a. **Absorption:** Clofazimine is well-absorbed when taken orally.

b. **Distribution:** It accumulates in various tissues, including skin, adipose tissue, and reticuloendothelial cells.

c. **Metabolism:** Clofazimine is primarily metabolized in the liver.

d. **Excretion:** It is excreted through feces, with minimal renal excretion.

3. **Half-life:** The elimination half-life of clofazimine can range from several weeks to months, contributing to its long duration of action.

4. **Dosage:** The dosage of clofazimine varies depending on the condition being treated. It is often used in multidrug therapy for leprosy and is taken as part of a combination regimen.

5. **Adverse Effects:** Common side effects of clofazimine can include gastrointestinal disturbances, skin discoloration (reddish-brown to dark brown), and occasionally, reversible pigmentation of mucous membranes.

CORTICOSTEROIDS:

1. **Pharmacodynamics:**

    a. Corticosteroids, such as prednisone or prednisolone, are synthetic drugs that mimic the actions of natural corticosteroid hormones produced by the adrenal glands.

    b. They have powerful anti-inflammatory and immunosuppressive properties. Corticosteroids act by suppressing the immune system's response to inflammation, reducing the release of inflammatory mediators, and inhibiting the function of immune cells involved in the inflammatory process.

2. **Pharmacokinetics:**

    a. **Absorption:** Corticosteroids can be administered orally, topically, intravenously, or by various other routes, and their absorption depends on the specific formulation.

3. **Metabolism:** Corticosteroids are metabolized in the liver, and their metabolism can be influenced by individual factors and concomitant use of other drugs.

4. **Excretion:** Corticosteroids and their metabolites are primarily excreted through the urine.

5. **Half-life:** The elimination half-life varies depending on the specific corticosteroid used.

6. **Dosage:** Dosage and administration of corticosteroids depend on the medical condition, the severity of inflammation, and the patient's individual response.

They are often prescribed for short-term use to manage acute inflammation and may be tapered to prevent withdrawal effects.

7. **Adverse Effects**: Corticosteroids have a wide range of potential side effects, including but not limited to immunosuppression, bone density loss (osteoporosis), weight gain, increased blood pressure, glucose intolerance, mood changes, and susceptibility to infections. Prolonged use or high doses can lead to more serious complications.

THALIDOMIDE:

Thalidomide is a medication with complex pharmacology, primarily known for its immunomodulatory properties. In short, here is an overview of the pharmacology of thalidomide:

1. Pharmacodynamics:

a. Thalidomide exerts its effects by modulating the immune system and inflammatory responses. It inhibits the production of pro-inflammatory cytokines, such as tumor necrosis factor-alpha (TNF-α), and enhances the release of anti-inflammatory cytokines.

b. It also has anti-angiogenic properties, which means it can inhibit the formation of new blood vessels.

2. Pharmacokinetics:

a. Thalidomide is well-absorbed after oral administration and reaches peak plasma concentrations within a few hours.

b. It undergoes extensive metabolism in the liver, primarily through hydroxylation and subsequent conjugation.

c. The drug is excreted in both urine and feces.

3. Half-life:

a. The elimination half-life of thalidomide is relatively short, typically around 5-7 hours.

4. Dosage:

a. The dosage of thalidomide depends on the specific medical condition being treated, such as leprosy reactions, multiple myeloma, or certain autoimmune disorders.

5. **Adverse Effects:**

    a. Thalidomide is known to have potentially severe side effects, including teratogenicity (causing birth defects if taken during pregnancy), peripheral neuropathy, and somnolence (drowsiness). Due to its teratogenic effects, thalidomide is subject to strict prescribing and dispensing regulations.

CHAPTER – 11

ANTIFUNGAL AGENTS

Mrs. Neelam Singh

Assistant Professor, Rajiv Gandhi Institute of Pharmacy, Faculty of Pharmaceutical Science & Technology, AKS University Satna, MP-India

ABSTRACT:

Antifungal agents are a class of medications used to treat fungal infections, which can range from superficial skin conditions to more severe systemic infections. These agents work by targeting specific components of fungal cells, thereby inhibiting their growth or killing them outright. There are several classes of antifungal drugs, including azoles, polyenes, echinocandins, allylamines, and others. Azoles, such as fluconazole and itraconazole, inhibit the synthesis of ergosterol, an essential component of fungal cell membranes. Polyenes, like amphotericin B and nystatin, bind to ergosterol and create pores in the fungal cell membrane, leading to cell death. Echinocandins, such as caspofungin and micafungin, inhibit the synthesis of β-glucan, a critical component of the fungal cell wall. Allylamines, including terbinafine and naftifine, inhibit squalene epoxidase, another enzyme involved in ergosterol synthesis. These antifungal agents are used to treat a variety of fungal infections, such as candidiasis, aspergillosis, cryptococcosis, and dermatophyte infections. The choice of antifungal drug depends on the type of infection, the causative organism, and patient-specific factors such as underlying health conditions and potential drug interactions. Effective management of fungal infections often requires a combination of pharmacologic therapy and supportive care to ensure complete eradication and prevent recurrence.

Introduction to Antifungal Agents

Fungal infections, or mycoses, are caused by fungi and can affect various parts of the body, ranging from superficial skin infections to severe systemic infections. Antifungal agents are medications specifically designed to treat these infections by either inhibiting fungal growth (fungistatic) or killing the fungi (fungicidal). The need for effective antifungal therapy has grown due to the increase in immunocompromised populations, such as those with HIV/AIDS, cancer, or undergoing immunosuppressive therapy, who are more susceptible to severe fungal infections.

Classification of Antifungal Agents

Antifungal agents can be classified based on their chemical structure, mechanism of action, and spectrum of activity. The main classes include:

1. **Azoles**
2. **Polyenes**
3. **Echinocandins**
4. **Allylamines**
5. **Other Antifungal Agents**

1. Azoles

Azoles are further divided into two subclasses: imidazoles and triazoles.

- **Imidazoles:**
    - **Examples:** Clotrimazole, Ketoconazole, Miconazole.
    - **Mechanism of Action:** Inhibit the enzyme lanosterol 14-α-demethylase, blocking ergosterol synthesis, an essential component of the fungal cell membrane.
- **Triazoles:**
    - **Examples:** Fluconazole, Itraconazole, Voriconazole, Posaconazole.
    - **Mechanism of Action:** Similar to imidazoles, triazoles also inhibit ergosterol synthesis but generally have a broader spectrum of activity and better pharmacokinetic properties.

2. Polyenes

- **Examples:** Amphotericin B, Nystatin.

- **Mechanism of Action:** Bind to ergosterol in the fungal cell membrane, creating pores that lead to cell leakage and death. They are primarily used for severe systemic infections (Amphotericin B) and topical applications (Nystatin).

3. Echinocandins

- **Examples:** Caspofungin, Micafungin, Anidulafungin.
- **Mechanism of Action:** Inhibit the synthesis of β-glucan, an essential component of the fungal cell wall, leading to cell lysis and death. They are particularly effective against Candida and Aspergillus species.

4. Allylamines

- **Examples:** Terbinafine, Naftifine.
- **Mechanism of Action:** Inhibit squalene epoxidase, an enzyme involved in ergosterol synthesis, leading to the accumulation of toxic squalene and disruption of the cell membrane. They are primarily used for dermatophyte infections (e.g., athlete's foot, ringworm).

5. Other Antifungal Agents

- **Griseofulvin:** Inhibits fungal cell mitosis by binding to microtubules. Used orally for dermatophyte infections.
- **Flucytosine:** Converts into 5-fluorouracil within the fungal cell, inhibiting DNA and RNA synthesis. Often used in combination with other antifungals for systemic infections.
- **Tolnaftate:** Used topically for dermatophyte infections. It distorts hyphae and stunts mycelial growth in susceptible fungi.

Fluconazole:

1. Mechanism of Action:

a. Fluconazole inhibits the enzyme lanosterol 14-alpha-demethylase, which is involved in the synthesis of ergosterol, a crucial component of fungal cell membranes. This inhibition disrupts the integrity of the fungal cell membrane.

2. **Spectrum of Activity:**
   a. Fluconazole is effective against a wide range of fungal pathogens, including Candida species (which cause infections like thrush and vaginal yeast infections) and Cryptococcus neoformans.

3. **Route of Administration:**
   a. Fluconazole is available in oral and intravenous formulations, providing flexibility in treatment approaches.

4. **Clinical Applications:**
   a. Commonly used for the treatment of systemic and superficial fungal infections.
   b. It is particularly useful in the treatment of Candida infections, including those that involve the central nervous system.

5. **Metabolism and Elimination:**
   a. Fluconazole is primarily metabolized in the liver, and the majority of the drug is excreted unchanged in the urine.

6. **Drug Interactions:**
   a. Fluconazole can inhibit the metabolism of other drugs, potentially leading to increased levels of co-administered medications.

Itraconazole:

1. **Mechanism of Action:**
   a. Itraconazole, like fluconazole, inhibits lanosterol 14-alpha-demethylase. It interferes with the synthesis of ergosterol, disrupting fungal cell membranes.

2. **Spectrum of Activity:**
   a. Itraconazole has a broader spectrum of antifungal activity compared to fluconazole. It is effective against various fungi, including Candida, Aspergillus, Blastomyces, Histoplasma, and others.

3. **Formulations:**

a. Itraconazole is available in both oral and intravenous formulations. The oral form is often used for chronic or less severe fungal infections.

4. Clinical Applications:

a. Used to treat a wide range of systemic fungal infections, including aspergillosis, blastomycosis, histoplasmosis, and dermatophyte infections.

5. Metabolism and Elimination:

a. Itraconazole undergoes extensive metabolism in the liver, and its active metabolites contribute to antifungal activity. It is eliminated mainly through feces.

6. Food Interactions:

a. Itraconazole absorption can be enhanced when taken with food, particularly a fatty meal.

Ketoconazole:

1. Mechanism of Action:

a. Ketoconazole is an azole antifungal that inhibits the synthesis of ergosterol, a key component of fungal cell membranes, by blocking the enzyme lanosterol 14-alpha-demethylase.

2. Spectrum of Activity:

a. Ketoconazole has a broad spectrum of antifungal activity and is effective against various fungi, including Candida species, dermatophytes, and some dimorphic fungi.

3. Route of Administration:

a. Ketoconazole is available in oral and topical formulations. The oral form is often used for systemic fungal infections.

4. Clinical Applications:

a. Historically, ketoconazole has been used to treat systemic fungal infections. However, due to the risk of serious hepatotoxicity and drug interactions, its systemic use has been largely replaced by other azole antifungals like fluconazole, itraconazole, and voriconazole.

5. Metabolism and Elimination:

    a. Ketoconazole undergoes extensive hepatic metabolism, and its metabolites are excreted in the urine and feces.

6. Drug Interactions:

    a. Ketoconazole is known for its potential to inhibit the metabolism of other drugs through the cytochrome P450 system, leading to drug interactions. This can result in increased levels of co-administered medications.

Voriconazole:

1. Mechanism of Action:

    a. Voriconazole is a second-generation triazole antifungal that inhibits the synthesis of ergosterol by blocking lanosterol 14-alpha-demethylase.

2. Spectrum of Activity:

    a. Voriconazole has a broad spectrum of activity against various fungi, including Candida species, Aspergillus species, and other molds.

3. Route of Administration:

    a. Voriconazole is available in both oral and intravenous formulations, providing flexibility in the treatment of systemic fungal infections.

4. Clinical Applications:

    a. Voriconazole is particularly effective against invasive aspergillosis and other serious fungal infections. It is often used in immunocompromised patients.

5. Metabolism and Elimination:

    a. Voriconazole undergoes extensive hepatic metabolism, primarily through the cytochrome P450 system. Individual variability in metabolism can affect plasma concentrations.

6. Drug Interactions:

a. Voriconazole also has the potential to interact with various drugs, including those metabolized by cytochrome P450 enzymes. Dose adjustments may be necessary when co-administering medications.

Amphotericin B:

1. Mechanism of Action:

a. Amphotericin B binds to ergosterol, a component of fungal cell membranes, forming pores that disrupt membrane integrity. This leads to leakage of cellular components, ultimately causing fungal cell death.

2. Spectrum of Activity:

a. Amphotericin B has a broad spectrum of antifungal activity and is effective against a wide range of fungi, including Candida species, Aspergillus species, Cryptococcus neoformans, and some dimorphic fungi.

3. Route of Administration:

a. Amphotericin B is typically administered intravenously due to poor oral absorption.

4. Clinical Applications:

a. It is often used in the treatment of severe systemic fungal infections, especially in immunocompromised patients. It may also be used for certain localized fungal infections.

5. Adverse Effects:

a. Amphotericin B is known for its potential to cause significant side effects, including infusion-related reactions (fever, chills), nephrotoxicity (kidney damage), and electrolyte imbalances.

6. Formulations:

a. Liposomal formulations of amphotericin B have been developed to reduce some of the side effects associated with the conventional formulation.

Nystatin:

1. Mechanism of Action:

a. Nystatin binds to ergosterol in fungal cell membranes, leading to the formation of pores and disruption of membrane integrity. This results in increased permeability and cell death.

2. Spectrum of Activity:

a. Nystatin is primarily effective against Candida species, including Candida albicans. It is commonly used for mucocutaneous and superficial fungal infections.

3. Route of Administration:

a. Nystatin is available in various formulations, including oral suspensions, topical creams, and ointments. It is usually administered topically or orally.

4. Clinical Applications:

a. Nystatin is commonly used for the treatment of oral thrush (Candida infection in the mouth) and other mucocutaneous candidiasis.

5. Adverse Effects:

a. Nystatin is generally well-tolerated when used topically or orally. However, systemic absorption is minimal, reducing the risk of significant adverse effects.

Caspofungin:

1. Mechanism of Action:

a. Caspofungin inhibits the synthesis of beta-glucan, an essential component of the fungal cell wall. By inhibiting the enzyme 1,3-beta-D-glucan synthase, caspofungin disrupts the integrity of the fungal cell wall, leading to cell death.

2. **Spectrum of Activity:**

a. Caspofungin has activity against a variety of Candida species, including Candida albicans, Candida glabrata, Candida tropicalis, and Aspergillus species.

3. **Route of Administration:**

a. Caspofungin is administered intravenously.

4. **Clinical Applications:**

a. It is used in the treatment of invasive aspergillosis, candidemia, esophageal candidiasis, and other serious fungal infections, particularly in patients who are refractory to or intolerant of other antifungal agents.

5. **Metabolism and Elimination**:

a. Caspofungin undergoes chemical degradation rather than hepatic metabolism. It is eliminated primarily through feces.

Micafungin:

1. **Mechanism of Action:**

a. Micafungin, like caspofungin, inhibits the synthesis of beta-glucan in the fungal cell wall.

2. **Spectrum of Activity:**

a. Micafungin has activity against a range of Candida species, including Candida albicans, Candida glabrata, Candida tropicalis, and Aspergillus species.

3. **Route of Administration:**

a. Micafungin is available in both intravenous and, in some regions, oral formulations.

4. **Clinical Applications:**

a. Micafungin is indicated for the treatment of candidemia, acute disseminated candidiasis, esophageal candidiasis, and prophylaxis of

Candida infections in patients undergoing hematopoietic stem cell transplantation.

5. Metabolism and Elimination:

a. Micafungin undergoes partial hepatic metabolism. The majority of the drug is excreted unchanged in the urine.

Terbinafine:

1. Mechanism of Action:

a. Terbinafine inhibits an enzyme called squalene epoxidase, which is involved in the synthesis of ergosterol, an essential component of fungal cell membranes. By blocking this enzyme, terbinafine disrupts the fungal cell membrane, leading to the death of the fungal cells.

2. Spectrum of Activity:

a. Terbinafine is particularly effective against dermatophyte fungi, which are responsible for many superficial fungal infections, such as athlete's foot (tinea pedis), ringworm (tinea corporis), and fungal nail infections (onychomycosis).

3. Route of Administration:

a. Terbinafine is available in oral and topical formulations. Oral terbinafine is commonly used for the treatment of fungal nail infections.

4. Metabolism and Elimination:

a. Terbinafine undergoes extensive hepatic metabolism, and the majority of the drug and its metabolites are excreted in the urine.

5. Clinical Applications:

a. Terbinafine is mainly used for dermatophyte infections of the skin, nails, and hair. It is not typically used for systemic fungal infections.

Flucytosine:

1. Mechanism of Action:

a. Flucytosine is converted to 5-fluorouracil within the fungal cells. 5-fluorouracil disrupts fungal RNA and DNA synthesis, leading to inhibition of fungal protein and nucleic acid synthesis.

2. Spectrum of Activity:

a. Flucytosine is primarily effective against yeasts, especially Candida species and Cryptococcus neoformans. It is often used in combination with other antifungal agents.

3. Route of Administration:

a. Flucytosine is usually administered orally.

4. Metabolism and Elimination:

a. Flucytosine is well-absorbed orally and is primarily excreted unchanged in the urine. It requires dosage adjustments in patients with renal impairment.

5. Clinical Applications:

a. Flucytosine is often used in combination therapy, particularly with amphotericin B, for the treatment of serious systemic fungal infections, such as cryptococcal meningitis and Candida infections.

Clotrimazole:

1. Mechanism of Action:

a. Clotrimazole belongs to the azole class of antifungals. It inhibits the synthesis of ergosterol, a key component of fungal cell membranes, by blocking the enzyme lanosterol 14-alpha-demethylase.

2. Spectrum of Activity:

a. Clotrimazole is effective against a variety of fungi, including Candida species and dermatophytes. It is commonly used for the treatment of superficial fungal infections such as vaginal yeast infections, oral thrush, and skin infections like athlete's foot and ringworm.

3. Route of Administration:

a. Clotrimazole is available in various formulations, including topical creams, powders, and oral lozenges. Topical formulations are commonly used for skin and mucosal infections.

4. **Metabolism and Elimination:**

a. Clotrimazole is primarily used topically, and systemic absorption is minimal. When used topically, it does not undergo significant metabolism, and any absorbed drug is excreted in the urine.

5. **Clinical Applications:**

a. Clotrimazole is widely used for the treatment of superficial fungal infections, both over-the-counter and by prescription.

Tavaborole:

1. **Mechanism of Action:**

a. Tavaborole is an oxaborole antifungal. It inhibits fungal protein synthesis by targeting leucyl-tRNA synthetase, an enzyme necessary for protein translation in the fungal cell.

2. **Spectrum of Activity:**

a. Tavaborole is primarily used for the treatment of onychomycosis (fungal infection of the toenails or fingernails) caused by dermatophyte fungi.

3. **Route of Administration:**

a. Tavaborole is available in a topical solution that is applied directly to the affected nails.

4. **Metabolism and Elimination:**

a. Tavaborole is applied topically, and systemic absorption is minimal. It is metabolized through oxidative pathways and is excreted in both urine and feces.

5. **Clinical Applications:**

a. Tavaborole is specifically indicated for the treatment of onychomycosis, providing an alternative to systemic antifungal medications for nail infections.

CHAPTER – 12

ANTIVIRAL DRUGS

Mr. Abu Tahir

Assistant Professor, Rajiv Gandhi Institute of Pharmacy, Faculty of Pharmaceutical Science & Technology, AKS University Satna, MP-India

ABSTRACT:

Antiviral drugs are medications designed to treat viral infections by inhibiting the replication and spread of viruses within the host organism. Unlike antibiotics, which target bacteria, antiviral drugs are specifically tailored to interfere with viral processes. These drugs work by targeting various stages of the viral life cycle, including viral entry, uncoating, replication, assembly, and release. Common antiviral drugs include acyclovir, which is used to treat herpes simplex virus infections, and oseltamivir, used for influenza. The development of antiretroviral therapy (ART) has significantly improved the management of HIV/AIDS, turning it into a manageable chronic condition. Antivirals such as remdesivir have also been pivotal in treating emerging viral infections like COVID-19. The challenge in antiviral drug development lies in the high mutation rates of viruses, which can lead to drug resistance. Therefore, combination therapies, which use multiple drugs with different mechanisms of action, are often employed to enhance efficacy and reduce the likelihood of resistance. The continued research and development of antiviral drugs are crucial in combating both existing and emerging viral threats, improving public health outcomes globally.

Introduction to Antiviral Drugs

Antiviral drugs are a class of medications specifically designed to treat viral infections by inhibiting the development and replication of viruses. Unlike bacteria, viruses are obligate intracellular parasites, meaning they require a host cell to replicate and propagate. This unique characteristic makes the development of antiviral drugs particularly challenging, as these medications must selectively target viral processes without causing significant harm to the host's cells. Antiviral therapy has been crucial in the management of various viral infections, including HIV/AIDS, hepatitis, influenza, and herpesvirus infections. With the rise of new and emerging viral diseases, the importance of effective antiviral treatments continues to grow.

Classification of Antiviral Drugs

Antiviral drugs can be classified based on their mechanism of action and the stage of the viral life cycle they target. The main classes include:

1. **Nucleoside and Nucleotide Analogues**

2. **Non-Nucleoside Polymerase Inhibitors**

3. **Protease Inhibitors**

4. **Entry and Fusion Inhibitors**

5. **Integrase Inhibitors**

6. **Neuraminidase Inhibitors**

7. **Other Antiviral Agents**

1. Nucleoside and Nucleotide Analogues

Examples: Acyclovir, Zidovudine (AZT), Lamivudine, Tenofovir

Mechanism of Action: These drugs mimic the natural nucleosides or nucleotides that are incorporated into viral DNA or RNA during replication. Once incorporated, they cause premature chain termination or introduce mutations, inhibiting viral replication.

2. Non-Nucleoside Polymerase Inhibitors

Examples: Efavirenz, Nevirapine

Mechanism of Action: These inhibitors bind directly to the viral RNA-dependent DNA polymerase (reverse transcriptase) or DNA-dependent RNA polymerase, causing conformational changes that inhibit the enzyme's activity without mimicking nucleosides.

3. Protease Inhibitors

Examples: Ritonavir, Saquinavir, Lopinavir

Mechanism of Action: Protease inhibitors target viral proteases, which are enzymes essential for the cleavage of viral polyprotein precursors into functional viral proteins. By inhibiting these proteases, the maturation of viral particles is disrupted.

4. Entry and Fusion Inhibitors

Examples: Enfuvirtide, Maraviroc

Mechanism of Action: These drugs prevent the virus from entering host cells by blocking the binding of the virus to the host cell receptors or inhibiting the fusion of the viral envelope with the host cell membrane.

5. Integrase Inhibitors

Examples: Raltegravir, Elvitegravir

Mechanism of Action: Integrase inhibitors block the viral enzyme integrase, which is required for the integration of viral DNA into the host genome, a critical step in the viral replication cycle.

6. Neuraminidase Inhibitors

Examples: Oseltamivir (Tamiflu), Zanamivir (Relenza)

Mechanism of Action: These drugs inhibit the viral enzyme neuraminidase, which is necessary for the release of new viral particles from infected cells. This inhibition prevents the spread of the virus to other cells.

7. Other Antiviral Agents

Examples: Interferons, Remdesivir

Mechanism of Action: Interferons are proteins that enhance the immune response against viral infections. Remdesivir, used for COVID-19, is a nucleoside analogue that inhibits viral RNA polymerase.

Pharmacology of Acyclovir

Chemical Structure:

Acyclovir is a synthetic nucleoside analogue of guanine.

Mechanism of Action:

Acyclovir is selectively activated by viral thymidine kinase, which phosphorylates acyclovir to acyclovir monophosphate. Cellular enzymes further convert it to acyclovir triphosphate, which is incorporated into viral DNA by viral DNA polymerase. This incorporation leads to premature chain termination, thereby inhibiting viral DNA synthesis and replication.

Pharmacokinetics:

- **Absorption:** Oral bioavailability is relatively low (15-30%). Intravenous and topical formulations are also available.
- **Distribution:** Widely distributed in body fluids, including the cerebrospinal fluid (CSF). It crosses the placenta and is excreted in breast milk.
- **Metabolism:** Acyclovir is minimally metabolized.
- **Excretion:** Primarily excreted unchanged in the urine by glomerular filtration and tubular secretion. The half-life ranges from 2 to 3 hours in patients with normal renal function.

Therapeutic Uses:

- Treatment of herpes simplex virus (HSV) infections, including genital herpes, herpes labialis, and HSV encephalitis.
- Treatment and prophylaxis of varicella-zoster virus (VZV) infections, including chickenpox and shingles.
- Prophylaxis in immunocompromised patients to prevent HSV and VZV infections.

Adverse Effects:

- **Common:** Nausea, diarrhea, headache.
- **Severe:** Renal toxicity (crystalluria), neurotoxicity (tremors, confusion), particularly with intravenous administration.
- **Local:** Inflammation and phlebitis at the injection site with intravenous use.

Pharmacology of Famciclovir

Chemical Structure:

Famciclovir is the diacetyl ester prodrug of penciclovir, a guanine analogue.

Mechanism of Action:

Famciclovir is rapidly converted to penciclovir in the liver. Penciclovir, similar to acyclovir, is phosphorylated by viral thymidine kinase to penciclovir monophosphate and then to penciclovir triphosphate by cellular kinases. Penciclovir triphosphate inhibits viral DNA polymerase, reducing viral DNA synthesis and replication without causing chain termination.

Pharmacokinetics:

- **Absorption:** Famciclovir has good oral bioavailability (about 77%). It is rapidly absorbed and converted to penciclovir.
- **Distribution:** Penciclovir is widely distributed in tissues. It is also excreted in breast milk.
- **Metabolism:** Famciclovir is metabolized to penciclovir by first-pass metabolism in the liver.
- **Excretion:** Penciclovir is excreted unchanged in the urine. The half-life of penciclovir is about 2 to 3 hours.

Therapeutic Uses:

- Treatment of acute herpes zoster (shingles).
- Treatment and suppression of recurrent genital herpes.
- Treatment of herpes labialis (cold sores).
- Prophylaxis and treatment of HSV infections in immunocompromised patients.

Adverse Effects:

- **Common:** Headache, nausea, diarrhea.
- **Severe:** Rarely, acute renal failure, particularly in patients with pre-existing renal impairment.
- **Other:** Rash, pruritus, and other hypersensitivity reactions.

Pharmacology of Tenofovir

Chemical Structure: Tenofovir is an acyclic nucleoside phosphonate analogue of adenosine monophosphate.

Mechanism of Action: Tenofovir is converted intracellularly to tenofovir diphosphate, which acts as a competitive inhibitor of HIV-1 reverse transcriptase and HBV polymerase. By incorporating into the viral DNA chain, tenofovir causes premature termination of DNA elongation, thereby inhibiting viral replication.

Pharmacokinetics:

- **Absorption:** Oral bioavailability is approximately 25-39% when taken on an empty stomach, and increases with a high-fat meal.
- **Distribution:** Widely distributed in the body, including into cerebrospinal fluid. It is also excreted in breast milk.
- **Metabolism:** Tenofovir is not extensively metabolized.
- **Excretion:** Primarily excreted unchanged in the urine via glomerular filtration and active tubular secretion. The half-life is approximately 17 hours.

Therapeutic Uses:

- Treatment of HIV-1 infection in combination with other antiretroviral agents.
- Treatment of chronic hepatitis B virus (HBV) infection.

Adverse Effects:

- **Common:** Nausea, vomiting, diarrhea, dizziness, rash.
- **Severe:** Renal toxicity (including acute renal failure and Fanconi syndrome), bone toxicity (osteomalacia and decreased bone mineral density).
- **Other:** Lactic acidosis and hepatomegaly with steatosis, particularly in patients with pre-existing liver disease.

Pharmacology of Zanamivir

Chemical Structure: Zanamivir is a neuraminidase inhibitor structurally related to sialic acid.

Mechanism of Action: Zanamivir inhibits the influenza virus neuraminidase enzyme, which is essential for the release of new viral particles from infected cells and for the virus's ability to spread. By blocking this enzyme, zanamivir prevents the virus from spreading in the respiratory tract, thereby limiting the infection.

Pharmacokinetics:

- **Absorption:** Zanamivir is administered via inhalation, which results in direct delivery to the respiratory tract. Systemic absorption is low.
- **Distribution:** After inhalation, zanamivir is distributed in the respiratory tract, with minimal systemic exposure.
- **Metabolism:** Zanamivir is not metabolized.
- **Excretion:** Excreted unchanged in the urine. The half-life of zanamivir is approximately 2.5 to 5 hours.

Therapeutic Uses:

- Treatment of acute, uncomplicated influenza A and B in patients who have been symptomatic for no more than 2 days.
- Prophylaxis of influenza A and B.

Adverse Effects:

- **Common:** Cough, throat discomfort, nasal symptoms.
- **Severe:** Bronchospasm and decline in lung function, especially in patients with underlying respiratory diseases such as asthma or chronic obstructive pulmonary disease (COPD).
- **Other:** Rare cases of allergic reactions, including orofacial edema.

Zanamivir:

1. **Mechanism of Action:** Zanamivir directly inhibits the neuraminidase enzyme on the surface of influenza viruses, similar to oseltamivir. By

preventing the release of new viral particles, zanamivir helps to reduce the severity and duration of influenza symptoms.

2. **Administration:** Zanamivir is available in an inhaled form, typically delivered using a device called a Diskhaler. It is not well absorbed through the gastrointestinal tract, so it is administered via inhalation to achieve higher concentrations in the respiratory tract.

3. **Pharmacokinetics:** Zanamivir has poor oral bioavailability, and the majority of the inhaled dose is deposited in the respiratory tract. It has a relatively short half-life of approximately 2-5 hours and is primarily excreted unchanged in the urine.

Raltegravir:

1. **Mechanism of Action:** Raltegravir inhibits the activity of the HIV integrase enzyme. HIV integrase is responsible for integrating the viral DNA into the host cell genome. By inhibiting this process, raltegravir prevents the replication of the virus within the host cell.

2. **Administration:** Raltegravir is administered orally, typically as raltegravir potassium. It is well-absorbed from the gastrointestinal tract, and its absorption is not significantly affected by food.

3. **Metabolism and Elimination:** Raltegravir undergoes glucuronidation in the liver, primarily by uridine diphosphate glucuronosyltransferase 1A1 (UGT1A1). The metabolites are eliminated through both feces and urine.

4. **Pharmacokinetics:** The drug has a relatively short half-life, requiring twice-daily dosing in most cases.

Elvitegravir:

1. **Mechanism of Action:** Elvitegravir also inhibits the integrase enzyme of HIV, preventing the integration of viral DNA into the host cell genome.

2. **Administration:** Elvitegravir is often co-formulated with other antiretroviral drugs in a fixed-dose combination. It is administered orally and is typically given with a boosting agent, cobicistat, to increase its bioavailability.

3. **Metabolism and Elimination:** Elvitegravir undergoes metabolism primarily by cytochrome P450 3A4 (CYP3A4) in the liver. Cobicistat, a pharmacokinetic enhancer, is used to inhibit CYP3A4 and increase the plasma concentrations of elvitegravir. The metabolites are eliminated through feces.

4. **Pharmacokinetics:** Elvitegravir has a longer half-life compared to raltegravir, allowing for once-daily dosing when used in combination with cobicistat.

Entecavir:

1. **Mechanism of Action:** Entecavir is a guanosine nucleoside analogue. It is phosphorylated intracellularly to its active form, entecavir triphosphate. This active metabolite competes with the natural substrate deoxyguanosine triphosphate for incorporation into the growing viral DNA chain. Once incorporated, it causes premature termination of the chain, inhibiting the reverse transcription process and blocking HBV replication.

2. **Administration:** Entecavir is administered orally and is well-absorbed from the gastrointestinal tract.

3. **Metabolism and Elimination:** Entecavir is primarily eliminated unchanged in the urine through a combination of glomerular filtration and active tubular secretion. The drug has a relatively long half-life, allowing for once-daily dosing in most cases.

Telbivudine:

1. **Mechanism of Action:** Telbivudine is a thymidine nucleoside analogue. Similar to entecavir, it undergoes phosphorylation to its active triphosphate form, which is incorporated into the growing viral DNA chain. This incorporation inhibits the reverse transcriptase enzyme, leading to chain termination and inhibition of HBV replication.

2. **Administration:** Telbivudine is administered orally, and it is well-absorbed from the gastrointestinal tract.

3. **Metabolism and Elimination:** Telbivudine is primarily eliminated unchanged in the urine. It does not undergo significant hepatic metabolism. The drug has a relatively long half-life, allowing for once-daily dosing.

Sofosbuvir:

1. **Mechanism of Action:** Sofosbuvir is a nucleotide analog inhibitor of the hepatitis C virus (HCV) RNA polymerase. Once inside the liver cells, it is converted into its active form, which is a substrate for the NS5B polymerase. The active form is incorporated into the growing HCV RNA chain, leading to chain termination and inhibition of viral replication.

2. **Administration:** Sofosbuvir is administered orally and is typically used in combination with other antiviral medications to form a complete regimen for the treatment of hepatitis C.

3. **Metabolism and Elimination:** Sofosbuvir is metabolized in the liver to its active form. The active metabolite has a long half-life, allowing for once-daily dosing. It is excreted primarily through the urine.

Remdesivir:

1. **Mechanism of Action**: Remdesivir is a broad-spectrum antiviral medication initially developed for Ebola virus infection. It is a nucleotide analog that inhibits the action of the viral RNA-dependent RNA polymerase. Remdesivir is thought to be incorporated into the viral RNA chain during replication, leading to premature termination and inhibition of viral replication.

2. **Administration**: Remdesivir is administered intravenously and is typically used in a hospital setting for the treatment of severe cases of COVID-19.

3. **Metabolism and Elimination:** Remdesivir undergoes metabolism to its active form, GS-441524. The active metabolite has a relatively long half-life, allowing for once-daily dosing. It is primarily eliminated through urine and feces.

CHAPTER – 13

ANTHELMINTICS

Ms. Shikha Singh

Assistant Professor, Rajiv Gandhi Institute of Pharmacy, Faculty of

Pharmaceutical Science & Technology, AKS University Satna, MP-India

ABSTRACT:

Anthelmintics are a class of drugs used to treat infections caused by helminths, or parasitic worms, which include nematodes (roundworms), trematodes (flukes), and cestodes (tapeworms). These medications work by targeting various biological processes essential for the survival and reproduction of these parasites. Common anthelmintics include albendazole, mebendazole, ivermectin, praziquantel, and pyrantel pamoate. Albendazole and mebendazole inhibit the polymerization of tubulin, impairing glucose uptake and depleting energy stores in helminths. Ivermectin increases the permeability of the parasite's cell membrane to chloride ions, leading to paralysis and death. Praziquantel induces severe spasms and paralysis of the worms' muscles by increasing calcium ion permeability. Pyrantel pamoate acts as a neuromuscular blocker, causing paralysis of the parasites. The choice of anthelmintic depends on the type of helminth infection and its location in the body. Effective treatment not only alleviates symptoms but also prevents the spread of infection and reduces the risk of complications. Continued research and development of anthelmintics are crucial to address emerging resistance and improve global health outcomes.

Introduction to Anthelmintics

Anthelmintics are a group of antiparasitic drugs designed to expel or destroy helminths (parasitic worms) from the host body. These parasites can cause a variety of diseases in humans and animals, impacting the gastrointestinal tract, blood, lymphatic system, and other tissues. Helminth infections are prevalent in many parts of the world, particularly in areas with poor sanitation and hygiene. Effective anthelmintic treatment is essential for controlling these infections, improving health, and preventing the spread of these parasites.

Classification of Anthelmintics

Anthelmintics can be classified based on their chemical structure, mechanism of action, and the type of helminth they target. The main classes include:

1. **Benzimidazoles**
2. **Avermectins and Milbemycins**
3. **Tetrahydropyrimidines**
4. **Praziquantel and Pyrantel**
5. **Salicylanilides and Substituted Phenols**
6. **Other Anthelmintics**

1. Benzimidazoles

Examples: Albendazole, Mebendazole, Thiabendazole

Mechanism of Action: Benzimidazoles bind to β-tubulin, inhibiting the polymerization of microtubules. This disruption affects cellular processes such as glucose uptake and energy production, leading to the depletion of energy stores and the death of the parasite.

Targeted Helminths: Effective against a broad spectrum of nematodes (roundworms) and some cestodes (tapeworms).

2. Avermectins and Milbemycins

Examples: Ivermectin, Abamectin, Milbemycin Oxime

Mechanism of Action: These drugs bind to glutamate-gated chloride channels, increasing the permeability of the cell membrane to chloride ions. This results in hyperpolarization of the nerve and muscle cells, causing paralysis and death of the parasite.

Targeted Helminths: Primarily effective against nematodes and ectoparasites (e.g., mites, lice).

3. Tetrahydropyrimidines

Examples: Pyrantel Pamoate, Oxantel

Mechanism of Action: Tetrahydropyrimidines act as depolarizing neuromuscular blocking agents, causing spastic paralysis of the helminths. The paralyzed worms are then expelled from the host's body.

Targeted Helminths: Effective against a variety of gastrointestinal nematodes.

4. Praziquantel and Pyrantel

Examples: Praziquantel, Pyrantel Pamoate

Mechanism of Action: Praziquantel increases the permeability of the cell membrane to calcium ions, causing muscle contraction, paralysis, and death of the parasite. Pyrantel pamoate acts as a neuromuscular blocker, leading to paralysis and expulsion of the worms.

Targeted Helminths: Praziquantel is effective against trematodes (flukes) and cestodes (tapeworms), while pyrantel pamoate is used for nematode infections.

5. Salicylanilides and Substituted Phenols

Examples: Niclosamide, Oxyclozanide

Mechanism of Action: These drugs disrupt oxidative phosphorylation in the parasite, inhibiting ATP production and leading to energy depletion and death of the parasite.

Targeted Helminths: Primarily effective against cestodes and trematodes.

6. Other Anthelmintics

Examples: Levamisole, Piperazine

Mechanism of Action: Levamisole acts as a nicotinic acetylcholine receptor agonist, causing spastic paralysis of the helminths. Piperazine induces flaccid paralysis by acting as a GABA agonist.

Targeted Helminths: Levamisole is used for nematode infections, while piperazine is effective against pinworms and roundworms.

ALBENDAZOLE:

Mechanism of Action:

a. Albendazole inhibits microtubule polymerization in the parasite, disrupting its microtubule structure. This interferes with the energy metabolism of the parasite and leads to immobilization and death.

Pharmacokinetics:

a. **Absorption:** Albendazole is poorly absorbed in the gastrointestinal tract.

b. **Metabolism:** It undergoes extensive hepatic metabolism to its active form, albendazole sulfoxide, which is responsible for its anthelmintic activity.

c. **Elimination:** The metabolites are primarily excreted in the bile.

Clinical Uses:

a. Albendazole is used to treat a variety of parasitic infections, including intestinal helminthiasis (such as hookworm, roundworm, and whipworm infections) and tissue helminthiasis (such as cysticercosis and hydatid disease).

MEBENDAZOLE:

Mechanism of Action:

a. Mebendazole acts by disrupting the microtubule structure in the parasites, inhibiting glucose uptake and disrupting the parasite's energy metabolism.

Pharmacokinetics:

a. **Absorption:** Mebendazole is poorly absorbed in the gastrointestinal tract.

b. **Metabolism:** It undergoes extensive hepatic metabolism to its active form.

c. **Elimination:** The drug and its metabolites are excreted in the feces.

Clinical Uses:

a. Mebendazole is commonly used to treat intestinal helminth infections, including infections caused by roundworms, hookworms, and whipworms.

LEVAMISOLE:

Mechanism of Action:

a. Levamisole is an immunomodulator and acts as a nicotinic acetylcholine receptor agonist. It stimulates the release of acetylcholine at the neuromuscular junction, leading to paralysis and expulsion of the worms.

Pharmacokinetics:

a. **Absorption**: Levamisole is well-absorbed after oral administration.

b. **Metabolism:** It undergoes hepatic metabolism.

c. **Elimination:** The drug and its metabolites are excreted in the urine.

Clinical Uses:

a. Levamisole is used to treat various worm infections, including roundworm and hookworm infections.

Adverse Effects:

a. Adverse effects may include nausea, vomiting, diarrhea, and rash.

b. Levamisole can cause agranulocytosis (a severe reduction in white blood cells), and regular monitoring of blood counts is recommended during treatment.

PIPERAZINE:

Mechanism of Action:

a. Piperazine paralyzes the helminths by blocking the response of the worm's musculature to acetylcholine.

Pharmacokinetics:

a. **Absorption:** Piperazine is well-absorbed after oral administration.

b. **Metabolism:** It has minimal metabolism in the body.

c. **Elimination:** Piperazine and its metabolites are primarily excreted in the urine.

Clinical Uses:

a. Piperazine is mainly used to treat infections caused by roundworms, particularly Ascaris lumbricoides.

Adverse Effects:

a. Piperazine is generally well-tolerated, but side effects may include nausea, vomiting, and dizziness.

IVERMECTIN:

Mechanism of Action:

a. Ivermectin acts as an agonist at the glutamate-gated chloride ion channels in invertebrates, leading to an increase in chloride ion permeability and hyperpolarization of the cell membrane. This results in paralysis and death of the targeted parasites.

Pharmacokinetics:

a. **Absorption:** Ivermectin is well-absorbed after oral administration.

b. **Distribution:** It has a large volume of distribution, and it mainly stays within the tissues.

c. **Metabolism:** Ivermectin undergoes hepatic metabolism.

d. **Elimination:** The drug and its metabolites are primarily excreted in the feces.

Clinical Uses:

a. Ivermectin is used to treat a variety of parasitic infections, including onchocerciasis (river blindness), strongyloidiasis, and certain types of skin conditions caused by parasitic mites.

Adverse Effects:

a. Adverse effects are generally mild and include headache, dizziness, and gastrointestinal symptoms.

b. In some cases, particularly when used in high doses, there have been reports of neurological effects.

ABAMECTIN:

Mechanism of Action:

a. Abamectin is a mixture of avermectins, and its mechanism of action is similar to that of Ivermectin. It acts on glutamate-gated chloride ion channels in invertebrates.

Pharmacokinetics:

a. **Absorption:** Abamectin is not well-absorbed after oral administration.

b. **Distribution:** It also has a large volume of distribution.

c. **Metabolism:** The metabolism of abamectin is not well-documented.

d. **Elimination:** The drug and its metabolites are primarily excreted in the feces.

Clinical Uses:

a. Abamectin is often used in veterinary medicine, particularly as an anthelmintic for livestock.

Adverse Effects:

a. Adverse effects are generally similar to those of Ivermectin, including mild gastrointestinal symptoms.

PYRANTEL PAMOATE:

Mechanism of Action:

a. Pyrantel pamoate acts as a depolarizing neuromuscular blocking agent in nematode parasites. It stimulates the release of acetylcholine at the neuromuscular junction, leading to spastic paralysis of the worms.

Pharmacokinetics:

a. **Absorption:** Pyrantel pamoate is poorly absorbed from the gastrointestinal tract.

b. **Distribution:** It remains largely within the gastrointestinal tract.

c. **Metabolism:** Pyrantel undergoes minimal metabolism.

d. **Elimination:** The drug and its metabolites are excreted in the feces.

Clinical Uses:

a. Pyrantel pamoate is commonly used to treat infections caused by intestinal nematodes, including roundworms (Ascaris lumbricoides), hookworms (Necator americanus, Ancylostoma duodenale), and pinworms (Enterobius vermicularis).

Adverse Effects:

a. Adverse effects are generally mild and may include nausea, vomiting, and abdominal cramps.

MORANTEL:

Mechanism of Action:

a. Morantel, like Pyrantel, acts as a depolarizing neuromuscular blocking agent in nematode parasites. It causes spastic paralysis by stimulating the release of acetylcholine.

Pharmacokinetics:

a. **Absorption**: Morantel is absorbed from the gastrointestinal tract.

b. **Distribution:** It remains largely within the gastrointestinal tract.

c. **Metabolism:** Morantel undergoes minimal metabolism.

d. **Elimination:** The drug and its metabolites are excreted in the feces.

Clinical Uses:

a. Morantel is used primarily in veterinary medicine, particularly in the treatment of intestinal nematode infections in livestock.

Adverse Effects:

a. Adverse effects are generally mild and may include gastrointestinal symptoms.

NICLOSAMIDE:

Mechanism of Action:

a. Niclosamide disrupts the energy metabolism of the parasite by inhibiting oxidative phosphorylation. It uncouples mitochondrial oxidative phosphorylation, leading to a decrease in ATP production, which is essential for the survival of the parasite.

Pharmacokinetics:

a. **Absorption:** Niclosamide is poorly absorbed from the gastrointestinal tract.

b. **Distribution:** It remains largely within the gastrointestinal tract.

c. **Metabolism:** Niclosamide undergoes minimal metabolism.

d. **Elimination:** The drug and its metabolites are primarily excreted in the feces.

Clinical Uses:

a. Niclosamide is used to treat intestinal tapeworm infections, such as those caused by Taenia solium (pork tapeworm) and Hymenolepis nana (dwarf tapeworm).

Adverse Effects:

a. Adverse effects are generally mild and may include gastrointestinal symptoms such as nausea and abdominal pain.

PRAZIQUANTEL:

Mechanism of Action:

a. Praziquantel increases the permeability of the schistosome cell membrane to calcium ions, leading to muscle paralysis, tegumental disruption, and subsequent death of the parasite. It is particularly effective against flatworms, including schistosomes and various types of tapeworms.

Pharmacokinetics:

a. **Absorption:** Praziquantel is well-absorbed from the gastrointestinal tract.

b. **Distribution:** It has a large volume of distribution.

c. **Metabolism:** Praziquantel undergoes hepatic metabolism.

d. **Elimination:** The drug and its metabolites are excreted in the urine.

Clinical Uses:

a. Praziquantel is used to treat a broad spectrum of parasitic infections, including schistosomiasis, cysticercosis, and infections caused by liver, lung, and intestinal flukes, as well as various types of tapeworms.

Adverse Effects:

a. Adverse effects are generally mild and may include dizziness, headache, and gastrointestinal symptoms. Allergic reactions are rare.

TRICLABENDAZOLE:

Mechanism of Action:

a. Triclabendazole is effective against liver flukes, particularly Fasciola hepatica. It disrupts the microtubule system in the parasites, causing a disturbance in their energy metabolism, which leads to paralysis and death.

Pharmacokinetics:

a. **Absorption:** Triclabendazole is well-absorbed after oral administration.

b. **Distribution:** It has a high affinity for liver tissues.

c. **Metabolism:** Triclabendazole undergoes extensive hepatic metabolism.

d. **Elimination:** The drug and its metabolites are excreted in the bile.

Clinical Uses:

a. Triclabendazole is specifically used to treat infections caused by liver flukes, such as Fasciola hepatica.

Adverse Effects:

a. Adverse effects are generally mild and may include gastrointestinal symptoms like nausea and abdominal pain.

OXYCLOZANIDE:

Mechanism of Action:

a. Oxyclozanide is effective against a variety of trematodes, including liver flukes. It interferes with the energy metabolism of the parasites, inhibiting oxidative phosphorylation and leading to their death.

Pharmacokinetics:

a. **Absorption:** Oxyclozanide is well-absorbed from the gastrointestinal tract.

b. **Distribution:** It distributes throughout the body.

c. **Metabolism:** The metabolism of oxyclozanide is not well-documented.

d. **Elimination:** The drug and its metabolites are excreted in the feces.

Clinical Uses:

a. Oxyclozanide is used to treat infections caused by liver flukes and other trematodes.

Adverse Effects:

a. Adverse effects are generally mild and may include gastrointestinal symptoms such as nausea and abdominal pain.

RAFOXANIDE:

Mechanism of Action:

a. Rafoxanide acts on the respiratory chain of the parasite, disrupting mitochondrial function. It interferes with the production of ATP in the parasite, leading to its death.

Pharmacokinetics:

a. **Absorption:** Rafoxanide is well-absorbed from the gastrointestinal tract.

b. **Distribution:** It distributes throughout the body.

c. **Metabolism:** Rafoxanide undergoes hepatic metabolism.

d. **Elimination:** The drug and its metabolites are primarily excreted in the feces.

Clinical Uses:

a. Rafoxanide is used in veterinary medicine to treat infections caused by liver flukes and certain gastrointestinal nematodes in ruminants.

Adverse Effects:

a. Adverse effects are generally mild and may include gastrointestinal symptoms.

CLOSANTEL:

Mechanism of Action:

a. Closantel interferes with the energy metabolism of the parasites, disrupting oxidative phosphorylation. It inhibits mitochondrial electron transport, leading to the depletion of ATP and subsequent paralysis and death of the parasites.

Pharmacokinetics:

a. **Absorption:** Closantel is well-absorbed after oral administration.

b. **Distribution:** It has a large volume of distribution.

c. **Metabolism:** Closantel undergoes hepatic metabolism.

d. **Elimination:** The drug and its metabolites are excreted in the feces.

Clinical Uses:

a. Closantel is used in veterinary medicine to treat infections caused by liver flukes, gastrointestinal nematodes, and certain external parasites in ruminants.

Adverse Effects:

a. Adverse effects are generally mild and may include gastrointestinal symptoms.

CHAPTER – 14

ANTIMALARIAL DRUGS

Dr. Gopal Garg

Professor, Rajiv Gandhi Institute of Pharmacy, Faculty of Pharmaceutical Science & Technology, AKS University Satna, MP-India

ABSTRACT:

Antimalarial drugs are medications used to prevent and treat malaria, a life-threatening disease caused by *Plasmodium* parasites transmitted through the bites of infected Anopheles mosquitoes. These drugs target different stages of the parasite's life cycle, including the liver and blood stages. Common antimalarial drugs include chloroquine, quinine, mefloquine, atovaquone-proguanil, and artemisinin-based combination therapies (ACTs). Chloroquine and mefloquine interfere with the parasite's ability to detoxify heme, a toxic byproduct of hemoglobin digestion. Quinine, a traditional remedy, disrupts the parasite's replication within red blood cells. ACTs, such as artemether-lumefantrine, are highly effective due to the rapid action of artemisinin derivatives combined with a partner drug to prevent resistance. Prophylactic drugs like atovaquone-proguanil and doxycycline are used to prevent infection in travelers to endemic areas. The development of drug resistance, particularly in *Plasmodium falciparum*, poses significant challenges, necessitating ongoing research for new treatments. Effective antimalarial therapy, combined with preventive measures like bed nets and insect repellents, is crucial for controlling and eventually eradicating malaria.

Introduction to Antimalarial Drugs

Malaria is a serious and sometimes fatal disease caused by *Plasmodium* parasites, which are transmitted to humans through the bites of infected

Anopheles mosquitoes. The disease remains a major health problem in many parts of the world, particularly in sub-Saharan Africa, Southeast Asia, and parts of South America. Antimalarial drugs are critical in both the treatment and prevention of malaria. These drugs work by targeting different stages of the parasite's life cycle, including the liver and blood stages, to reduce the parasite load and alleviate symptoms. Effective antimalarial therapy, in combination with vector control measures such as insecticide-treated bed nets and indoor residual spraying, is essential in the global fight against malaria.

Classification of Antimalarial Drugs

Antimalarial drugs can be classified based on their chemical structure, mechanism of action, and the stage of the *Plasmodium* life cycle they target. The main classes include:

1. **Aminoquinolines**
2. **Artemisinin Derivatives**
3. **Antifolate Drugs**
4. **Hydroxynaphthoquinones**
5. **Antibiotics**
6. **Other Antimalarials**

1. Aminoquinolines

Examples: Chloroquine, Hydroxychloroquine, Mefloquine

Mechanism of Action: Aminoquinolines interfere with the parasite's ability to detoxify heme, a byproduct of hemoglobin digestion within red blood cells. Accumulation of toxic heme leads to parasite death.

Targeted Stages: Blood schizonticides, effective against asexual erythrocytic forms of *Plasmodium*.

Clinical Use: Chloroquine is used for treating non-resistant *Plasmodium falciparum* and other *Plasmodium* species. Mefloquine is used for both treatment and prophylaxis, particularly in areas with chloroquine-resistant *P. falciparum.*

2. Artemisinin Derivatives

Examples: Artemether, Artesunate, Dihydroartemisinin

Mechanism of Action: Artemisinin derivatives produce free radicals within the parasite by reacting with heme, leading to oxidative damage and death of the parasite.

Targeted Stages: Rapid-acting blood schizonticides, effective against asexual erythrocytic forms and early gametocytes of *Plasmodium.*

Clinical Use: Used in combination therapies (ACTs) to treat uncomplicated and severe malaria. Examples include artemether-lumefantrine and artesunate-mefloquine.

3. Antifolate Drugs

Examples: Sulfadoxine-Pyrimethamine (Fansidar), Proguanil, Pyrimethamine

Mechanism of Action: Antifolate drugs inhibit enzymes involved in folate synthesis, crucial for DNA synthesis and cell division in the parasite.

Targeted Stages: Blood schizonticides and some liver stage activity.

Clinical Use: Used in combination with other antimalarials for treatment and prophylaxis. Sulfadoxine-pyrimethamine is commonly used in intermittent preventive treatment in pregnancy (IPTp).

4. Hydroxynaphthoquinones

Examples: Atovaquone

Mechanism of Action: Atovaquone inhibits the parasite's mitochondrial electron transport chain, disrupting energy production.

Targeted Stages: Blood and liver schizonticide.

Clinical Use: Used in combination with proguanil (atovaquone-proguanil) for both treatment and prophylaxis of malaria.

5. Antibiotics

Examples: Doxycycline, Clindamycin, Azithromycin

Mechanism of Action: Antibiotics interfere with protein synthesis in the parasite by targeting its ribosomes.

Targeted Stages: Blood schizonticides; primarily used in combination with other antimalarials.

Clinical Use: Doxycycline is commonly used for malaria prophylaxis in travelers. Clindamycin is used in combination with quinine or artesunate for treatment.

6. Other Antimalarials

Examples: Quinine, Primaquine, Tafenoquine

Mechanism of Action:

- **Quinine:** Interferes with heme polymerization, similar to aminoquinolines.
- **Primaquine and Tafenoquine:** Disrupt mitochondrial function and generate reactive oxygen species.

Targeted Stages:

- **Quinine:** Blood schizonticide, effective against severe malaria.
- **Primaquine and Tafenoquine:** Effective against liver stages (hypnozoites of *P. vivax* and *P. ovale*) and gametocytes.

Clinical Use:

- **Quinine:** Used for severe malaria and as a second-line treatment.
- **Primaquine and Tafenoquine:** Used for radical cure of *P. vivax* and *P. ovale* to prevent relapse and to prevent transmission.

Chloroquine

Chemical Structure: Chloroquine is a 4-aminoquinoline compound.

Mechanism of Action: Chloroquine acts by inhibiting the heme polymerase enzyme, which converts toxic heme (released during hemoglobin digestion) into non-toxic hemozoin in the parasite's food vacuole. Accumulation of toxic heme results in oxidative damage and death of the parasite.

Pharmacokinetics:

- **Absorption:** Chloroquine is well absorbed orally.
- **Distribution:** It is widely distributed in body tissues, including the liver, spleen, kidneys, and lungs. It also accumulates in melanin-containing tissues like the skin and retina.
- **Metabolism:** Metabolized in the liver to active metabolites.
- **Excretion:** Excreted primarily via the kidneys. The elimination half-life is about 1-2 months due to extensive tissue binding.

Therapeutic Uses:

- Treatment and prophylaxis of malaria caused by *Plasmodium vivax*, *P. ovale*, *P. malariae*, and chloroquine-sensitive *P. falciparum*.
- Treatment of extraintestinal amebiasis.
- Anti-inflammatory effects for rheumatoid arthritis and lupus erythematosus.

Adverse Effects:

- **Common:** Gastrointestinal disturbances, headache, dizziness, and pruritus.
- **Severe:** Retinopathy, cardiotoxicity (especially with long-term use), and potential for hypoglycemia.

Artemisinin

Chemical Structure: Artemisinin is a sesquiterpene lactone containing a peroxide bridge, derived from the sweet wormwood plant (*Artemisia annua*).

Mechanism of Action: The peroxide bridge in artemisinin is activated by iron, leading to the generation of free radicals within the parasite. These free radicals cause extensive oxidative damage to parasite proteins and membranes, leading to rapid parasite death.

Pharmacokinetics:

- **Absorption:** Artemisinin and its derivatives (artemether, artesunate) are well absorbed orally and intramuscularly.
- **Distribution:** Widely distributed in the body, including the brain.
- **Metabolism:** Rapidly metabolized in the liver to dihydroartemisinin, the active metabolite.
- **Excretion:** Excreted primarily in the urine. The half-life is relatively short, ranging from 1 to 3 hours.

Therapeutic Uses:

- Treatment of uncomplicated and severe malaria caused by *Plasmodium falciparum*.
- Often used in combination with other antimalarials (artemisinin-based combination therapies, ACTs) to prevent resistance.

Adverse Effects:

- **Common:** Nausea, vomiting, diarrhea, dizziness.
- **Severe:** Rare but can include neurotoxicity and cardiotoxicity, especially with prolonged use or high doses.

Hydroxychloroquine

Chemical Structure: Hydroxychloroquine is a 4-aminoquinoline, chemically similar to chloroquine but with a hydroxyl group.

Mechanism of Action: Similar to chloroquine, hydroxychloroquine inhibits heme polymerase, leading to the accumulation of toxic heme in the parasite's food vacuole. It also has immunomodulatory effects, making it useful in treating autoimmune diseases.

Pharmacokinetics:

- **Absorption:** Well absorbed orally.
- **Distribution:** Extensively distributed in body tissues, including the skin, liver, kidneys, and eyes. It crosses the placenta and is found in breast milk.
- **Metabolism:** Partially metabolized in the liver to active metabolites.
- **Excretion:** Excreted primarily via the kidneys. The elimination half-life is approximately 40-50 days due to extensive tissue binding.

Therapeutic Uses:

- Treatment and prophylaxis of malaria, particularly in chloroquine-sensitive areas.
- Treatment of rheumatoid arthritis and systemic lupus erythematosus.
- Potential off-label uses in other autoimmune conditions.

Adverse Effects:

- **Common:** Gastrointestinal disturbances, headache, dizziness, and pruritus.
- **Severe:** Retinopathy (risk increases with cumulative dose), cardiotoxicity, muscle weakness, and potential for hypoglycemia.

ARTEMETHER:

1. Mechanism of Action:

a. Artemether is a derivative of artemisinin and acts by forming free radicals in the presence of iron. This can damage the proteins and membranes of the malaria parasite, leading to its destruction.

2. Pharmacokinetics:

a. **Absorption:** Artemether is rapidly absorbed after oral administration.

b. **Distribution:** It has a short half-life and is quickly distributed to tissues.

c. **Metabolism:** Artemether undergoes metabolism primarily in the liver.

d. **Excretion:** The drug and its metabolites are excreted in the urine.

3. Clinical Uses:

a. Artemether is often used in combination with lumefantrine as part of artemisinin-based combination therapies (ACTs).

b. It is specifically effective against Plasmodium falciparum, including drug-resistant strains.

c. ACTs, including artemether-based combinations, are recommended as the first-line treatment for uncomplicated falciparum malaria due to their rapid parasite clearance.

SULFADOXINE-PYRIMETHAMINE (SP):

1. Mechanism of Action:

a. Sulfadoxine: Sulfadoxine is a dihydropteroate synthase inhibitor, which interferes with the synthesis of folic acid in the malaria parasite. Folic acid is essential for the synthesis of DNA and RNA.

b. Pyrimethamine: Pyrimethamine inhibits dihydrofolate reductase, another enzyme involved in the synthesis of folic acid. The combination of sulfadoxine and pyrimethamine results in a synergistic effect, disrupting folate metabolism and inhibiting the growth of the malaria parasite.

2. **Pharmacokinetics:**

   a. **Absorption:** Both components are well-absorbed after oral administration.

   b. **Distribution:** They are widely distributed in tissues.

   c. **Metabolism:** Metabolism occurs in the liver.

   d. **Excretion:** Both drugs and their metabolites are excreted in the urine.

3. **Clinical Uses:**

   a. SP has been used for the treatment of uncomplicated malaria caused by Plasmodium falciparum.

   b. It has also been used for intermittent preventive treatment in pregnant women and infants in areas with high malaria transmission.

PRIMAQUINE:

1. **Mechanism of Action:**

   a. Primaquine's exact mechanism of action is not fully understood. It is believed to interfere with the metabolism of the malarial parasite, particularly in the liver stage, and may also induce oxidative stress leading to the destruction of the parasite.

2. **Pharmacokinetics:**

   a. **Absorption:** Primaquine is well-absorbed after oral administration.

   b. **Distribution:** It is distributed throughout the body.

   c. **Metabolism:** Metabolism occurs primarily in the liver.

   d. **Excretion:** Primaquine and its metabolites are excreted in the urine.

3. **Clinical Uses:**

a. Primaquine is primarily used for the radical cure of Plasmodium vivax and Plasmodium ovale malaria, as it targets the liver stages of the parasite.

b. It is also used for the prevention of relapse in individuals infected with P. vivax or P. ovale.

PROGUANIL:

1. Mechanism of Action:

a. Proguanil is a synthetic antimalarial drug that is a prodrug. Its active form is cycloguanil.

b. Cycloguanil inhibits the dihydrofolate reductase enzyme of the malaria parasite. This enzyme is essential for the synthesis of purines and pyrimidines, which are necessary for DNA replication and ultimately the survival of the parasite.

2. Clinical Use:

a. Proguanil is often used in combination with atovaquone, and the combination is known as atovaquone/proguanil (Malarone). This combination is used for both the prevention and treatment of malaria.

3. Pharmacokinetics:

a. Proguanil is well-absorbed orally.

b. It undergoes hepatic metabolism to its active form, cycloguanil.

4. Adverse Effects:

a. Proguanil is generally well-tolerated, but potential side effects may include gastrointestinal disturbances and mouth ulcers.

QUININE:

1. Mechanism of Action:

a. Quinine is a natural alkaloid derived from the bark of the cinchona tree.

b. It acts primarily by inhibiting the hemozoin biocrystallization process within the parasitized erythrocyte. Hemozoin is a byproduct of hemoglobin digestion by the malaria parasite, and its inhibition leads to the accumulation of toxic heme within the parasite, causing its death.

2. **Clinical Use:**

   a. Quinine has been used for many years in the treatment of malaria. It's often used in combination with other antimalarial drugs to reduce the risk of resistance.

3. **Pharmacokinetics:**

   a. Quinine is administered orally or intravenously.

   b. It undergoes hepatic metabolism, and its elimination half-life varies.

4. **Adverse Effects:**

   a. Quinine can cause a range of side effects, including cinchonism (headache, nausea, vomiting, tinnitus), hypoglycemia, and, in rare cases, serious adverse events like cardiac arrhythmias.

DOXYCYCLINE:

1. **Mechanism of Action:**

   a. Doxycycline is a tetracycline antibiotic.

   b. It inhibits bacterial protein synthesis by binding to the 30S ribosomal subunit, preventing the addition of amino acids to the growing peptide chain.

2. **Clinical Use:**

   a. In the context of malaria, doxycycline is often used for the prevention of malaria in travelers to areas where certain types of malaria parasites are resistant to other antimalarial drugs.

   b. It is also used for the treatment of malaria in combination with other antimalarial drugs.

3. **Pharmacokinetics:**

   a. Doxycycline is well-absorbed after oral administration.

   b. It has a relatively long half-life, allowing for once-daily dosing.

4. Adverse Effects:

a. Common side effects include gastrointestinal disturbances, photosensitivity, and the risk of yeast infections.

b. It should not be used in pregnant women or young children due to the risk of tooth discoloration.

MEFLOQUINE:

1. Mechanism of Action:

a. Mefloquine is a synthetic antimalarial drug.

b. Its exact mechanism of action is not completely understood, but it is believed to interfere with the parasites' ability to detoxify heme, leading to the accumulation of toxic heme metabolites within the parasite.

2. Clinical Use:

a. Mefloquine is used both for the prevention and treatment of malaria.

b. It is particularly useful in areas where malaria parasites are resistant to other antimalarial drugs.

3. Pharmacokinetics:

a. Mefloquine is well-absorbed after oral administration.

b. It has a long half-life, allowing for weekly dosing for malaria prophylaxis.

4. Adverse Effects:

a. Adverse effects may include gastrointestinal disturbances, dizziness, headache, and vivid dreams.

b. Rarely, mefloquine can cause neuropsychiatric side effects, such as anxiety, depression, and seizures. Therefore, individuals with a history of psychiatric disorders may be advised against using mefloquine.

CLINDAMYCIN:

1. Mechanism of Action:

a. Clindamycin is a lincosamide antibiotic.

b. It inhibits bacterial protein synthesis by binding to the 50S ribosomal subunit and preventing the addition of amino acids to the growing peptide chain.

2. Clinical Use:

a. Clindamycin is primarily used for the treatment of bacterial infections, especially those caused by anaerobic bacteria.

b. In the context of malaria, it is sometimes used as an alternative treatment for severe cases or when other medications are not well-tolerated.

3. Pharmacokinetics:

a. Clindamycin is available in oral, intravenous, and topical formulations.

b. It is well-absorbed after oral administration, and it penetrates well into various tissues, making it effective against infections in different body systems.

4. Adverse Effects:

a. Common side effects include gastrointestinal disturbances, rash, and the risk of Clostridium difficile infection.

b. Severe allergic reactions are rare but can occur.

LUMEFANTRINE:

1. Mechanism of Action:

a. Lumefantrine is an artemisinin-based combination therapy (ACT), specifically combined with artemether in the medication Coartem.

b. It works in conjunction with artemether to disrupt the growth and reproduction of the malaria parasites in the erythrocytic stage.

2. Clinical Use:

a. Lumefantrine, in combination with artemether, is used for the treatment of uncomplicated malaria, particularly caused by Plasmodium falciparum.

b. ACTs are recommended by the World Health Organization as a first-line treatment for uncomplicated malaria due to their efficacy.

3. Pharmacokinetics:

a. Lumefantrine is administered orally.

b. It has a relatively long elimination half-life, which helps to sustain therapeutic levels in the body.

4. Adverse Effects:

a. Common side effects include gastrointestinal symptoms, headache, and dizziness.

b. It is generally well-tolerated, but allergic reactions and rare instances of QT interval prolongation have been reported.

PIPERAQUINE:

1. Mechanism of Action:

a. Piperaquine is a bisquinoline antimalarial agent.

b. It inhibits heme polymerase activity, preventing the detoxification of heme and leading to the accumulation of toxic heme metabolites in the malaria parasite.

2. Clinical Use:

a. Piperaquine is often used in combination with other antimalarial drugs, such as dihydroartemisinin, in artemisinin-based combination therapies (ACTs).

b. ACTs are recommended as first-line treatments for uncomplicated malaria caused by Plasmodium falciparum.

3. Pharmacokinetics:

a. Piperaquine is administered orally.

b. It has a long elimination half-life, allowing for once-daily dosing in combination therapies.

4. Adverse Effects:

a. Common side effects include gastrointestinal symptoms, dizziness, and changes in electrocardiogram (ECG) readings.

b. It is generally well-tolerated, but prolonged QT interval on ECG has been reported in some cases.

PYRIMETHAMINE:

1. Mechanism of Action:

a. Pyrimethamine is a dihydrofolate reductase inhibitor.

b. It inhibits the enzyme dihydrofolate reductase, which is involved in the synthesis of tetrahydrofolic acid, a precursor to DNA synthesis in the malaria parasite.

2. Clinical Use:

a. Pyrimethamine is often used in combination with sulfadoxine, forming a combination known as sulfadoxine/pyrimethamine (SP).

b. This combination is used for the intermittent preventive treatment of malaria in pregnant women and infants in areas with high levels of malaria transmission.

3. Pharmacokinetics:

a. Pyrimethamine is administered orally.

b. It undergoes hepatic metabolism and has a relatively long elimination half-life.

4. Adverse Effects:

a. Common side effects include gastrointestinal disturbances, rash, and allergic reactions.

b. Pyrimethamine should be used with caution in individuals with folate deficiency, as it can exacerbate folate deficiency symptoms.

ATOVAQUONE:

1. Mechanism of Action:

a. Atovaquone is a hydroxynaphthoquinone.

b. It inhibits the mitochondrial electron transport chain in the malaria parasite, specifically targeting the cytochrome bc1 complex. This disruption interferes with the parasite's ability to generate adenosine triphosphate (ATP) and leads to the death of the parasite.

2. Clinical Use:

a. Atovaquone is commonly used in combination with proguanil (atovaquone/proguanil or Malarone) for the prevention and treatment of malaria.

b. It is also used in the treatment of Toxoplasma gondii and Pneumocystis jirovecii infections in certain patient populations.

3. Pharmacokinetics:

a. Atovaquone is well-absorbed orally.

b. It has a relatively long elimination half-life, allowing for once-daily dosing.

4. Adverse Effects:

a. Common side effects include gastrointestinal symptoms such as nausea, vomiting, and diarrhea.

b. It is generally well-tolerated, but elevated liver enzyme levels have been reported in some cases.

ARTEMETHER-LUMEFANTRINE (COARTEM):

1. Mechanism of Action:

a. Artemether is an artemisinin derivative that rapidly clears the majority of parasites, while lumefantrine, a derivative of aryl-amino alcohol, has a slower action and helps to eliminate remaining parasites.

b. Artemether-lumefantrine (Coartem) is an artemisinin-based combination therapy (ACT) used for the treatment of uncomplicated malaria.

c. The combination works by rapidly reducing the parasite burden (artemether) and then eliminating residual parasites over a longer period (lumefantrine).

2. **Clinical Use:**

   a. Coartem is a first-line treatment for uncomplicated malaria, especially in areas where Plasmodium falciparum is prevalent.

   b. ACTs, including Coartem, are recommended by the World Health Organization due to their high efficacy.

3. **Pharmacokinetics:**

   a. Artemether-lumefantrine is administered orally.

   b. Lumefantrine has a relatively long elimination half-life, allowing for a specific dosing schedule.

4. **Adverse Effects:**

   a. Common side effects include gastrointestinal symptoms, headache, and dizziness.

   b. It is generally well-tolerated, but rare instances of QT interval prolongation have been reported.

CHAPTER – 15

ANTIAMOEBIC AGENTS

Mrs. Neha Soni

Assistant Professor, Rajiv Gandhi Institute of Pharmacy, Faculty of
Pharmaceutical Science & Technology, AKS University Satna, MP-India

ABSTRACT:

Antiamoebic agents are a class of drugs used to treat infections
caused by amoebae, primarily *Entamoeba histolytica*, the causative
agent of amoebiasis. These infections can range from asymptomatic
colonization to severe invasive diseases, including amoebic dysentery and
liver abscess. The main classes of antiamoebic drugs include luminal
agents, systemic agents, and mixed agents, which target different stages
of the parasite's lifecycle. Luminal agents like paromomycin and
iodoquinol act within the intestinal lumen to eliminate cysts and
trophozoites. Systemic agents such as metronidazole and tinidazole
penetrate tissues to treat invasive infections. Mixed agents, like
nitazoxanide, are effective in both the intestinal lumen and tissues.
Metronidazole, the most commonly used antiamoebic, disrupts DNA
synthesis in anaerobic organisms. These agents are often used in
combination to ensure complete eradication of the parasite, especially in
cases of invasive disease. Effective treatment is crucial to prevent
complications and transmission. Despite their efficacy, the emergence of
drug resistance and adverse effects remain challenges, necessitating
ongoing research and development of new antiamoebic therapies.

Introduction to Antiamoebic Agents

Amoebiasis is an infection caused by the protozoan parasite *Entamoeba
histolytica*, which primarily affects the intestines and can lead to severe
dysentery, colitis, and extraintestinal manifestations such as liver abscesses.

Antiamoebic agents are medications designed to treat these infections by targeting different stages of the amoeba's lifecycle, including cysts and trophozoites in the intestinal lumen and tissues. Effective treatment of amoebiasis is crucial to alleviate symptoms, prevent complications, and stop the spread of the parasite.

Classification of Antiamoebic Agents

Antiamoebic agents can be classified based on their site of action and the stage of the parasite they target. The main classes include:

1. **Luminal Agents**
2. **Systemic Agents**
3. **Mixed Agents**

1. Luminal Agents

Examples: Paromomycin, Iodoquinol, Diloxanide Furoate

Mechanism of Action: Luminal agents act within the intestinal lumen to eliminate both cysts and trophozoites of *Entamoeba histolytica*. They are not absorbed significantly from the gastrointestinal tract, which limits their action to the lumen.

Therapeutic Use: These agents are primarily used to treat asymptomatic carriers and to prevent relapse after treatment of invasive amoebiasis with systemic agents.

Adverse Effects: Paromomycin can cause gastrointestinal disturbances, while iodoquinol can lead to neurotoxicity and optic neuritis with prolonged use.

2. Systemic Agents

Examples: Metronidazole, Tinidazole, Chloroquine, Dehydroemetine

Mechanism of Action: Systemic agents are absorbed into the bloodstream and distributed throughout the body, allowing them to target invasive amoebic infections in tissues, such as liver abscesses and colitis. Metronidazole and tinidazole disrupt DNA synthesis in anaerobic organisms by producing reactive nitrogen species.

Therapeutic Use: These agents are used to treat invasive amoebiasis, including amoebic liver abscess and severe intestinal infections.

Adverse Effects: Metronidazole and tinidazole can cause gastrointestinal disturbances, metallic taste, headache, and rarely, neurotoxicity. Alcohol should be avoided during treatment due to the risk of a disulfiram-like reaction.

3. Mixed Agents

Examples: Nitazoxanide, Secnidazole, Ornidazole

Mechanism of Action: Mixed agents are effective against both luminal and tissue stages of the parasite. Nitazoxanide interferes with the pyruvate-ferredoxin oxidoreductase enzyme-dependent electron transfer reaction, essential for anaerobic energy metabolism.

Therapeutic Use: These agents are used for both symptomatic intestinal infections and tissue infections, offering a broader spectrum of action.

Adverse Effects: Generally well-tolerated, but can cause gastrointestinal disturbances and, rarely, allergic reactions.

Specific Agents in Detail

1. Metronidazole

- **Mechanism of Action:** Disrupts DNA synthesis by producing toxic metabolites in anaerobic conditions.
- **Therapeutic Use:** First-line treatment for invasive amoebiasis, including amoebic liver abscess.
- **Adverse Effects:** Nausea, vomiting, metallic taste, headache, and potential neurotoxicity.

2. Paromomycin

- **Mechanism of Action:** Binds to the 30S ribosomal subunit, inhibiting protein synthesis in the parasite.
- **Therapeutic Use:** Effective luminal agent for asymptomatic carriers and post-systemic treatment to prevent relapse.
- **Adverse Effects:** Gastrointestinal disturbances.

3. Iodoquinol

- **Mechanism of Action:** Exact mechanism is unclear, but it is effective in the intestinal lumen.
- **Therapeutic Use:** Used for luminal infections.
- **Adverse Effects:** Neurotoxicity, optic neuritis with prolonged use.

4. Nitazoxanide

- **Mechanism of Action:** Inhibits pyruvate-ferredoxin oxidoreductase enzyme-dependent electron transfer.
- **Therapeutic Use:** Effective against both luminal and tissue stages.
- **Adverse Effects:** Generally mild gastrointestinal symptoms.

METRONIDAZOLE

Metronidazole is an antimicrobial agent with a broad spectrum of activity, primarily against anaerobic bacteria and some protozoa. Here are key aspects of the pharmacology of metronidazole:

1. Mechanism of Action:

Metronidazole exerts its antimicrobial effects through a multi-step process involving reduction and formation of cytotoxic products. The drug is taken up by susceptible organisms and undergoes chemical reduction by intracellular electron transport proteins. This reduction process leads to the formation of reactive intermediates that disrupt DNA structure, leading to inhibition of nucleic acid synthesis and DNA strand breakage. This mechanism is particularly effective against anaerobic microorganisms that lack protective enzymes against reactive oxygen species.

2. Spectrum of Activity:

Metronidazole is effective against a wide range of anaerobic bacteria, including Bacteroides, Clostridium, Fusobacterium, and Peptostreptococcus species. It is also active against certain protozoa, especially Entamoeba histolytica, Giardia lamblia, and Trichomonas vaginalis.

3. Absorption and Distribution:

Metronidazole is well absorbed from the gastrointestinal tract. It achieves good tissue penetration, including the central nervous system (CNS) and various body fluids. The drug crosses the blood-brain barrier, making it effective for treating anaerobic infections in the CNS.

4. Metabolism and Elimination:

Metronidazole undergoes extensive metabolism in the liver, and its metabolites are excreted in the urine. The elimination half-life is relatively short, typically around 8 hours, but may be prolonged in patients with hepatic dysfunction.

5. Clinical Uses:

a. Metronidazole is used in the treatment of various infections, including:

b. Anaerobic bacterial infections, such as intra-abdominal infections, skin and soft tissue infections, and bacterial vaginosis.

c. Protozoal infections, including amoebiasis, giardiasis, and trichomoniasis.

d. Helicobacter pylori eradication in combination with other antibiotics for peptic ulcer disease.

6. Adverse Effects:

Common side effects include nausea, vomiting, metallic taste, and gastrointestinal upset. Neurological side effects, such as peripheral neuropathy and seizures, are rare but can occur with prolonged use or high doses.

7. Drug Interactions:

Metronidazole can interact with certain drugs, including disulfiram (causing a disulfiram-like reaction), warfarin (potentiating anticoagulant effects), and alcohol (leading to a disulfiram-like reaction).

8. Precautions and Contraindications:

Metronidazole should be used with caution in patients with hepatic impairment. It is contraindicated in the first trimester of pregnancy due to potential teratogenic effects

TINIDAZOLE

Tinidazole is an antiprotozoal and antibacterial medication with a structure similar to metronidazole. It shares some similarities in its mechanism of action and spectrum of activity with metronidazole but has certain pharmacokinetic differences. Here is an overview of the pharmacology of tinidazole:

1. **Mechanism of Action:**

Tinidazole, like metronidazole, is a 5-nitroimidazole derivative. Its antimicrobial activity is based on the reduction of its nitro group by intracellular transport proteins within microorganisms. The reduced intermediates formed disrupt the DNA structure of the microorganisms, leading to inhibition of nucleic acid synthesis and eventual cell death.

2. **Spectrum of Activity:**

Tinidazole has a broad spectrum of activity against anaerobic bacteria and protozoa. It is effective against various pathogens, including Trichomonas vaginalis (causing trichomoniasis), Giardia lamblia (causing giardiasis), and Entamoeba histolytica (causing amoebiasis). Tinidazole is also active against certain anaerobic bacteria, similar to metronidazole.

3. **Absorption and Distribution:**

Tinidazole is well absorbed after oral administration, and its absorption is not significantly affected by food. It has good tissue penetration, and therapeutic concentrations are achieved in various body tissues and fluids, including the gastrointestinal tract.

4. **Metabolism and Elimination:**

Tinidazole undergoes hepatic metabolism, primarily through conjugation, and its metabolites are excreted in the urine. The elimination half-life is approximately 12-14 hours.

5. Clinical Uses:

Tinidazole is used in the treatment of various infections, including:

a. **Trichomoniasis:** A sexually transmitted infection caused by Trichomonas vaginalis.

b. **Giardiasis:** An intestinal infection caused by Giardia lamblia.

c. **Amoebiasis:** An infection caused by Entamoeba histolytica.

d. **Bacterial vaginosis:** An overgrowth of harmful bacteria in the vagina.

6. Adverse Effects:

Common side effects of tinidazole include nausea, metallic taste, and gastrointestinal upset. Neurological side effects are rare but can occur, including headache and dizziness. Like metronidazole, the concurrent use of alcohol should be avoided due to the potential for a disulfiram-like reaction.

7. Precautions and Contraindications:

Tinidazole should be used with caution in patients with hepatic impairment. It is contraindicated in the first trimester of pregnancy, similar to metronidazole.

PAROMOMYCIN

Paromomycin is an aminoglycoside antibiotic with activity against various parasites, including certain protozoa and helminths. Here is an overview of the pharmacology of paromomycin:

1. Mechanism of Action:

Paromomycin's primary mechanism of action involves binding to the 30S ribosomal subunit of the parasite's ribosome. By interfering with protein synthesis, it disrupts the translation of mRNA, leading to inhibition of protein production. This ultimately results in the death of the parasite.

2. **Spectrum of Activity:**

Paromomycin is effective against a variety of parasites, including:

   a. **Entamoeba histolytica:** The causative agent of amoebiasis.

   b. **Giardia lamblia:** A protozoan causing giardiasis.

   c. **Cryptosporidium parvum:** An intestinal parasite causing cryptosporidiosis.

   d. **Leishmania species**: Parasites causing leishmaniasis.

3. **Absorption and Distribution:**

Paromomycin is poorly absorbed from the gastrointestinal tract when administered orally. Therefore, it is generally administered orally for the treatment of intestinal infections. When used to treat systemic infections, it may be administered intravenously.

4. **Metabolism and Elimination:**

Paromomycin is not significantly metabolized in the body. It is excreted primarily unchanged in the feces after oral administration. In cases where intravenous administration is used, it is excreted mainly in the urine.

5. **Clinical Uses:**

Paromomycin is used in the treatment of various parasitic infections, including:

   a. **Amoebiasis:** Intestinal infection caused by Entamoeba histolytica.

   b. **Giardiasis:** Infection of the small intestine caused by Giardia lamblia.

   c. **Cryptosporidiosis:** Infection of the gastrointestinal tract caused by Cryptosporidium parvum.

   d. **Leishmaniasis:** A group of infections caused by various species of the Leishmania parasite.

6. **Adverse Effects:**

Common side effects of paromomycin include gastrointestinal symptoms such as nausea, vomiting, and diarrhea. Since it is not significantly absorbed from the gastrointestinal tract, systemic side effects are generally minimal compared to other aminoglycosides.

7. Precautions and Contraindications:

Paromomycin should be used with caution in individuals with renal impairment. It is contraindicated in patients with a known hypersensitivity to aminoglycosides.

DILOXANIDE FUROATE

Diloxanide furoate is an antiprotozoal medication used in the treatment of intestinal infections, particularly those caused by the amoeba Entamoeba histolytica. Here is an overview of the pharmacology of diloxanide furoate:

1. Mechanism of Action:

Diloxanide furoate exerts its antiprotozoal effects by inhibiting the growth and multiplication of Entamoeba histolytica in the intestinal lumen. While the exact mechanism of action is not fully understood, it is believed that diloxanide furoate is metabolized to its active form, diloxanide, in the intestines. Diloxanide then acts locally, preventing the amoeba from dividing and causing damage to the intestinal tissues.

2. Absorption and Distribution:

Diloxanide furoate is administered orally and is poorly absorbed from the gastrointestinal tract. The drug remains largely in the intestinal lumen, where it exerts its therapeutic effects against the amoeba. Due to its poor absorption, systemic distribution is minimal.

3. Metabolism and Elimination:

Diloxanide furoate is metabolized in the intestinal mucosa to its active form, diloxanide. The majority of the drug is excreted in the feces, primarily as unchanged diloxanide.

4. Clinical Uses:

Diloxanide furoate is used in the treatment of asymptomatic cyst passers or individuals with mild intestinal amoebiasis caused by Entamoeba histolytica. It is often used in combination with tissue amoebicides, such as metronidazole, which act on the invasive forms of the amoeba in tissues.

5. Adverse Effects:

Diloxanide furoate is generally well-tolerated. Common side effects are mild and may include gastrointestinal symptoms such as nausea, vomiting, and diarrhea. Allergic reactions are rare.

6. Precautions and Contraindications:

Diloxanide furoate is contraindicated in patients with known hypersensitivity to the drug. It is generally considered safe for use during pregnancy and lactation, but as with any medication, the potential benefits and risks should be carefully evaluated.

7. Dosage and Administration:

The dosage of diloxanide furoate is typically determined based on the severity of the infection and the individual's weight. The medication is usually administered orally.

IODOQUINOL

Iodoquinol is an antiprotozoal medication used in the treatment of certain intestinal parasitic infections. Here's an overview of the pharmacology of iodoquinol:

1. Mechanism of Action:

The exact mechanism of action of iodoquinol is not fully understood. However, it is believed to act by interfering with the energy metabolism of the parasites, leading to their death. Iodoquinol is particularly effective against certain protozoa and is used in the treatment of infections such as amoebiasis.

2. Absorption and Distribution:

Iodoquinol is poorly absorbed from the gastrointestinal tract after oral administration. Most of the drug remains in the intestinal lumen, where it exerts its therapeutic effects against the parasites. Due to its poor absorption, systemic distribution is limited.

3. Metabolism and Elimination:

Iodoquinol undergoes some degree of metabolism in the liver. The majority of the drug and its metabolites are excreted in the feces. A small portion may be excreted in the urine.

4. Clinical Uses:

Iodoquinol is primarily used in the treatment of intestinal infections caused by Entamoeba histolytica, a protozoan parasite that can cause amoebiasis. It is effective against the luminal forms of the parasite in the intestines. However, iodoquinol is generally not used as a first-line treatment for invasive amoebiasis; tissue amoebicides such as metronidazole are often preferred for such cases.

5. Adverse Effects:

Common side effects of iodoquinol include gastrointestinal symptoms such as nausea, vomiting, and diarrhea. Neurological side effects are rare but have been reported, particularly with prolonged use or high doses. Neurotoxicity may manifest as peripheral neuropathy, optic neuropathy, or other neurological symptoms.

6. Precautions and Contraindications:

Iodoquinol should be used with caution in individuals with a history of neurological disorders. It is contraindicated in patients with optic neuropathy or hypersensitivity to the drug.

7. Dosage and Administration:

The dosage of iodoquinol is typically determined based on the specific infection being treated and the patient's weight. It is usually administered orally.

METRONIDAZOLE + DILOXANIDE FUROATE

Metronidazole and diloxanide furoate are often prescribed in combination for the treatment of amoebic infections, particularly amoebiasis caused by the protozoan parasite Entamoeba histolytica. Here's an overview of the pharmacology of this combination:

Metronidazole:

1. **Mechanism of Action:**
   a. Metronidazole is a 5-nitroimidazole derivative.
   b. It enters the microbial cell, is reduced by intracellular electron transport proteins, and generates cytotoxic intermediates.
   c. These intermediates disrupt DNA structure, leading to inhibition of nucleic acid synthesis and DNA strand breakage.

2. **Spectrum of Activity:**
   a. Metronidazole is effective against anaerobic bacteria and certain protozoa, including Entamoeba histolytica.
   b. It is widely used for various infections, including amoebiasis, bacterial vaginosis, and certain anaerobic bacterial infections.

3. **Absorption and Distribution:**
   a. Metronidazole is well absorbed from the gastrointestinal tract.
   b. It achieves good tissue penetration, including the central nervous system (CNS).

4. **Metabolism and Elimination:**
   a. Metronidazole undergoes hepatic metabolism, and its metabolites are excreted in the urine.
   b. The elimination half-life is relatively short, around 8 hours.

Diloxanide Furoate:

1. Mechanism of Action:

a. Diloxanide furoate inhibits the growth and multiplication of Entamoeba histolytica in the intestinal lumen.

b. The active form, diloxanide, acts locally to prevent the amoeba from dividing and causing damage to the intestinal tissues.

2. Absorption and Distribution:

a. Diloxanide furoate is poorly absorbed from the gastrointestinal tract.

b. It remains largely in the intestinal lumen, exerting its effects against the amoeba locally.

3. Metabolism and Elimination:

a. Diloxanide furoate is metabolized in the intestinal mucosa to its active form, diloxanide.

b. The majority of the drug is excreted in the feces, primarily as unchanged diloxanide.

Combination Therapy:

1. Rationale:

a. Combining metronidazole with diloxanide furoate is often done to target both the invasive and luminal forms of Entamoeba histolytica.

b. Metronidazole acts systemically to target the amoeba in tissues, while diloxanide furoate acts locally in the intestinal lumen.

2. Clinical Uses:

a. This combination is used in the treatment of amoebiasis to ensure a more comprehensive and effective eradication of the parasite.

3. Adverse Effects:

a. Adverse effects are generally those associated with each individual drug, including gastrointestinal symptoms, metallic taste, and potential neurological side effects with metronidazole.

4. Precautions and Monitoring:

a. The combination should be used under the guidance of a healthcare professional.

b. Monitoring for adverse effects, especially with metronidazole, is important during the course of treatment.

CHAPTER – 16

CHEMOTHERAPY – II

Mr. Sumit Kumar Pandey

Assistant Professor, Rajiv Gandhi Institute of Pharmacy, Faculty of

Pharmaceutical Science & Technology, AKS University Satna, MP-India

ABSTRACT:

Chemotherapy, a common treatment for cancer, can have a profound impact on the immune system, making patients more susceptible to infections, including urinary tract infections (UTIs) and sexually transmitted diseases (STDs). The drugs used in chemotherapy often lower white blood cell counts, which are crucial for fighting off infections. As a result, even minor infections can become severe and require prompt medical attention. UTIs, caused by bacteria entering the urinary tract, can lead to symptoms like pain, burning during urination, and frequent urges to urinate. In immunocompromised patients, these infections can quickly spread to the kidneys and bloodstream, posing significant health risks. Similarly, the weakened immune response can make chemotherapy patients more vulnerable to contracting STDs, which can further complicate their overall health status. Preventive measures, such as practicing good hygiene, staying hydrated, and engaging in safe sexual practices, are essential. Regular medical check-ups and prompt reporting of any symptoms to healthcare providers are also critical for timely diagnosis and treatment. Managing the risk of infections during chemotherapy requires a comprehensive approach that includes patient education, preventive strategies, and vigilant monitoring.

Introduction:

Chemotherapy, a cornerstone of cancer treatment, involves the use of potent drugs to target and eliminate cancer cells. However, this aggressive approach also affects healthy cells, particularly those in the immune system, leaving patients more vulnerable to various infections. Among these, urinary tract infections (UTIs) and sexually transmitted diseases (STDs) are of particular concern. The immunosuppressive nature of chemotherapy reduces the body's ability to fend off pathogens, increasing the risk of infections that can complicate treatment and recovery. Understanding the link between chemotherapy and these infections is crucial for developing effective preventive and management strategies, ensuring better patient outcomes and quality of life during this challenging period.

Chemotherapy is a medical treatment that involves the use of drugs to kill or inhibit the growth of rapidly dividing cells, such as cancer cells. The goal of chemotherapy is to destroy cancer cells throughout the body or prevent their further growth and division. While cancer cells are the primary target, chemotherapy can also affect normal, healthy cells that divide quickly, such as those in the bone marrow, digestive tract, and hair follicles. This can lead to side effects such as fatigue, nausea, hair loss, and a weakened immune system.

URINARY TRACT INFECTIONS (UTIS):

A Urinary Tract Infection (UTI) is a bacterial infection that affects any part of the urinary system, which includes the kidneys, bladder, ureters, and urethra. Most UTIs involve the lower urinary tract, which comprises the bladder and the urethra. UTIs are more common in women than in men.

Urinary tract infections (UTIs) are commonly treated with various classes of antibiotics, each with specific pharmacological properties tailored to eliminate the causative bacteria. Below are some classifications and pharmacology of drugs used to treat UTIs:

1. Sulfonamides

Example: Trimethoprim-sulfamethoxazole (Bactrim, Septra)
Pharmacology: Sulfonamides inhibit the synthesis of dihydrofolic acid, a form of folic acid that bacteria need for DNA synthesis and growth. Trimethoprim inhibits dihydrofolate reductase, leading to a synergistic effect when combined with sulfamethoxazole. They are often used as first-line treatment for uncomplicated UTIs due to their effectiveness against a broad range of pathogens.

2. Quinolones

Example: Ciprofloxacin (Cipro), Levofloxacin (Levaquin)
Pharmacology: Quinolones, or fluoroquinolones, inhibit bacterial DNA gyrase and topoisomerase IV, enzymes critical for DNA replication and cell division. They are broad-spectrum antibiotics effective against both Gram-negative and Gram-positive bacteria, making them suitable for complicated UTIs and cases resistant to other antibiotics.

3. Beta-lactams

Example: Amoxicillin-clavulanate (Augmentin), Ceftriaxone (Rocephin)
Pharmacology: Beta-lactams, including penicillins and cephalosporins, interfere with bacterial cell wall synthesis by binding to penicillin-binding proteins, leading to cell lysis and death. The addition of clavulanate, a beta-lactamase inhibitor, extends the spectrum of amoxicillin by preventing bacterial resistance.

4. Nitrofurans

Example: Nitrofurantoin (Macrobid, Macrodantin)
Pharmacology: Nitrofurantoin is reduced by bacterial enzymes to reactive intermediates that damage bacterial DNA, ribosomal proteins, and other

macromolecules. It is primarily used for treating uncomplicated UTIs due to its high urinary concentration and effectiveness against common uropathogens.

5. Aminoglycosides

Example: Gentamicin, Amikacin

Pharmacology: Aminoglycosides bind to the bacterial 30S ribosomal subunit, causing misreading of mRNA and inhibition of protein synthesis. They are effective against Gram-negative bacteria and are often used in severe or complicated UTIs, particularly in hospitalized patients.

6. Fosfomycin

Example: Fosfomycin tromethamine (Monurol)

Pharmacology: Fosfomycin inhibits bacterial cell wall synthesis by inactivating the enzyme enolpyruvyl transferase, which is critical for peptidoglycan formation. It is often used as a single-dose treatment for uncomplicated UTIs due to its broad-spectrum activity and low resistance rates.

7. Tetracyclines

Example: Doxycycline (Vibramycin)

Pharmacology: Tetracyclines bind to the 30S ribosomal subunit, preventing the attachment of aminoacyl-tRNA to the ribosomal acceptor site, thereby inhibiting protein synthesis. They are effective against a variety of bacteria and are sometimes used for UTIs caused by atypical pathogens.

8. Carbapenems

Example: Imipenem-cilastatin (Primaxin), Meropenem (Merrem)

Pharmacology: Carbapenems inhibit bacterial cell wall synthesis and are highly resistant to beta-lactamases. They have a broad spectrum of activity and are often reserved for multidrug-resistant bacterial infections, including complicated UTIs.

SEXUALLY TRANSMITTED DISEASES (STDS):

Sexually transmitted diseases (STDs) are treated with various classes of antibiotics and antiviral medications, each with specific pharmacological actions tailored to eliminate or suppress the causative pathogens. Below are the classifications and pharmacology of drugs commonly used to treat STDs:

1. Penicillins

Example: Penicillin G, Penicillin V

Pharmacology: Penicillins inhibit bacterial cell wall synthesis by binding to penicillin-binding proteins, leading to cell lysis and death. Penicillin G is the first-line treatment for syphilis caused by *Treponema pallidum* due to its efficacy and low resistance rates.

2. Cephalosporins

Example: Ceftriaxone (Rocephin)

Pharmacology: Cephalosporins, similar to penicillins, interfere with bacterial cell wall synthesis. Ceftriaxone is used to treat gonorrhea due to its effectiveness against *Neisseria gonorrhoeae*, including strains resistant to other antibiotics.

3. Macrolides

Example: Azithromycin (Zithromax)

Pharmacology: Macrolides bind to the 50S ribosomal subunit, inhibiting bacterial protein synthesis. Azithromycin is used to treat chlamydia and is also effective against *Neisseria gonorrhoeae* when combined with ceftriaxone.

4. Tetracyclines

Example: Doxycycline (Vibramycin)

Pharmacology: Tetracyclines bind to the 30S ribosomal subunit, preventing the attachment of aminoacyl-tRNA to the ribosomal acceptor site, thereby inhibiting protein synthesis. Doxycycline is used to treat chlamydia, syphilis, and *Mycoplasma genitalium* infections.

5. Fluoroquinolones

Example: Ciprofloxacin (Cipro), Levofloxacin (Levaquin)

Pharmacology: Fluoroquinolones inhibit bacterial DNA gyrase and topoisomerase IV, enzymes critical for DNA replication and cell division. They are used for treating chlamydia and gonorrhea, although resistance has limited their use.

6. Nitroimidazoles

Example: Metronidazole (Flagyl), Tinidazole (Tindamax)

Pharmacology: Nitroimidazoles are reduced in anaerobic bacteria and protozoa to reactive intermediates that damage DNA. They are the treatment of choice for trichomoniasis caused by *Trichomonas vaginalis* and bacterial vaginosis.

7. Antivirals

Example: Acyclovir (Zovirax), Valacyclovir (Valtrex), Famciclovir (Famvir)

Pharmacology: Antivirals inhibit viral DNA polymerase, preventing viral replication. These drugs are used to manage herpes simplex virus (HSV) infections, reducing the frequency and severity of outbreaks.

8. Antifungals

Example: Fluconazole (Diflucan)

Pharmacology: Antifungals inhibit ergosterol synthesis, disrupting fungal cell membrane integrity. Fluconazole is used to treat candidiasis, including vulvovaginal candidiasis.

9. Nucleoside Reverse Transcriptase Inhibitors (NRTIs)

Example: Tenofovir (Viread), Emtricitabine (Emtriva)
Pharmacology: NRTIs are incorporated into the viral DNA by reverse transcriptase, causing premature chain termination. They are used in combination therapies for HIV infection.

10. Non-nucleoside Reverse Transcriptase Inhibitors (NNRTIs)

Example: Efavirenz (Sustiva), Nevirapine (Viramune)
Pharmacology: NNRTIs bind directly to reverse transcriptase, causing a conformational change that inhibits its activity. They are part of combination therapies for HIV treatment.

CHAPTER – 17

CHEMOTHERAPY OF MALIGNANCY

Mrs. Durgesh Kumari Gupta

Assistant Professor, Rajiv Gandhi Institute of Pharmacy, Faculty of

Pharmaceutical Science & Technology, AKS University Satna, MP-India

ABSTRACT:

Chemotherapy is a pivotal treatment modality in the fight against malignancies, leveraging potent drugs to target and eradicate cancer cells. It operates by disrupting the cellular mechanisms essential for cancer cell proliferation and survival, thereby inhibiting tumor growth. These drugs can be administered orally, intravenously, or through other routes, allowing for flexibility in treatment plans. Chemotherapy regimens are often tailored to the specific type and stage of cancer, with protocols designed to maximize efficacy while minimizing adverse effects. Despite its benefits, chemotherapy is accompanied by a range of side effects due to its impact on rapidly dividing healthy cells, such as those in the bone marrow, gastrointestinal tract, and hair follicles. The choice of chemotherapy agents and their combinations is guided by the cancer's histological characteristics, genetic markers, and the patient's overall health. Advances in pharmacogenomics have enabled more personalized chemotherapy approaches, improving outcomes and reducing toxicity. Chemotherapy can be used as a primary treatment or in conjunction with surgery and radiation therapy, enhancing the overall efficacy of cancer management. Neoadjuvant chemotherapy aims to shrink tumors before surgical intervention, while adjuvant chemotherapy targets residual cancer cells post-surgery. Supportive care measures, such as antiemetics, growth factors, and hydration therapy, are critical in managing the side effects and maintaining the patient's quality of life during treatment. Regular monitoring and adjustments to the chemotherapy regimen help mitigate adverse reactions and ensure optimal therapeutic responses. Research continues to evolve, with new chemotherapy agents and combination therapies being developed to overcome resistance and improve survival rates. As a cornerstone of oncology, chemotherapy remains a dynamic and essential component in the comprehensive treatment of malignancies, offering hope and extending lives for many cancer patients.

Introduction to Chemotherapy of Malignancy

Chemotherapy is a cornerstone in the treatment of malignancies, utilizing powerful drugs to target and destroy cancer cells. Unlike localized treatments such as surgery and radiation therapy, chemotherapy works systemically, making it effective against cancer cells that have spread throughout the body. The primary objective of chemotherapy is to eradicate cancer cells, reduce tumor size, prevent metastasis, and alleviate symptoms. Chemotherapy can be used alone or in combination with other treatments to enhance overall efficacy. Despite its therapeutic benefits, chemotherapy can affect healthy cells, leading to side effects that require careful management. Advances in chemotherapy drugs and personalized medicine continue to improve the precision and effectiveness of cancer treatment.

Chemotherapy of malignancy, often referred to simply as chemotherapy, is a medical treatment approach aimed at using drugs to destroy or inhibit the growth of cancer cells. Malignancy refers to the property of being cancerous or having the potential to invade and spread to other tissues in an uncontrolled manner. Chemotherapy is a systemic treatment, meaning it affects the entire body, and it is commonly used to treat various types of cancers.

Classification of Chemotherapy Drugs

Chemotherapy drugs can be classified based on their chemical structure, mechanism of action, and cell cycle specificity. Here are some of the main categories:

1. **Alkylating Agents**
   - o **Examples:** Cyclophosphamide, Ifosfamide, Melphalan
   - o **Mechanism:** These drugs work by adding alkyl groups to DNA, leading to DNA cross-linking and strand breaks, which ultimately inhibit DNA replication and transcription, causing cell death. They are effective throughout the cell cycle but are particularly potent during the DNA synthesis phase (S-phase).
2. **Antimetabolites**
   - o **Examples:** Methotrexate, 5-Fluorouracil (5-FU), Cytarabine
   - o **Mechanism:** Antimetabolites resemble natural substances within the cell, interfering with DNA and RNA synthesis by substituting for normal building blocks of RNA and DNA. This results in faulty DNA synthesis and cell death, particularly affecting rapidly dividing cells in the S-phase of the cell cycle.
3. **Mitotic Inhibitors**
   - o **Examples:** Paclitaxel, Docetaxel, Vincristine, Vinblastine
   - o **Mechanism:** These drugs inhibit cell division by disrupting the microtubule structures that are necessary for mitosis (M-phase). They prevent cells from successfully completing mitosis, leading to cell death.
4. **Topoisomerase Inhibitors**
   - o **Examples:** Doxorubicin, Etoposide, Irinotecan
   - o **Mechanism:** These drugs interfere with the enzymes topoisomerase I and II, which are essential for DNA replication and repair. Inhibition of these enzymes results in DNA strand breaks and cell death.
5. **Antitumor Antibiotics**
   - o **Examples:** Doxorubicin, Bleomycin, Mitomycin C

- o **Mechanism:** Derived from natural products, these drugs intercalate into DNA strands, inhibiting RNA synthesis and causing breaks in DNA. They are effective in various phases of the cell cycle.

6. **Hormonal Agents**
- o **Examples:** Tamoxifen, Letrozole, Leuprolide
- o **Mechanism:** These drugs are used in cancers that are hormone-dependent, such as breast and prostate cancers. They work by blocking hormone receptors or decreasing hormone production, thereby inhibiting cancer cell growth.

7. **Targeted Therapy**
- o **Examples:** Imatinib, Trastuzumab, Erlotinib
- o **Mechanism:** These drugs target specific molecules involved in cancer cell growth and survival, such as tyrosine kinases or HER2 receptors. They offer a more precise approach to cancer treatment with potentially fewer side effects compared to traditional chemotherapy.

8. **Immunotherapy**
- o **Examples:** Pembrolizumab, Nivolumab, Ipilimumab
- o **Mechanism:** Immunotherapy drugs enhance the body's immune response against cancer cells. They work by targeting immune checkpoints, modulating immune cell activity, or using engineered immune cells to attack cancer.

Introduction to Chemotherapy of Malignancy

Chemotherapy is a cornerstone in the treatment of malignancies, utilizing powerful drugs to target and destroy cancer cells. Unlike localized treatments such as surgery and radiation therapy, chemotherapy works systemically, making it effective against cancer cells that have spread throughout the body. The primary objective of chemotherapy is to eradicate cancer cells, reduce tumor size, prevent metastasis, and alleviate symptoms. Chemotherapy can be used alone or in combination with other treatments to enhance overall efficacy. Despite its therapeutic benefits, chemotherapy can affect healthy cells, leading to side effects that require careful management. Advances in chemotherapy drugs and personalized medicine continue to improve the precision and effectiveness of cancer treatment.

Classification of Chemotherapy Drugs

Chemotherapy drugs can be classified based on their chemical structure, mechanism of action, and cell cycle specificity. Here are some of the main categories:

1. **Alkylating Agents**
   - **Examples:** Cyclophosphamide, Ifosfamide, Melphalan
   - **Mechanism:** These drugs work by adding alkyl groups to DNA, leading to DNA cross-linking and strand breaks, which ultimately inhibit DNA replication and transcription, causing cell death. They are effective throughout the cell cycle but are particularly potent during the DNA synthesis phase (S-phase).

2. **Antimetabolites**
   - **Examples:** Methotrexate, 5-Fluorouracil (5-FU), Cytarabine
   - **Mechanism:** Antimetabolites resemble natural substances within the cell, interfering with DNA and RNA synthesis by substituting for normal building blocks of RNA and DNA. This results in faulty DNA synthesis and cell death, particularly affecting rapidly dividing cells in the S-phase of the cell cycle.

3. **Mitotic Inhibitors**
   - **Examples:** Paclitaxel, Docetaxel, Vincristine, Vinblastine
   - **Mechanism:** These drugs inhibit cell division by disrupting the microtubule structures that are necessary for mitosis (M-phase).

They prevent cells from successfully completing mitosis, leading to cell death.

4. **Topoisomerase Inhibitors**

o **Examples:** Doxorubicin, Etoposide, Irinotecan

o **Mechanism:** These drugs interfere with the enzymes topoisomerase I and II, which are essential for DNA replication and repair. Inhibition of these enzymes results in DNA strand breaks and cell death.

5. **Antitumor Antibiotics**

o **Examples:** Doxorubicin, Bleomycin, Mitomycin C

o **Mechanism:** Derived from natural products, these drugs intercalate into DNA strands, inhibiting RNA synthesis and causing breaks in DNA. They are effective in various phases of the cell cycle.

6. **Hormonal Agents**

o **Examples:** Tamoxifen, Letrozole, Leuprolide

o **Mechanism:** These drugs are used in cancers that are hormone-dependent, such as breast and prostate cancers. They work by blocking hormone receptors or decreasing hormone production, thereby inhibiting cancer cell growth.

7. **Targeted Therapy**

o **Examples:** Imatinib, Trastuzumab, Erlotinib

o **Mechanism:** These drugs target specific molecules involved in cancer cell growth and survival, such as tyrosine kinases or HER2 receptors. They offer a more precise approach to cancer treatment with potentially fewer side effects compared to traditional chemotherapy.

8. **Immunotherapy**

o **Examples:** Pembrolizumab, Nivolumab, Ipilimumab

- o **Mechanism:** Immunotherapy drugs enhance the body's immune response against cancer cells. They work by targeting immune checkpoints, modulating immune cell activity, or using engineered immune cells to attack cancer.

Pharmacology of Chemotherapy Drugs

Chemotherapy drugs are used to treat various malignancies, and understanding their pharmacology is essential for optimizing their therapeutic effects while minimizing adverse reactions. Here's a detailed look at their mechanisms of action, pharmacokinetics, adverse effects, and uses:

1. Alkylating Agents

Examples: Cyclophosphamide, Ifosfamide, Melphalan

Mechanism of Action:

Alkylating agents add alkyl groups to DNA bases, causing DNA cross-linking and strand breaks. This interferes with DNA replication and transcription, leading to cell cycle arrest and apoptosis.

Pharmacokinetics:

- **Absorption:** Often administered intravenously or orally.
- **Distribution:** Widely distributed in the body, including the central nervous system for some agents.
- **Metabolism:** Metabolized primarily in the liver.
- **Excretion:** Excreted mainly via urine.

Adverse Effects:

- Myelosuppression (bone marrow suppression)
- Nausea and vomiting
- Alopecia (hair loss)
- Hemorrhagic cystitis (especially with cyclophosphamide and ifosfamide)

Uses:

- Hodgkin's and non-Hodgkin's lymphomas
- Breast cancer

- Ovarian cancer
- Multiple myeloma

2. Antimetabolites

Examples: Methotrexate, 5-Fluorouracil (5-FU), Cytarabine

Mechanism of Action:

Antimetabolites mimic natural substrates and interfere with DNA and RNA synthesis. For example, methotrexate inhibits dihydrofolate reductase, reducing the synthesis of thymidylate and purines necessary for DNA synthesis.

Pharmacokinetics:

- **Absorption:** Oral and intravenous administration.
- **Distribution:** Methotrexate can cross the blood-brain barrier.
- **Metabolism:** Hepatic metabolism; some drugs are activated intracellularly.
- **Excretion:** Renal excretion is significant.

Adverse Effects:

- Myelosuppression
- Mucositis (inflammation of the mucous membranes)
- Hepatotoxicity
- Renal toxicity (particularly with methotrexate)

Uses:

- Leukemias
- Breast cancer
- Gastrointestinal cancers
- Osteosarcoma

3. Mitotic Inhibitors

Examples: Paclitaxel, Docetaxel, Vincristine, Vinblastine

Mechanism of Action:

Mitotic inhibitors disrupt microtubule dynamics, preventing mitosis. Taxanes (paclitaxel, docetaxel) stabilize microtubules, while vinca alkaloids (vincristine, vinblastine) inhibit microtubule formation.

Pharmacokinetics:

- **Absorption:** Administered intravenously.
- **Distribution:** Widely distributed; high affinity for tubulin.
- **Metabolism:** Hepatic metabolism (cytochrome P450 enzymes).
- **Excretion:** Primarily biliary excretion.

Adverse Effects:

- Myelosuppression
- Peripheral neuropathy
- Alopecia
- Hypersensitivity reactions (particularly with paclitaxel)

Uses:

- Breast cancer
- Ovarian cancer
- Lung cancer
- Hodgkin's lymphoma

4. Topoisomerase Inhibitors

Examples: Doxorubicin, Etoposide, Irinotecan

Mechanism of Action:

Topoisomerase inhibitors interfere with DNA replication by stabilizing the transient breaks made by topoisomerase enzymes, leading to DNA damage and apoptosis.

Pharmacokinetics:

- **Absorption:** Intravenous administration.
- **Distribution:** Widely distributed; doxorubicin has high tissue binding.
- **Metabolism:** Hepatic metabolism; irinotecan is a prodrug converted to active SN-38.

- **Excretion:** Primarily biliary and renal excretion.

Adverse Effects:

- Myelosuppression
- Cardiotoxicity (especially doxorubicin)
- Gastrointestinal toxicity (diarrhea with irinotecan)
- Secondary malignancies

Uses:

- Breast cancer
- Lung cancer
- Ovarian cancer
- Leukemias

5. Antitumor Antibiotics

Examples: Doxorubicin, Bleomycin, Mitomycin C

Mechanism of Action:

These drugs intercalate into DNA, inhibiting RNA synthesis and causing DNA strand breaks. They generate free radicals that damage cellular components.

Pharmacokinetics:

- **Absorption:** Administered intravenously.
- **Distribution:** Extensive tissue binding; doxorubicin accumulates in the heart.
- **Metabolism:** Primarily hepatic.
- **Excretion:** Biliary and renal excretion.

Adverse Effects:

- Myelosuppression
- Cardiotoxicity (doxorubicin)
- Pulmonary toxicity (bleomycin)
- Mucositis

Uses:

- Breast cancer

- Lung cancer
- Lymphomas
- Sarcomas

6. Hormonal Agents

Examples: Tamoxifen, Letrozole, Leuprolide

Mechanism of Action:

Hormonal agents block hormone receptors or decrease hormone production. Tamoxifen is an estrogen receptor antagonist, while letrozole is an aromatase inhibitor, and leuprolide is a GnRH agonist that suppresses gonadotropin release.

Pharmacokinetics:

- **Absorption:** Oral administration.
- **Distribution:** High protein binding.
- **Metabolism:** Hepatic metabolism.
- **Excretion:** Renal and biliary excretion.

Adverse Effects:

- Hot flashes
- Bone loss (aromatase inhibitors)
- Cardiovascular risk (tamoxifen)
- Tumor flare (leuprolide)

Uses:

- Breast cancer
- Prostate cancer

7. Targeted Therapy

Examples: Imatinib, Trastuzumab, Erlotinib

Mechanism of Action:

Targeted therapies specifically inhibit molecules involved in cancer cell signaling and growth. Imatinib inhibits BCR-ABL tyrosine kinase, trastuzumab targets HER2, and erlotinib inhibits EGFR.

Pharmacokinetics:

- **Absorption:** Oral administration.

- **Distribution:** Varies by drug; trastuzumab is administered intravenously.

- **Metabolism:** Primarily hepatic (cytochrome P450 enzymes for small molecules).

- **Excretion:** Biliary and renal excretion.

Adverse Effects:

- Diarrhea

- Rash (EGFR inhibitors)

- Cardiomyopathy (trastuzumab)

- Edema (imatinib)

Uses:

- Chronic myeloid leukemia (CML)

- Breast cancer (HER2-positive)

- Non-small cell lung cancer (NSCLC)

8. Immunotherapy

Examples: Pembrolizumab, Nivolumab, Ipilimumab

Mechanism of Action:

Immunotherapy drugs enhance the immune response against cancer cells by blocking immune checkpoints (PD-1, CTLA-4) or modulating immune activity.

Pharmacokinetics:

- **Absorption:** Intravenous administration.

- **Distribution:** Extensive distribution in the body.

- **Metabolism:** Degraded by proteolytic enzymes.

- **Excretion:** Renal and hepatic pathways.

Adverse Effects:

- Immune-related adverse events (irAEs) such as colitis, dermatitis, and hepatitis

- Fatigue

- Endocrinopathies

Uses:

- Melanoma
- Non-small cell lung cancer
- Renal cell carcinoma
- Hodgkin's lymphoma

CHAPTER – 18

IMMUNOPHARMACOLOGY

Mr. Santosh Kumar

Assistant Professor, Rajiv Gandhi Institute of Pharmacy, Faculty of Pharmaceutical Science & Technology, AKS University Satna, MP-India

ABSTRACT:

Immunopharmacology, the study of drugs that influence the immune system, is a critical field in both understanding and manipulating immune responses for therapeutic benefit. This branch of pharmacology encompasses a wide range of substances, including immunosuppressants, immunostimulants, and immunomodulators, each playing a pivotal role in treating various diseases. Immunosuppressants, such as corticosteroids, calcineurin inhibitors, and monoclonal antibodies, are essential in preventing organ transplant rejection and treating autoimmune diseases by dampening overactive immune responses. On the other hand, immunostimulants like vaccines and adjuvants boost the immune system's ability to fight infections and certain cancers by enhancing antigen-specific responses.The advent of biologics, such as monoclonal antibodies and cytokine inhibitors, has revolutionized the treatment of autoimmune diseases, providing targeted approaches that minimize broad immunosuppression. For example, drugs like infliximab and etanercept inhibit tumor necrosis factor-alpha (TNF-α), a key cytokine in inflammatory processes, offering significant relief in conditions like rheumatoid arthritis and Crohn's disease. Additionally, checkpoint inhibitors, a class of immunomodulatory drugs, have shown remarkable success in oncology by unleashing the immune system to target cancer cells more effectively. Agents like pembrolizumab and nivolumab block inhibitory pathways, such as PD-1/PD-L1, enhancing T-cell activity against tumors. Immunopharmacology also addresses the challenge of balancing efficacy and safety. Immunosuppressive therapies, while crucial for preventing transplant rejection, can increase susceptibility to infections and malignancies. Similarly, immunostimulatory therapies must be carefully managed to avoid triggering excessive inflammation or autoimmunity. Advances in precision medicine and biomarker research are enabling more personalized approaches, tailoring immunotherapies to individual patient profiles for optimized outcomes. The integration of immunopharmacology with other fields, such as genomics and bioinformatics, continues to drive innovation, paving the way for new treatments that harness the power of the immune system with unprecedented specificity and control.

Introduction:

Immunopharmacology is the scientific discipline focused on the study of drugs that modulate the immune system's function. This field is critical for understanding how various pharmacological agents can enhance or suppress immune responses to treat a wide array of diseases. By investigating the interactions between the immune system and therapeutic agents, immunopharmacology provides insights into the mechanisms of action, efficacy, and potential adverse effects of these drugs. It encompasses a diverse range of substances, including immunosuppressants, which are used to prevent transplant rejection and treat autoimmune disorders; immunostimulants, which boost the immune system to fight infections and cancers; and immunomodulators, which adjust the immune response to achieve a desired therapeutic outcome. The advancements in immunopharmacology have led to significant breakthroughs in medicine, particularly in the areas of oncology, infectious diseases, and chronic inflammatory conditions. As our understanding of the immune system deepens, the field of immunopharmacology continues to evolve, driving the development of innovative treatments that harness the power of the immune system with greater precision and effectiveness.

IMMUNOSTIMULANTS

Introduction to Immunostimulants

Immunostimulants are a class of drugs designed to enhance or stimulate the body's immune response. These agents are particularly valuable in conditions where the immune system is weakened or requires a boost to combat infections, cancer, or other diseases. Immunostimulants work by activating or increasing the activity of immune cells, enhancing the body's natural defense mechanisms. They play a crucial role in prophylactic and therapeutic settings, including vaccination, cancer immunotherapy, and treatment of chronic infections. By understanding the mechanisms and applications of immunostimulants, healthcare providers can better utilize these agents to improve patient outcomes in various clinical scenarios.

Classification of Immunostimulants

Immunostimulants can be broadly classified into the following categories:

1. **Vaccines**
   - **Examples:** Hepatitis B vaccine, Influenza vaccine
   - **Function:** Stimulate the immune system to produce a specific response against pathogens, providing immunity and preventing disease.
2. **Cytokines**
   - **Examples:** Interferons (IFNs), Interleukins (IL-2)
   - **Function:** Enhance the immune response by promoting the activity of immune cells such as T-cells, NK cells, and macrophages.
3. **Adjuvants**
   - **Examples:** Alum, Monophosphoryl lipid A

- o **Function:** Enhance the body's immune response to an antigen, often used in combination with vaccines to improve efficacy.

4. **Colony-Stimulating Factors (CSFs)**
   - o **Examples:** Granulocyte colony-stimulating factor (G-CSF), Granulocyte-macrophage colony-stimulating factor (GM-CSF)
   - o **Function:** Stimulate the production and differentiation of bone marrow progenitor cells into mature blood cells.

5. **Immune Checkpoint Inhibitors**
   - o **Examples:** Pembrolizumab, Nivolumab
   - o **Function:** Block inhibitory pathways in immune cells, enhancing the immune system's ability to fight cancer.

6. **Bacterial Derivatives**
   - o **Examples:** Bacillus Calmette-Guérin (BCG)
   - o **Function:** Stimulate the immune system through the activation of macrophages and other immune cells, often used in cancer immunotherapy.

Pharmacology of Immunostimulants

Vaccines

- **Mechanism of Action:** Vaccines introduce an antigen (inactivated or attenuated pathogen, or subunit) to the body, prompting the immune system to produce specific antibodies and memory cells that provide long-term immunity.
- **Pharmacokinetics:**
  - o **Absorption:** Usually administered via intramuscular, subcutaneous, or oral routes.
  - o **Distribution:** Distributed throughout the body, primarily affecting lymphoid tissues.

o **Metabolism:** Not applicable; vaccines act by eliciting an immune response.

o **Excretion:** The antigen is processed and eliminated by the immune system.

- **Adverse Effects:** Local site reactions (redness, swelling), fever, fatigue, allergic reactions (rare).

- **Uses:** Prevention of infectious diseases (e.g., measles, mumps, rubella, influenza).

Cytokines

- **Mechanism of Action:** Cytokines are signaling proteins that modulate immune cell activity. Interferons enhance antiviral responses, while interleukins stimulate T-cell proliferation and activation.

- **Pharmacokinetics:**

o **Absorption:** Administered intravenously or subcutaneously.

o **Distribution:** Widely distributed, particularly in immune tissues.

o **Metabolism:** Rapidly metabolized in the liver and kidneys.

o **Excretion:** Primarily renal excretion.

- **Adverse Effects:** Flu-like symptoms (fever, chills, fatigue), myalgia, hypotension, hepatotoxicity.

- **Uses:** Treatment of chronic viral infections (e.g., hepatitis B and C), cancer therapy (e.g., melanoma, renal cell carcinoma).

Adjuvants

- **Mechanism of Action:** Adjuvants enhance the immune response to an antigen by activating innate immune receptors and promoting antigen presentation.

- **Pharmacokinetics:**

- o **Absorption:** Co-administered with vaccines.
- o **Distribution:** Localized at the injection site, with some systemic distribution.
- o **Metabolism:** Not metabolized; act locally to enhance immune response.
- o **Excretion:** Biodegradable components are phagocytosed and eliminated.
- **Adverse Effects:** Local inflammation, mild systemic reactions.
- **Uses:** Boosting efficacy of vaccines.

Colony-Stimulating Factors (CSFs)

- **Mechanism of Action:** CSFs stimulate the proliferation and differentiation of hematopoietic progenitor cells into mature leukocytes, enhancing the immune response and aiding recovery after chemotherapy-induced myelosuppression.
- **Pharmacokinetics:**
  - o **Absorption:** Administered subcutaneously or intravenously.
  - o **Distribution:** Distributed to bone marrow and other tissues.
  - o **Metabolism:** Rapidly cleared by the liver and kidneys.
  - o **Excretion:** Renal excretion.
- **Adverse Effects:** Bone pain, fever, fatigue, injection site reactions.
- **Uses:** Management of neutropenia in cancer patients, bone marrow transplantation.

Immune Checkpoint Inhibitors

- **Mechanism of Action:** These drugs block inhibitory receptors (e.g., PD-1, CTLA-4) on T-cells, enhancing T-cell activity against cancer cells.
- **Pharmacokinetics:**

- o **Absorption:** Administered intravenously.
- o **Distribution:** Wide distribution in the body.
- o **Metabolism:** Degraded by proteolytic enzymes.
- o **Excretion:** Not fully characterized; eliminated via natural protein degradation pathways.
- **Adverse Effects:** Immune-related adverse events (colitis, dermatitis, hepatitis, endocrinopathies).
- **Uses:** Treatment of various cancers, including melanoma, non-small cell lung cancer, renal cell carcinoma.

Bacterial Derivatives

- **Mechanism of Action:** BCG and similar agents activate macrophages and other immune cells, leading to a heightened immune response against cancer cells.
- **Pharmacokinetics:**
- o **Absorption:** Administered intravesically (for bladder cancer) or intradermally.
- o **Distribution:** Localized at the site of administration.
- o **Metabolism:** Not metabolized; act locally to stimulate immune cells.
- o **Excretion:** Phagocytosed and eliminated by immune cells.
- **Adverse Effects:** Local inflammation, fever, allergic reactions.
- **Uses:** Immunotherapy for bladder cancer, potential use in other malignancies and infectious diseases.

IMMUNOSUPPRESSANT

Introduction to Immunosuppressant Drugs

Immunosuppressant drugs are essential in medicine for their ability to suppress or modulate the immune system. They are widely used to prevent rejection of transplanted organs and tissues, manage autoimmune diseases, and treat conditions where an overactive immune response causes harm. By dampening immune activity, these drugs help reduce inflammation, control autoimmune reactions, and improve the success of organ transplantation. Understanding their classification and pharmacology is crucial for optimizing their therapeutic benefits while managing potential risks and side effects.

Classification of Immunosuppressant Drugs

Immunosuppressants can be classified into several categories based on their mechanism of action:

1. **Calcineurin Inhibitors**
   - **Examples:** Cyclosporine, Tacrolimus
   - **Mechanism:** Inhibit calcineurin, a phosphatase necessary for T-cell activation and cytokine production.
   - **Uses:** Prevention of organ transplant rejection, treatment of autoimmune diseases like rheumatoid arthritis and psoriasis.

2. **Antimetabolites**
   - **Examples:** Azathioprine, Methotrexate
   - **Mechanism:** Interfere with DNA synthesis and cell proliferation, particularly in rapidly dividing immune cells.
   - **Uses:** Maintenance therapy post-transplantation, treatment of autoimmune disorders such as systemic lupus erythematosus (SLE).

3. **Corticosteroids**
   - **Examples:** Prednisone, Prednisolone
   - **Mechanism:** Act on multiple pathways to suppress inflammation and immune responses.

- o **Uses:** Broad spectrum in autoimmune diseases, acute transplant rejection, and as adjunctive therapy in many conditions.

4. **Biological Agents (Monoclonal Antibodies)**

- o **Examples:** Rituximab, Basiliximab
- o **Mechanism:** Target specific immune cells or molecules involved in immune activation or modulation.
- o **Uses:** Targeted therapy in autoimmune diseases and prevention of rejection in transplant recipients.

5. **mTOR Inhibitors**

- o **Examples:** Sirolimus, Everolimus
- o **Mechanism:** Inhibit the mammalian target of rapamycin (mTOR), reducing T-cell proliferation and cytokine production.
- o **Uses:** Used in combination with other immunosuppressants in organ transplantation and some autoimmune diseases.

Pharmacology of Immunosuppressant Drugs

Calcineurin Inhibitors (Cyclosporine, Tacrolimus)

- **Mechanism of Action:** Inhibit calcineurin, blocking the transcription of interleukin-2 (IL-2) and other cytokines essential for T-cell activation.
- **Pharmacokinetics:**
- o **Absorption:** Oral administration; variable bioavailability.
- o **Distribution:** Widely distributed, with significant tissue penetration.
- o **Metabolism:** Hepatic metabolism (CYP3A4 enzymes).
- o **Excretion:** Primarily biliary and renal excretion.
- **Adverse Effects:** Nephrotoxicity, hypertension, hyperglycemia, neurotoxicity.

Antimetabolites (Azathioprine, Methotrexate)

- **Mechanism of Action:** Azathioprine is metabolized into active metabolites that interfere with purine synthesis, inhibiting lymphocyte proliferation. Methotrexate inhibits dihydrofolate reductase, reducing DNA and RNA synthesis.
- **Pharmacokinetics:**
  - **Absorption:** Oral administration; variable bioavailability.
  - **Distribution:** Wide tissue distribution.
  - **Metabolism:** Hepatic metabolism.
  - **Excretion:** Renal excretion.
- **Adverse Effects:** Bone marrow suppression, hepatotoxicity, gastrointestinal disturbances.

Corticosteroids (Prednisone, Prednisolone)

- **Mechanism of Action:** Bind to glucocorticoid receptors, modifying gene expression and inhibiting inflammatory pathways.
- **Pharmacokinetics:**
  - **Absorption:** Oral administration; rapid and complete absorption.
  - **Distribution:** Wide tissue distribution, including the brain.
  - **Metabolism:** Hepatic metabolism.
  - **Excretion:** Renal excretion.
- **Adverse Effects:** Immunodeficiency, osteoporosis, hypertension, hyperglycemia, mood changes.

Biological Agents (Rituximab, Basiliximab)

- **Mechanism of Action:** Rituximab targets CD20 antigen on B-cells, depleting them. Basiliximab binds to IL-2 receptor, inhibiting T-cell activation.

- **Pharmacokinetics:**
- o **Absorption:** Administered intravenously.
- o **Distribution:** Varies by agent; distributed to tissues.
- o **Metabolism:** Metabolized by proteolytic enzymes.
- o **Excretion:** Metabolites excreted via renal and hepatic pathways.
- **Adverse Effects:** Infusion reactions, increased risk of infections, immunosuppression-related malignancies.

mTOR Inhibitors (Sirolimus, Everolimus)

- **Mechanism of Action:** Inhibit mTOR pathway, blocking T-cell activation and proliferation in response to cytokines.
- **Pharmacokinetics:**
- o **Absorption:** Oral administration; variable bioavailability.
- o **Distribution:** Extensive tissue distribution.
- o **Metabolism:** Hepatic metabolism.
- o **Excretion:** Renal excretion.
- **Adverse Effects:** Hyperlipidemia, thrombocytopenia, delayed wound healing.

PROTEIN DRUGS

Introduction to Protein Drugs

Protein drugs represent a class of pharmaceuticals derived from proteins or peptides that play crucial roles in regulating biological processes. These drugs are designed to mimic or augment natural protein functions in the body, offering targeted therapeutic effects for a wide range of diseases and conditions. Due to their specificity and biological activity, protein drugs have revolutionized treatment approaches, particularly in areas such as oncology, immunology, and endocrinology. Understanding their classification and pharmacology is essential for their effective utilization in clinical practice.

Classification of Protein Drugs

Protein drugs can be classified into several categories based on their structure and therapeutic targets:

1. **Monoclonal Antibodies (mAbs)**
   o **Examples:** Rituximab, Trastuzumab, Infliximab
   o **Function:** Target specific antigens or receptors on cells, modulating immune responses or inhibiting signaling pathways involved in disease progression.
   o **Uses:** Treatment of cancer, autoimmune disorders, and inflammatory diseases.

2. **Cytokines and Growth Factors**
   o **Examples:** Interferons (IFNs), Interleukins (ILs), Erythropoietin (EPO)
   o **Function:** Regulate immune responses, cell growth, and differentiation.
   o **Uses:** Immunotherapy, hematopoietic support, treatment of chronic diseases.

3. **Enzyme Replacement Therapies (ERTs)**
   o **Examples:** Alglucosidase alfa, L-asparaginase
   o **Function:** Replace deficient or absent enzymes in metabolic disorders, facilitating normal biochemical processes.
   o **Uses:** Treatment of lysosomal storage disorders, enzyme deficiencies.

4. **Hormones and Hormone Antagonists**
   o **Examples:** Insulin, Growth hormone, Gonadotropin-releasing hormone (GnRH) agonists
   o **Function:** Regulate physiological processes such as metabolism, growth, and reproduction.
   o **Uses:** Diabetes management, growth disorders, fertility treatments.

5. **Fusion Proteins and Therapeutic Peptides**

- o **Examples:** Etanercept, Abatacept, GLP-1 agonists
- o **Function:** Combine functional domains of different proteins to target specific disease pathways or receptors.
- o **Uses:** Treatment of autoimmune diseases, diabetes, and metabolic disorders.

Pharmacology of Protein Drugs

Protein drugs exhibit distinct pharmacological characteristics compared to small molecule drugs:

- **Mechanism of Action:** Protein drugs typically exert their effects by binding to specific receptors or molecules, modulating biochemical pathways, or replacing deficient proteins/enzymes.
- **Pharmacokinetics:**
- o **Absorption:** Administered via injection (intravenous, subcutaneous) due to poor oral bioavailability.
- o **Distribution:** Distribution varies depending on protein size, charge, and receptor binding.
- o **Metabolism:** Metabolized by proteolytic enzymes or cleared by the reticuloendothelial system.
- o **Excretion:** Excreted primarily via renal clearance or metabolism in the liver.
- **Adverse Effects:** Common adverse effects include immune reactions (e.g., infusion reactions for mAbs), hypersensitivity reactions, and potential immunogenicity leading to neutralizing antibodies.
- **Uses and Therapeutic Considerations:** Protein drugs are used for targeted therapy due to their specificity, often requiring careful dosing, monitoring of immune responses, and management of potential adverse effects. They are pivotal in personalized medicine approaches, tailoring treatment to individual patient profiles and disease characteristics.

MONOCLONAL ANTIBODIES

Monoclonal antibodies (mAbs) are laboratory-produced molecules that are engineered to mimic the immune system's ability to fight off harmful pathogens, such as viruses or cancer cells. These antibodies are designed to recognize and bind to specific proteins, and they have become a crucial class of therapeutic agents in various medical fields. Monoclonal antibodies (mAbs) are a class of protein therapeutics produced from identical immune cells that are clones of a unique parent cell. These antibodies are designed to target specific antigens, receptors, or proteins in the body, offering precise therapeutic effects across a wide range of medical conditions. Here's an overview covering their development, mechanism of action, therapeutic applications, and challenges:

Development of Monoclonal Antibodies

Monoclonal antibodies are developed through hybridoma technology or recombinant DNA technology:

- **Hybridoma Technology:** Involves fusing a specific antibody-producing B cell with a myeloma cell to create immortalized hybrid cells that produce identical antibodies.
- **Recombinant DNA Technology:** Utilizes genetic engineering to produce monoclonal antibodies by inserting DNA sequences encoding the antibody into host cells such as mammalian cells or yeast.

Mechanism of Action

Monoclonal antibodies exert their therapeutic effects through several mechanisms:

- **Binding and Neutralization:** Bind to specific antigens or receptors on cells, blocking their function or neutralizing harmful effects.

- **Cellular Depletion:** Trigger immune responses to eliminate cells expressing the target antigen, such as cancer cells or pathogen-infected cells.
- **Signal Blockade:** Inhibit signaling pathways involved in disease progression, such as inflammatory cytokines or growth factor receptors.

Therapeutic Applications

Monoclonal antibodies have diverse therapeutic applications across various medical fields:

- **Cancer Treatment:** Target cancer-specific antigens (e.g., HER2 in breast cancer) or immune checkpoints (e.g., PD-1/PD-L1 inhibitors) to enhance immune responses against tumors.
- **Autoimmune Diseases:** Suppress immune activity by targeting cytokines (e.g., TNF-alpha inhibitors for rheumatoid arthritis) or immune cells (e.g., B-cell depletion in multiple sclerosis).
- **Infectious Diseases:** Neutralize pathogens (e.g., SARS-CoV-2 antibodies for COVID-19) or enhance immune responses against viral infections.
- **Other Conditions:** Treatments for cardiovascular diseases, transplantation, and neurological disorders are also being explored.

Challenges and Considerations

- **Immunogenicity:** Some monoclonal antibodies may induce immune responses, leading to neutralizing antibodies that reduce efficacy over time.
- **Manufacturing Complexity:** Production requires advanced biotechnological processes, leading to high costs and potential supply chain challenges.

- **Administration Route:** Most monoclonal antibodies are administered via intravenous infusion or subcutaneous injection due to their large size and poor oral bioavailability.

Future Directions

Ongoing research focuses on improving monoclonal antibody therapies by:

- **Enhancing Specificity:** Developing antibodies with higher target specificity to minimize off-target effects.
- **Reducing Immunogenicity:** Engineering antibodies to reduce immunogenic responses and prolong therapeutic efficacy.
- **Expanding Applications:** Exploring new targets and combinations with other therapies to enhance treatment outcomes and patient responses.

TARGET DRUGS TO ANTIGEN, SIMILAR

Targeting drugs to specific antigens or antigens that are similar involves leveraging the specificity of monoclonal antibodies (mAbs) and other targeted therapies. Here's how drugs can be targeted to antigens or similar molecules:

1. **Monoclonal Antibodies (mAbs):**
   - **Specific Binding:** mAbs are designed to bind to specific antigens on cells or soluble antigens in the bloodstream.
   - **Therapeutic Applications:** Targeting cancer-specific antigens (e.g., HER2 in breast cancer, CD20 in lymphoma), immune checkpoint inhibitors (e.g., PD-1/PD-L1), and inflammatory cytokines (e.g., TNF-alpha).
   - **Mechanism:** By binding to these targets, mAbs can block signaling pathways, induce cellular responses (e.g., antibody-dependent cellular cytotoxicity, ADCP), or deliver payloads (e.g., toxins, radioisotopes) directly to the antigen-expressing cells.
2. **Antibody-Drug Conjugates (ADCs):**

o **Design:** Combines a monoclonal antibody with a cytotoxic drug or payload.

o **Targeting:** The antibody component targets specific antigens on cancer cells, while the drug component delivers a cytotoxic payload directly to the target cells.

o **Examples:** Trastuzumab emtansine (T-DM1) targets HER2-positive breast cancer cells, delivering a cytotoxic agent.

3. **Bispecific Antibodies:**

o **Structure:** Engineered to bind simultaneously to two different antigens or epitopes.

o **Applications:** Redirect T cells to target specific cells (e.g., CD19/CD3 bispecific antibodies in leukemia), or simultaneously block two different signaling pathways.

4. **Vaccines:**

o **Antigen-Specific:** Stimulate the immune system to produce antibodies against specific antigens, providing immunity against infectious diseases (e.g., SARS-CoV-2 vaccines targeting the spike protein).

5. **Small Molecule Drugs:**

o **Targeted Therapies:** Designed to inhibit specific molecules or pathways that are overactive in diseases, such as kinase inhibitors in cancer therapy targeting specific mutant kinases.

6. **Peptide Therapeutics:**

o **Design:** Peptides can be designed to mimic antigenic epitopes or bind specifically to receptors on cells.

o **Applications:** Used in diagnostics (e.g., peptide-based imaging agents) or therapeutics (e.g., peptide hormones).

Targeting drugs to antigens or similar molecules enhances specificity and reduces off-target effects, leading to improved therapeutic outcomes and reduced toxicity compared to traditional treatments. This approach is central to precision medicine, where treatments are tailored to individual patient characteristics and disease profiles.

CHAPTER – 19

PRINCIPLES OF TOXICOLOGY

Mr. Ram Prasad Sahu

Assistant Professor, Rajiv Gandhi Institute of Pharmacy, Faculty of

Pharmaceutical Science & Technology, AKS University Satna, MP-India

ABSTRACT:

Toxicology is the study of the adverse effects of chemicals or physical agents on living organisms. Its principles are fundamental in assessing and managing risks associated with exposure to potentially harmful substances. Key principles of toxicology include:

1. **Dose-Response Relationship:** Toxicologists study how the severity of a toxic effect changes with the dose or concentration of the substance. This relationship helps determine safe exposure limits and therapeutic doses.

2. **Exposure Routes:** Toxicants can enter the body through ingestion, inhalation, dermal contact, or injection. Understanding how different routes affect toxicity helps in assessing risks and designing safety measures.

3. **Absorption, Distribution, Metabolism, and Excretion (ADME):** These processes determine how toxicants are absorbed into the body, distributed to tissues, metabolized into less harmful or more toxic compounds, and excreted. ADME studies are crucial in understanding toxicokinetics.

4. **Mechanisms of Toxicity:** Toxicologists investigate how toxicants exert their harmful effects at the molecular, cellular, and organ levels. This includes interactions with biological targets, disruption of cellular functions, and induction of oxidative stress or inflammation.

5. **Toxicity Testing and Risk Assessment:** Methods such as animal studies, in vitro assays, and computational models are used to predict and evaluate

the potential toxicity of chemicals. Risk assessment integrates toxicological data with exposure information to determine safe exposure levels for humans and the environment.

6. **Variability in Susceptibility:** Individuals vary in their susceptibility to toxicants due to genetic factors, age, health status, and environmental influences. Understanding these differences helps in assessing population risks and implementing targeted interventions.

7. **Health Effects:** Toxicologists study the range of adverse health effects caused by toxicants, including acute effects (immediate harm) and chronic effects (long-term consequences like cancer or reproductive disorders).

8. **Emerging Toxicants:** As new chemicals and technologies emerge, toxicologists evaluate their potential risks and develop strategies to mitigate harm. This includes studying environmental pollutants, pharmaceuticals, and industrial chemicals.

9. **Regulatory Guidelines:** Toxicological data informs regulatory agencies in setting safety standards, establishing permissible exposure limits (PELs), and developing guidelines for chemical management and environmental protection.

10. **Ethical Considerations:** Toxicologists adhere to ethical principles in conducting research and risk assessment, ensuring transparency, accountability, and consideration of societal impacts.

Introduction:

Toxicology is the scientific study of the adverse effects of chemical, physical, or biological agents on living organisms and the ecosystem, including the prevention and amelioration of such effects. The principles of toxicology encompass several key concepts:

1. Dose-Response Relationship:

a. The relationship between the amount of a substance (dose) and its effects on an organism.

b. It helps to determine the toxic effects at different levels of exposure.

2. Exposure:

a. The route, duration, and frequency of contact between an organism and a toxic substance.

b. Different routes of exposure include ingestion, inhalation, dermal contact, and injection.

3. Absorption, Distribution, Metabolism, and Elimination (ADME):

a. The processes that describe how a toxic substance enters, moves within, and leaves the body.

b. Understanding these processes helps in predicting and explaining the distribution and fate of toxicants.

4. Bioavailability:

a. The fraction of an administered dose of a substance that reaches the systemic circulation in an unchanged form.

b. It influences the degree to which a substance exerts its toxic effects.

5. Toxicokinetics and Toxicodynamics:

a. Toxicokinetics deals with the absorption, distribution, metabolism, and excretion of toxicants in the body.

b. Toxicodynamics involves the study of the mechanisms by which toxicants produce their effects on living organisms.

6. Target Organ Toxicity:

a. Different toxicants may have specific affinities for certain organs or tissues, leading to selective toxicity.

b. Understanding target organ toxicity is crucial in assessing the potential harm of a substance.

7. Acute and Chronic Toxicity:

a. Acute toxicity refers to the adverse effects that occur shortly after exposure to a single, high dose of a substance.

b. Chronic toxicity involves the long-term exposure to lower levels of a substance, leading to persistent or delayed toxic effects.

8. Risk Assessment:

a. The process of evaluating the potential for adverse effects resulting from exposure to a specific substance or agent.

b. It involves hazard identification, dose-response assessment, exposure assessment, and risk characterization.

9. Threshold and Non-threshold Effects:

a. Threshold effects occur only above a certain dose, while non-threshold effects can occur at any dose.

b. Regulatory standards often focus on preventing exposures that could lead to non-threshold effects.

10. Interindividual Variability:

a. Recognizing that individuals may respond differently to the same exposure due to factors such as age, genetics, and pre-existing health conditions.

Toxicity refers to the potential of a substance to cause harm to living organisms. The nature and duration of exposure determine the type of toxicity observed. Here are definitions and basic knowledge of acute, subacute, and chronic toxicity:

Acute Toxicity

Definition: Acute toxicity refers to the adverse effects of a substance that occur shortly after a single or short-term exposure. It typically manifests within hours or days after exposure.

Characteristics:

- **Rapid Onset:** Symptoms appear quickly after exposure.

- **Short Duration:** Effects are usually transient and resolve once exposure ceases or the substance is eliminated from the body.
- **High Dose Sensitivity:** Often characterized by a steep dose-response curve, where higher doses lead to more severe effects.

Examples: Acute toxicity can result from ingesting a large quantity of a toxic substance (e.g., overdose of medication) or exposure to a high concentration of a chemical (e.g., accidental inhalation of a toxic gas).

Subacute Toxicity

Definition: Subacute toxicity refers to adverse effects that occur after repeated exposure to a substance for several weeks or months but less than 90 days.

Characteristics:

- **Repetitive Exposure:** Effects result from repeated or continuous exposure over a defined period.
- **Less Immediate:** Onset of symptoms may be delayed compared to acute toxicity.
- **Variable Severity:** Effects can range from mild to moderate, depending on the dose and duration of exposure.

Examples: Subacute toxicity may occur from prolonged exposure to certain medications, environmental pollutants, or workplace chemicals.

Chronic Toxicity

Definition: Chronic toxicity refers to adverse effects that develop after prolonged or repeated exposure to a substance over an extended period, typically lasting for more than 90 days.

Characteristics:

- **Long-Term Exposure:** Effects develop gradually over months or years of continuous or intermittent exposure.
- **Persistent Effects:** Symptoms may persist even after exposure has ceased.

- **Low Dose Sensitivity:** Often characterized by a low dose-response curve, where lower doses over extended periods can lead to cumulative damage or adverse health effects.

Examples: Chronic toxicity can result from long-term exposure to environmental contaminants (e.g., heavy metals, pesticides), occupational hazards (e.g., asbestos), or pharmaceuticals used over extended periods.

Differentiation and Importance

- **Differentiation:** Acute, subacute, and chronic toxicity differ primarily in the duration and frequency of exposure, as well as the nature and severity of effects.
- **Importance:** Understanding these categories helps toxicologists assess risks associated with various substances, design appropriate safety guidelines and exposure limits, and implement strategies for minimizing harm to human health and the environment.

DEFINITION AND BASIC KNOWLEDGE OF GENOTOXICITY, CARCINOGENICITY, TERATOGENICITY AND MUTAGENICITY

Genotoxicity

Definition: Genotoxicity refers to the ability of a substance to damage genetic material (DNA or chromosomes) within cells, potentially leading to mutations.

Characteristics:

- **Mechanism:** Genotoxic substances may directly interact with DNA, causing breaks or modifications, or interfere with cellular processes involved in DNA repair.
- **Consequences:** Genetic damage can lead to mutations, chromosomal abnormalities, and potentially contribute to cancer development or hereditary disorders.
- **Testing:** Genotoxicity is assessed through in vitro tests (e.g., Ames test) and in vivo studies to evaluate DNA damage and mutation induction.

Examples: Chemicals like benzene, aflatoxins, and some chemotherapy drugs are known genotoxic agents.

Carcinogenicity

Definition: Carcinogenicity refers to the ability of a substance to cause cancer in living organisms.

Characteristics:

- **Induction of Cancer:** Carcinogens initiate or promote the development of malignant tumors.

- **Mechanism:** Carcinogens may act through genotoxic mechanisms (direct DNA damage), epigenetic alterations, or disrupting cellular signaling pathways.

- **Classification:** Carcinogens are classified based on sufficient evidence from animal studies, epidemiological data, or mechanistic studies.

- **Regulation:** Regulatory agencies classify substances as carcinogens and establish exposure limits to minimize cancer risks.

Examples: Known carcinogens include tobacco smoke (containing polycyclic aromatic hydrocarbons), asbestos fibers, and certain pesticides.

Teratogenicity

Definition: Teratogenicity refers to the ability of a substance to cause developmental abnormalities or birth defects in embryos or fetuses when exposed during pregnancy.

Characteristics:

- **Effect on Development:** Teratogens disrupt normal fetal development, leading to structural or functional abnormalities in organs or tissues.

- **Timing of Exposure:** Effects can depend on the timing and duration of exposure during pregnancy's critical stages of organogenesis.

- **Testing:** Teratogenic potential is evaluated through animal studies and epidemiological observations.

- **Prevention:** Pregnant women are advised to avoid known teratogens to minimize risks to fetal development.

Examples: Thalidomide, alcohol, certain medications (e.g., isotretinoin), and environmental toxins (e.g., methylmercury) are known teratogens.

Mutagenicity

Definition: Mutagenicity refers to the ability of a substance to induce mutations in the genetic material (DNA) of cells.

Characteristics:

- **Types of Mutations:** Mutagens can cause point mutations, deletions, insertions, or chromosomal rearrangements.
- **Mechanism:** Mutagens may directly damage DNA or interfere with DNA replication or repair mechanisms.
- **Testing:** Mutagenicity is assessed using various assays, including bacterial tests (e.g., Ames test) and mammalian cell assays.
- **Implications:** Mutagenic substances are of concern due to their potential to increase cancer risk and hereditary disorders.

Examples: Chemicals such as benzene, aflatoxins, and ionizing radiation (e.g., X-rays) are known mutagens.

Importance in Toxicology

Understanding genotoxicity, carcinogenicity, teratogenicity, and mutagenicity is crucial in:

- **Risk Assessment:** Evaluating potential health risks associated with exposure to chemicals and environmental agents.
- **Regulation:** Establishing safety standards, exposure limits, and regulatory guidelines to protect human health.
- **Drug Development:** Assessing the safety of pharmaceuticals and chemicals during preclinical and clinical trials.
- **Public Health:** Educating the public and healthcare professionals about potential hazards and preventive measures.

General principles of treatment of Poisoning:

General Principles of Treatment of Poisoning

Treating poisoning involves several key principles aimed at minimizing the absorption of toxins, enhancing their elimination, managing symptoms, and providing supportive care. Here are the general principles:

1. **Assessment and Stabilization:**

o **Assessment:** Quickly assess the patient's condition, including vital signs, level of consciousness, and symptoms.

o **Stabilization:** Ensure adequate airway, breathing, and circulation (ABCs). Address any immediate life-threatening conditions.

2. **Decontamination:**

o **Gastric Lavage:** Used for recent ingestions within 1 hour, involves flushing the stomach with saline solution to remove toxins.

o **Activated Charcoal:** Administered orally to adsorb toxins in the gastrointestinal tract, reducing absorption.

o **Skin Decontamination:** Remove contaminated clothing and wash exposed skin to prevent further absorption.

3. **Enhanced Elimination:**

o **Urinary Alkalinization:** Adjust urine pH to enhance elimination of acidic drugs.

o **Enhanced Elimination Techniques:** Use methods like hemodialysis or hemoperfusion for certain toxins that are not effectively cleared by the kidneys.

4. **Antidotes:**

o Administer specific antidotes if available and appropriate for the toxin involved (e.g., naloxone for opioid overdose, atropine for organophosphate poisoning).

5. **Supportive Care:**

- o **Symptomatic Treatment:** Manage symptoms such as seizures, hypotension, or respiratory depression with medications and supportive measures.
- o **Monitoring:** Continuously monitor vital signs, electrolytes, and organ function.
- o **Fluid and Electrolyte Management:** Correct imbalances and maintain adequate hydration.

6. **Prevention of Absorption:**
   - o **Chelation Therapy:** Use specific agents (e.g., EDTA for heavy metal poisoning) to bind and facilitate excretion of toxic metals.

7. **Psychosocial Support:**
   - o Provide reassurance and psychological support to patients and their families during and after treatment.

Clinical Symptoms and Management of Barbiturates Poisoning

Clinical Symptoms:

- **Central Nervous System Depression:** Barbiturates depress the central nervous system, leading to symptoms such as drowsiness, confusion, slurred speech, and impaired coordination.
- **Respiratory Depression:** Severe cases may present with respiratory depression, hypoventilation, or respiratory arrest.
- **Hypotension:** Barbiturates can cause hypotension due to vasodilation and decreased cardiac output.
- **Coma:** Severe poisoning can progress to coma and respiratory failure.

Management:

1. **Immediate Actions:**
   - o **ABCs:** Ensure airway patency, adequate ventilation, and cardiovascular support as needed.
   - o **Decontamination:** Consider gastric lavage or administration of activated charcoal if ingestion is recent and significant.

2. **Supportive Care:**

- **Monitoring:** Continuous monitoring of vital signs, respiratory status, and neurological function.
- **Ventilatory Support:** Provide mechanical ventilation if respiratory depression is severe.
- **Fluid Resuscitation:** Maintain adequate fluid balance and correct electrolyte abnormalities.

3. **Specific Treatment:**

- **Enhanced Elimination:** Consider hemodialysis in severe cases to enhance elimination.
- **Antidote:** There is no specific antidote for barbiturates. Treatment is mainly supportive and symptomatic.

4. **Seizure Management:**

- **Anticonvulsants:** Administer benzodiazepines (e.g., diazepam) or barbiturate antagonists (e.g., flumazenil) cautiously to control seizures.

5. **Monitoring and Complications:**

- **Neurological Monitoring:** Assess for signs of increasing intracranial pressure and cerebral edema.
- **Cardiovascular Monitoring:** Watch for arrhythmias, hypotension, and signs of shock.

6. **Psychosocial Support:**

- Provide emotional support to the patient and their family, especially if there are concerns about intentional overdose.

Clinical Symptoms and Management of Morphine Poisoning

Clinical Symptoms:

- **Central Nervous System Depression:** Morphine, an opioid, depresses the central nervous system, leading to drowsiness, confusion, and sedation.

- **Respiratory Depression:** Severe poisoning can cause respiratory depression, hypoventilation, or even respiratory arrest.
- **Miosis:** Constricted pupils are a hallmark sign of opioid toxicity.
- **Hypotension:** Morphine can cause vasodilation and reduced cardiac output, resulting in low blood pressure.
- **Bradycardia:** Slowed heart rate may occur due to morphine's effects on the autonomic nervous system.

Management:

1. **Immediate Actions:**
   - **ABCs:** Ensure airway patency, adequate ventilation, and cardiovascular support as needed.
   - **Decontamination:** Consider gastric lavage or administration of activated charcoal if ingestion was recent and substantial.

2. **Supportive Care:**
   - **Monitoring:** Continuously monitor vital signs, respiratory status, and neurological function.
   - **Ventilatory Support:** Provide mechanical ventilation if respiratory depression is severe.
   - **Fluid Resuscitation:** Maintain adequate fluid balance and correct electrolyte abnormalities.

3. **Specific Treatment:**
   - **Naloxone Administration:** Naloxone is a specific opioid antagonist used to reverse the effects of morphine overdose. It competitively binds to opioid receptors, displacing morphine and restoring respiratory and CNS function.
     - **Dosing:** Initial dose of naloxone may be repeated until desired response (e.g., respiratory rate >10 breaths/minute) is achieved. Continuous infusion may be required in severe cases.

- **Caution:** Monitor for potential withdrawal symptoms (e.g., agitation, hypertension, tachycardia) once naloxone is administered.

4. **Seizure Management:**

o Administer benzodiazepines (e.g., diazepam) to manage seizures if they occur.

5. **Monitoring and Complications:**

o **Neurological Monitoring:** Assess for signs of increasing intracranial pressure and cerebral edema.

o **Cardiovascular Monitoring:** Watch for arrhythmias, hypotension, and signs of shock.

6. **Psychosocial Support:**

o Provide emotional support to the patient and their family, particularly if there are concerns about intentional overdose or addiction issues.

Clinical Symptoms and Management of Organophosphorous Compounds Poisoning

Clinical Symptoms:

- **Cholinergic Overstimulation:** Organophosphates inhibit acetylcholinesterase, leading to excessive accumulation of acetylcholine.

o **Muscarinic Effects:** Salivation, lacrimation, urination, defecation (SLUD syndrome), miosis (pinpoint pupils), bronchoconstriction, and bradycardia.

o **Nicotinic Effects:** Muscle fasciculations, weakness, and potentially paralysis.

o **Central Nervous System Effects:** Headache, dizziness, confusion, seizures, and coma in severe cases.

Management:

1. **Immediate Actions:**

- o **ABCs:** Ensure airway patency, adequate ventilation, and cardiovascular support as needed.
  - o **Decontamination:** Remove contaminated clothing and wash exposed skin. Administer activated charcoal if ingestion is recent and substantial.

2. **Specific Treatment:**
   - o **Atropine:** Antagonizes muscarinic effects by blocking acetylcholine receptors. Administer in incremental doses to control symptoms such as bradycardia, bronchoconstriction, and excessive secretions.
   - o **Pralidoxime (2-PAM):** Reactivates inhibited acetylcholinesterase, helping to restore enzyme function and reduce cholinergic effects. Administer in conjunction with atropine, particularly for moderate to severe poisoning.

3. **Supportive Care:**
   - o **Ventilatory Support:** Provide respiratory support with oxygen and mechanical ventilation if needed.
   - o **Seizure Management:** Administer benzodiazepines (e.g., diazepam) to control seizures if they occur.

4. **Monitoring and Complications:**
   - o **Neurological Monitoring:** Assess for signs of neurological deterioration, seizures, or coma.
   - o **Cardiovascular Monitoring:** Monitor for arrhythmias and hemodynamic instability.

Clinical Symptoms and Management of Lead, Arsenic, and Mercuric Poisoning

Lead Poisoning:

- **Clinical Symptoms:** Depend on the level and duration of exposure. Includes abdominal pain, constipation, anemia, nephropathy, and neurologic effects (e.g., encephalopathy).
- **Management:** Remove the source of exposure. Chelation therapy with agents like EDTA or dimercaptosuccinic acid (DMSA) may be indicated for elevated blood lead levels.

Arsenic Poisoning:

- **Clinical Symptoms:** Initial symptoms include nausea, vomiting, abdominal pain, and diarrhea. Chronic exposure may lead to skin changes, peripheral neuropathy, and malignancies.
- **Management:** Discontinue exposure. Chelation therapy with dimercaprol or DMSA may be considered for severe cases.

Mercury Poisoning:

- **Clinical Symptoms:** Depend on the form of mercury (elemental, inorganic, or organic). Includes gastrointestinal symptoms, neurological symptoms (e.g., tremors, ataxia), and renal toxicity.
- **Management:** Remove the source of exposure. Chelation therapy with agents like dimercaprol or DMSA may be considered for severe cases.

CHAPTER – 20

CHRONOPHARMACOLOGY

Mr. Satyendra Garg

Assistant Professor, Rajiv Gandhi Institute of Pharmacy, Faculty of

Pharmaceutical Science & Technology, AKS University Satna, MP-India

ABSTRACT:

Chronopharmacology is a specialized field within pharmacology that explores how biological rhythms and the timing of drug administration influence pharmacokinetics, pharmacodynamics, and therapeutic outcomes. This discipline recognizes that the human body operates on intricate biological clocks, orchestrating physiological processes such as metabolism, hormone secretion, and cellular activity in a rhythmic manner. These rhythms are governed by the circadian clock, which follows a roughly 24-hour cycle, and other ultradian rhythms that occur more frequently. The timing of drug intake can significantly impact how drugs are absorbed, distributed, metabolized, and eliminated by the body. Biological factors such as changes in gastrointestinal motility, liver enzyme activity, renal function, and cellular receptor sensitivity exhibit diurnal variations, influencing drug efficacy and toxicity. Therefore, understanding these temporal variations is crucial for optimizing drug therapy to achieve maximum therapeutic benefits while minimizing adverse effects. Chronopharmacology not only focuses on the optimal timing of drug administration but also investigates how biological rhythms affect drug response in various disease states and patient populations. This field has practical implications across medical specialties, guiding the development of personalized treatment strategies tailored to individual circadian rhythms. By harnessing the principles of chronopharmacology, healthcare providers can improve patient outcomes, enhance drug effectiveness, and contribute to the advancement of precision medicine practices.

Introduction:

Chronopharmacology is the study of the effects of drugs on the body in relation to the time of day or biological rhythms. It recognizes that the body's physiological processes, such as metabolism, hormone production, and organ function, follow daily rhythms known as circadian rhythms. These rhythms are influenced by the body's internal biological clock, which is synchronized with the 24-hour day-night cycle.

Chronopharmacology is the study of how biological rhythms and the timing of drug administration influence drug pharmacokinetics and pharmacodynamics, as well as their therapeutic and adverse effects on the body. This field recognizes that many physiological processes, including metabolism, hormone secretion, and enzyme activity, fluctuate in a rhythmic manner throughout the day. Here are key aspects and implications of chronopharmacology:

1. **Biological Rhythms:** The human body operates on various biological rhythms, such as the circadian rhythm (approximately 24-hour cycle) and ultradian rhythms (cycles shorter than 24 hours). These rhythms influence factors like sleep-wake cycles, body temperature, and hormone production.

2. **Drug Absorption and Distribution:** Timing of drug administration can affect the absorption and distribution of drugs in the body. For instance, gastrointestinal motility and blood flow to organs vary throughout the day, impacting how drugs are absorbed and distributed.

3. **Metabolism and Elimination:** Enzyme activity involved in drug metabolism and renal clearance can exhibit diurnal variations. This can affect the rate at which drugs are metabolized and eliminated from the body, influencing their duration of action and potential toxicity.

4. **Chronotherapy:** Chronopharmacology emphasizes the optimization of drug administration timing to maximize therapeutic efficacy and

minimize adverse effects. Tailoring drug regimens to align with the body's biological rhythms can improve patient outcomes.

5. **Circadian Variation in Drug Response:** The body's sensitivity to drugs may vary throughout the day due to changes in receptor sensitivity, cellular responsiveness, and physiological function. Timing drug administration to coincide with peak efficacy or minimal side effects is crucial.

6. **Clinical Applications:** Chronopharmacology has implications across various medical specialties, including cardiovascular medicine, oncology, psychiatry, and anesthesia. For example, timing antihypertensive medications to coincide with morning blood pressure surges can enhance efficacy.

7. **Shift Work and Disease States:** Individuals working night shifts or experiencing disrupted circadian rhythms due to travel (jet lag) may experience altered drug responses. Understanding these variations is important in managing drug therapy in such populations.

8. **Chronotoxicology:** This branch of chronopharmacology examines how the timing of toxicant exposure influences toxicity outcomes. It considers circadian variations in detoxification processes and organ susceptibility to toxicants.

9. **Chronopharmacokinetics:** Studies focusing on the timing of drug absorption, distribution, metabolism, and elimination provide insights into optimizing drug dosing schedules for maximal therapeutic benefit.

10. **Experimental Design:** Research in chronopharmacology often involves carefully designed studies to assess drug effects at different times of day, considering factors such as sleep-wake cycles, meal times, and environmental lighting conditions.

DEFINITIONS OF RHYTHM AND CYCLES

Rhythm:

In the context of chronopharmacology, the term "rhythm" is often used to describe the temporal patterns and fluctuations in various physiological processes that influence the pharmacokinetics (absorption, distribution, metabolism, and excretion) and pharmacodynamics (effects on the body) of drugs. Here are detailed definitions of rhythm in the context of chronopharmacology:

1. **Circadian Rhythm:**

a. **Definition:** Circadian rhythms are biological rhythms that follow a roughly 24-hour cycle, corresponding to the Earth's day-night cycle. These rhythms are regulated by the body's internal circadian clock and influence various physiological processes, including body temperature, hormone production, and sleep-wake cycles.

b. **Relevance to Chronopharmacology:** The circadian rhythm plays a crucial role in determining the optimal timing for drug administration. Many physiological functions, such as liver metabolism and kidney function, exhibit circadian variations, affecting the way drugs are processed and eliminated from the body.

2. **Ultradian Rhythm:**

a. **Definition:** Ultradian rhythms are shorter biological cycles, typically occurring more than once in a 24-hour period. Examples include the pulsatile release of certain hormones and cycles of rapid eye movement (REM) during sleep.

b. **Relevance to Chronopharmacology:** Ultradian rhythms contribute to the complexity of drug responses. For instance, the pulsatile release of hormones may affect the sensitivity of target tissues to drugs at different times, influencing therapeutic outcomes.

3. **Infradian Rhythm:**

a. **Definition:** Infradian rhythms have a longer duration than the 24-hour circadian cycle, often extending over days, weeks, or months. Examples include the menstrual cycle in females.

b. **Relevance to Chronopharmacology:** Infradian rhythms are important in considering the variability of drug responses over longer time frames. For example, hormonal fluctuations during the menstrual cycle may impact the pharmacokinetics and pharmacodynamics of certain medications.

Cycles:

Chronopharmacology is a branch of pharmacology that studies the effects of drugs and their administration timing in relation to the body's circadian rhythms or biological clock. Circadian rhythms are the natural, internal processes that regulate various physiological and behavioral processes in living organisms, including the sleep-wake cycle, body temperature, hormone secretion, and metabolism. In the context of chronopharmacology, cycles play a crucial role in understanding how the timing of drug administration can influence their efficacy and potential side effects. Here are some key cycles involved in chronopharmacology:

1. Circadian Rhythms:

a. **Definition:** Circadian rhythms are approximately 24-hour cycles that regulate the physiological processes in living organisms, influenced by external cues like light and temperature.

b. **Relevance:** The body's response to drugs can vary based on the time of day due to fluctuations in physiological parameters, such as hormone levels, organ function, and drug metabolism. Understanding circadian rhythms is essential for optimizing drug administration schedules.

2. Sleep-Wake Cycle:

a. **Definition:** The sleep-wake cycle is a circadian rhythm that regulates the alternating periods of wakefulness and sleep.

b. **Relevance:** Some drugs may have different effects or side effects depending on whether they are administered during waking or sleeping hours. The sleep-wake cycle can influence drug absorption, distribution, and metabolism.

3. **Biological Clock:**

a. **Definition:** The biological clock is an internal timing mechanism that regulates the body's circadian rhythms.

b. **Relevance:** The biological clock influences the timing of physiological processes, including drug metabolism and responsiveness of target tissues to drugs. It helps determine the optimal time for drug administration to maximize therapeutic effects and minimize side effects.

4. **Hormonal Cycles:**

a. **Definition:** Hormonal cycles refer to the rhythmic fluctuations in hormone levels throughout the day.

b. **Relevance:** Hormones play a crucial role in mediating the effects of drugs. For instance, the efficacy of certain drugs may be influenced by the variations in cortisol, insulin, or other hormones. Timing drug administration to coincide with specific hormonal peaks can enhance therapeutic outcomes.

5. **Metabolic Cycles:**

a. **Definition:** Metabolic cycles involve fluctuations in metabolic processes throughout the day, affecting drug metabolism and elimination.

b. **Relevance:** The body's ability to metabolize drugs can vary based on the time of day, impacting drug bioavailability and clearance.

Knowledge of metabolic cycles helps in optimizing drug dosing schedules.

BIOLOGICAL CLOCK AND THEIR SIGNIFICANCE LEADING TO CHRONOTHERAPY

The biological clock, also known as the circadian clock, is an internal timing system that regulates various physiological and behavioral processes in living organisms. This clock is synchronized with the 24-hour day-night cycle and is influenced by external cues, primarily light. The master circadian clock in humans is located in the suprachiasmatic nucleus (SCN) of the hypothalamus. Peripheral clocks are also present in various tissues throughout the body, allowing for the coordination of biological processes.

Significance of the Biological Clock in Chronotherapy:

1. **Circadian Rhythms and Drug Metabolism:**

    a. The activity of drug-metabolizing enzymes in the liver follows a circadian rhythm. For example, the expression of certain cytochrome P450 enzymes, responsible for metabolizing many drugs, fluctuates throughout the day.

    b. **Significance:** Administering drugs during peak enzyme activity can enhance metabolism and clearance, optimizing drug efficacy and reducing the risk of side effects.

2. **Cellular Sensitivity and Chronopharmacodynamics:**

    a. The responsiveness of target tissues to drugs can vary depending on the time of day. This is often due to fluctuations in receptor expression and cellular sensitivity.

    b. **Significance:** Administering drugs when target tissues are most responsive can maximize therapeutic effects while minimizing the required dosage, reducing the risk of toxicity.

3. **Hormonal Regulation and Chronopharmacology:**

a. Hormones, such as cortisol, insulin, and growth hormone, exhibit circadian rhythms. These hormones play a crucial role in modulating various physiological processes.

b. **Significance:** Timing drug administration to coincide with specific hormonal peaks or troughs can enhance drug efficacy and minimize side effects. For example, administering corticosteroids in alignment with the body's natural cortisol rhythm may improve anti-inflammatory effects.

4. **Chronopharmacokinetics:**

a. Circadian rhythms influence drug absorption, distribution, and elimination. Factors like gastric emptying, blood flow to organs, and renal function show rhythmic variations.

b. **Significance:** Understanding these pharmacokinetic variations helps determine the optimal timing for drug administration to achieve the desired therapeutic effect.

5. **Chronotoxicology and Minimizing Side Effects:**

a. The biological clock can influence the tolerance of tissues to toxic effects of drugs. Some tissues may be more vulnerable to drug toxicity at certain times.

b. **Significance:** Chronotoxicology aims to minimize side effects by administering drugs when the affected tissues are less susceptible to toxicity.

6. **Individual Variability and Personalized Chronotherapy:**

a. There is considerable inter-individual variability in circadian rhythms, emphasizing the importance of personalized approaches in chronotherapy.

b. **Significance**: Tailoring drug administration schedules based on an individual's biological clock can optimize treatment outcomes by accounting for variations in drug metabolism, efficacy, and tolerability.

7. **Circadian Disruption and Disease Susceptibility:**

    a. Disruption of circadian rhythms, as seen in shift work or irregular sleep patterns, is associated with an increased risk of various health conditions.

    b. **Significance:** Chronotherapy aims to minimize circadian disruption by aligning drug administration with the patient's natural circadian rhythm, potentially reducing the risk of adverse health effects.

BIOLOGICAL SIGNIFICANCE LEADING TO CHRONOTHERAPY:

Biological clocks refer to internal mechanisms that regulate biological processes and behaviors in living organisms. These clocks enable organisms to anticipate and adapt to recurring environmental changes, such as the light-dark cycle of day and night. The most well-known biological clock in humans is the circadian rhythm, which operates on approximately a 24-hour cycle and influences various physiological functions, including sleep-wake patterns, hormone secretion, metabolism, and body temperature regulation.

Significance Leading to Chronotherapy:

1. **Optimal Drug Efficacy and Safety:** Biological rhythms impact drug pharmacokinetics and pharmacodynamics. Understanding the timing of peak drug effectiveness and minimizing side effects is crucial for chronotherapy. For example, administering medications during times of peak disease activity or minimizing drug levels during periods of low tolerance can optimize treatment outcomes.

2. **Personalized Treatment Strategies:** Chronotherapy allows for personalized medicine approaches that consider individual biological rhythms. By aligning drug administration with the patient's circadian

rhythms, healthcare providers can tailor treatment regimens to enhance efficacy and minimize adverse effects.

3. **Enhanced Patient Compliance:** Adhering to the body's natural rhythms can improve patient compliance with medication schedules. For instance, timing medications to coincide with daily routines such as meals or sleep can facilitate adherence to treatment plans.

4. **Management of Chronic Diseases:** Certain chronic conditions, such as asthma, cardiovascular disease, and psychiatric disorders, exhibit diurnal variations in symptoms and disease activity. Chronotherapy aims to optimize drug delivery to match these fluctuations, improving symptom control and quality of life.

5. **Minimization of Side Effects:** Circadian variations in drug metabolism and toxicity can influence the likelihood and severity of adverse effects. Timing drug administration to align with periods of reduced sensitivity or enhanced detoxification capacity can minimize the risk of side effects.

6. **Research and Development:** Advances in chronobiology and chronopharmacology drive innovation in drug development. Researchers explore new formulations and delivery systems that release medications in a time-dependent manner, enhancing therapeutic efficacy and patient outcomes.